Library of Congress Cataloging in Publication
Data

Freeman, Thomas, 1919-
    Childhood psychopathology and adult psy-
choses.

    Bibliography: p.
    1. Child psychiatry. 2. Psychoses. I. Title.
[DNLM: 1. Psychoses—In adulthood. 2. Psycho-
pathology—In infancy and childhood. 3. Psycho-
analytic theory. WM200 F855c]
RJ499.F76   616.8'9   75-31854
ISBN 0-8236-0775-5

Childhood [

and Adu[

THOMAS [

M.D., F.R.C.P.E.

Consultant Psychiatrist,
Antrim, Northern
Hampstead Child-Thera

PREFACE BY ANN.

INTERNATIONAL UNIVERSITIES

New York

CONTENTS

Preface

The concept of childhood psychosis has been under debate in the psychiatric literature for several decades, with opinions widely divergent from each other. Some authors have maintained that manifestations such as estrangement from reality, retreat to a delusional world, breakdown of secondary-process thinking, etc., can occur at any age. Others have asserted that these are derangements restricted to the mature personality and that any comparable phenomena in early childhood signify arrests, failures, and defects in the developmental processes themselves.

It is this controversial subject to which the author of this book addresses himself. As he has done in former publications, he bases his work on the careful metapsychological dissection of adult clinical pictures and proceeds from these to the application of the same mode of thinking to childhood symptomatology. His study is, thus, essentially a comparative one.

What emerges from his efforts is a clearer formulation of and some light thrown on problems that, up to now, have remained unsolved. There is always the vital question whether the hidden mental processes underlying the relevant manifest symptoms in adults and children are identical or different in nature. There is the present inability, even in our most painstaking examinations of individual child developments, to detect and describe the signs that herald psychotic outbreaks at later ages. There is, further, the urgent need for evidential proof to confirm or refute the analytic reconstructions of the earliest childhood events, as they are currently arrived at during therapeutic work with adult psychotics.

It is to be hoped that Dr. Freeman's book will convince the reader that neither the exploration of deviant children as such, nor that of adult psychotics by itself, can produce the answers. As he demonstrates, it is only the merging of the two areas of work that leads to the advance in knowledge we are seeking.

Anna Freud
London

Acknowledgments

I want to thank Miss Anna Freud and Mrs. Dorothy Burlingham for giving direction to my work. Their encouragement and stimulus to thought has been supplemented by many helpful suggestions made by my colleagues Dr. Clifford Yorke, Dr. Stanley Wiseberg, and Dr. Christopher Dare. I must also acknowledge my indebtedness to Dr. Maurits Katan for opportunities to gain a deeper understanding of his theoretical views. I am grateful to Dr. R. Berstock, Miss I. Elkan, and Mrs. H. Kennedy for clinical data drawn from patients under their care at the Hampstead Clinic. Finally, I want to thank my wife for her consistent interest in my psychoanalytic and psychiatric work.

The studies reported in this book have been carried out in connection with a research project undertaken by the Hampstead Child-Therapy Clinic, London, and financed under Grant 5R01 05683 by the National Institutes of Mental Health, Washington, D.C.

Introduction

The present work is an extension of the systematic psychoanalytic studies of adult psychoses described in a previous publication (Freeman, 1973). In that work the clinical phenomena were conceptualized in metapsychological terms with the help of a profile schema introduced by Anna Freud and her co-workers and then suitably amended by the author.

The profiles amply confirmed the long-held belief that many striking similarities exist between adult psychotic phenomena and the mental life of healthy and disturbed children. Patients related to nurses, doctors, ancillary workers, and other patients as need-satisfying objects, as supports in the task of drive control, and as objects for identification. In all this they thought and acted like healthy children. The morbid process had exposed developmental phases belonging to the first years of life. Where the therapy was successful, the psychiatrist and nurses, like the parents, served as external objects encouraging the conversion of narcissistic into object libido.

Over and above this, however, unexpected similarities were found between the symptomatology of adult patients and the behavior of children suddenly separated from their mothers (A. Freud and Burlingham, 1943).

The withdrawal from others, lack of affect, and motility disorders characteristic of the schizophrenic patient mirrored what had been observed in motherless children. Even the nonrecognition, indifference, or hostility the hospitalized patient often exhibits to his visitors had its counterpart in the way in which the young children reacted to their mother's return. Denial of object loss, when it occurred, was similar in its expression in both adult patients and "separated" children.

The delusional content of patients suffering from schizophrenic and manic-depressive psychoses often consisted of fantasies typical of the Oedipus complex and latency period. Conflicts, anxieties, and defenses characteristic of libidinal phases could be discerned, which in their expression were identical to those observed in children and adults suffering from neuroses. These observations prompted a closer examination of normal and abnormal childhood mental life within the context of the study of adult psychotic states. Encouraged by the results of a comparison between the psychoses of childhood and those of adult life (Freeman, 1973), the author investigated the extent to which manic-depressive and paranoid syndromes, on the one hand, and neurotic and borderline states in children, on the other hand, might have a descriptive and metapsychological similarity. The results of these inquiries comprise the content of the first four chapters of this book.

In Chapters 5 and 6 the metapsychological approach is used to evaluate a number of clinical and theoretical problems as they arise in connection with psychotic illness in adults. In the clinical field there are studies of the prepsychotic phase, states of partial remission, and persecutory ideas. In the theoretical sphere there is a review and examination of the problem of predisposition to schizophrenia and to psychosis in general.

It is to be hoped that this work will stimulate interest in the common ground between the psychopathology of childhood and the psychoses of adulthood.

CHAPTER 1

Comparisons Between Normal
and Pathological Manifestations
in Early Childhood
and Adult Psychoses

In studies concerned with abnormal mental states attention inevitably turns to those normal expressions of childhood mental development presenting the greatest similarities to pathological phenomena. This trend is even more pronounced in an investigation whose avowed aim is to delineate, in the mentally abnormal child and adult, those forms of healthy mental activity whose origins belong in early childhood. The introduction of the concept of the "developmental line" (A. Freud, 1965) provides a better means of describing and studying the different phases of childhood mental life. Instead of regarding the developmental sequences occurring in one or another mental function as primarily due to either drive or ego maturation, they can be viewed as stages of a developmental line. Each stage results from an interaction between the drives and the ego.

Anna Freud (1965) takes as a prototype of the developmental line the advance from "dependency to emotional self-reliance and adult object relationships" (p. 64). The line begins with the phase of biological unity

1

between mother and child. This is followed by the beginning of object relations, where the task of the object is to provide for the satisfaction of bodily needs. The phase of object constancy emerges with the establishment of permanent object representation. Here the representation of the mother is positively toned as a consequence of repeated acts of need satisfaction.

With the increasing differentiation of self and object, the next phase of the line (the pre-oedipal, anal-sadistic stage) appears. This is characterized by clinging attitudes and a need to control and dominate the love object. It is during the early period of this stage that requests and demands from the parents are met with resistiveness and negativism; the child seems unable to accede to any of the requests needed for such daily routines as washing and dressing.

The transition to the oedipal period finds the child preoccupied with the wish to possess the parent of the opposite sex and jealous of the parent of the same sex. Exhibitionism and curiosity are characteristic of this stage of object relations. In the ensuing latency period there is not only a reduction in the intensity of the drive derivatives, but also the beginning of sublimated activities. Signs of disillusionment with the parents are reflected in family romance fantasies (see Chapter 6). In preadolescence behavior reminiscent of the phase of need satisfaction appears, while in adolescence itself there is the establishment of genital primacy, with the libidinal drives being turned from the parents to objects outside the family.

The early stages of the developmental line "from dependency to emotional self-reliance and adult object relationships" are characterized by all those uses a child makes of the parental objects so that development may proceed in an optimal manner. These uses include the narcissistic unity with the mother, where "no distinction is made between self and environment" (A. Freud, 1965, p. 46), where the mother provides the conditions necessary for the satisfaction of bodily needs, where the parents act as external objects facilitating the transformation of narcissistic libido into object libido, where the parents function as an aid to the child in the task of drive control, and where they act as models for identification.

In describing the child's progress in terms of developmental lines, Anna Freud (1965) takes the development to body independence as the "physical" counterpart to the advance to emotional independence and adult object relations. Body independence is just as hard won as "emotional and moral self-reliance." This is to be seen in those phenomena revealing that in early infancy not only is there confusion on the infant's side concerning body boundaries but, in addition, the degree of differentiation between the self and the external object is dependent on subjective experiences of pleasure and unpleasure rather than on reality considerations—"while the mother's breast or face, hands, or hair, may be treated (or maltreated) by the infant as parts of his own organization, his hunger, his tiredness, his discomforts are her concern as much as they are his own" (A. Freud, 1965, p. 69).

This egocentric state is paramount in the period prior to the advent of object constancy. The mother is without an independent existence and is only recognized in accordance with the child's bodily needs and drive expectancies. In consequence, the infant's awareness and "judgment" of the external object's behavior is wholly assessed in terms of whether or not needs are met and discomforts relieved:

> Every preoccupation of the mother, her concerns with other members of the family, with work or outside interests, her depressions, illnesses, absences, even her death, are transformed thereby into experiences of rejection and desertion.... in short, as a hostile act to which the child in his turn answers with hostility and disappointment expressed either in excessive demandingness or in emotional withdrawal with its adverse consequences [A. Freud, 1965, pp. 58-59].

Three developmental lines are postulated to describe progress to body independence (see also Chapter 3). The first line — "from suckling to rational eating" (A. Freud, 1965, p. 69) — begins with the infant's hunger, his inevitable bodily discomforts, the mother's anxieties, the reactions incurred in the child by weaning from the breast or bottle and the beginning of self-feeding. It is at this time that difficulties in the mother-child relation appear because of the infant's tendency to equate food and mother. A further stage of the line arrives when attitudes derived from anal trends intrude, with the emergence of food fads, negativism, etc. With the appearance of the Oedipus complex, sexual theories find representation and so influence the function of eating through "fantasies of impregnation through the mouth (fear of poison), pregnancy (fear of getting fat), anal birth (fear of intake and output), as well as by reaction formations against cannibalism and sadism..." (A. Freud, 1965, p. 71). This sexualization of eating gradually disappears with the onset of the latency period.

The second developmental line in the movement to body independence is the progress "from wetting and soiling to bladder and bowel control" (A. Freud, 1965, p. 72). In contrast to the emergence of rational eating, the change to bladder and bowel control requires the alteration of instinctual aims. While the need to eat and the satisfaction in eating does not demand a change in the oral drives, with bladder and bowel control anal and urethral drives must be extensively modified. Four stages are distinguished in the developmental line concerned with bladder and bowel control. The duration of the first stage during which soiling and wetting occur freely, is determined entirely by the mother. This may therefore last from several days to two to three years. The second stage, however, is initiated by maturational rather than environmental influences — namely, by the transition of drive dominance from the oral to the anal zone. Feces are cathected with both libido and aggression and this leads to an intense ambivalence to the object world. The mother's behavior is in accord with her own unconscious attitudes to anality. The third stage is that of bowel and bladder control. At this point there is an identification with the mother's standards. These controls are vulnerable to dissolution because they remain based on an object relation. Complete, autonomous functioning only emerges after the passing of the Oedipus complex. This final development occurs once "the concern for cleanliness is disconnected from object ties and attains the status of a fully neutralized, autonomous ego and superego concern" (A. Freud, 1965, p. 75).

The last developmental line to be traced out with regard to body independence is the transition "from irresponsibility to responsibility in body management" (A. Freud, 1965, p. 75). The assumption by the child of responsibility for the care of his body is closely connected with the emergence of the ego functions and reality testing. Interest, regard, and concern for the safety of the body depend on the presence of the "pain barrier" and on the acquisition of an adequate libidinal cathexis of the body. The latter is based on the mother having cathected the infant's body. The child's subsequent attitude to his body is therefore closely connected to the earliest periods of object relation with the implications this has for the distribution of libido between the self-representations, on the one hand, and object representations, on the other.

The developmental lines described and others not referred to here, such as "from egocentricity to companionship" and "from the body to the toy and from play to work" (A. Freud, 1965, pp. 78-79), are concerned with the development of psychosocial functions. Thus, the descriptive and metapsychological accounts of each developmental line include references to all the mental processes operative and interacting at a particular developmental phase. A developmental line becomes increasingly informative when there is detailed knowledge of how a specific drive develops or how an ego function comes to assume its final form. This is illustrated by Mittelman's (1954) study of motility in infants and children.

Like others concerned with changes in the form of cognition, affect, and motility occurring during childhood, Mittelman's study confirms the general hypothesis regarding mental development implicit in the concepts of the primary and secondary processes. While mental functions are at the level of the primary process, drive, affect, and motility are syncretic in their expression and such cognition as occurs is the outcome of this mode of mental activity. Drive arousal in the young child, whether libidinal or aggressive, is always accompanied by overactivity and affect.

The mental life of a child, at any particular age, results from the interaction between developmental lines. Variations between children are due to the extent to which advances have been made along individual developmental lines and how they integrate with one another. Ideally there should be a simultaneous advance along all the developmental lines, but this expectation is not always fulfilled. Some children are more advanced along one line compared to another. The potential for progress on a developmental line and the final achievement result from constitutional and environmental influences. The psychoanalytic study and treatment of children has already led to the description of those environmental events that, under given internal as well as external conditions, have the capability of bringing about deleterious effects on progress along one or more developmental lines.

Relevant in this respect is Nagera's (1966) concept of "developmental interference." In his words: "A 'developmental interference' can be defined as whatever disturbs the typical unfolding of development. The term may be reserved to describe those situations that involve gross external (environmental) interference with certain needs and rights of the child or situations in which unjustified demands are made of the child" (p. 28). Some developmental interferences are accidental, others are "purposive" in that they spring from unhealthy attitudes and psychopathology in the parents. Outstanding among the developmental interferences is separation of the child from the mother at a period when he is not yet able to sustain the consequences of object loss (separations may result from hospitalization of the child or the mother). Other causes are overrigid feeding and toilet training regimes; childhood illness of an upsetting nature; mental distress, such as depression in the mother; death of a parent or sibling; genital seduction; physical overstimulation, as in primal-scene experiences; oral or anal overstimulation; and surgical treatments.

Nagera (1966) points out that developmental interferences are by their very nature conflicts between the needs of the child and his environment. They therefore belong to that series of events occurring in the development of every child and described by Anna Freud (1965) as resulting from external conflicts — conflicts between the child's wishes and parental restrictions and demands. Developmental conflicts are another form of external conflict in that they arise whenever the manifestations of a developmental phase — anal or oedipal — result in clashes with the parents. In contrast to developmental interferences, "developmental conflicts are usually phase specific and of a transitory nature" (Nagera, 1966, p. 45).

Functions newly acquired by the healthy child are not, initially, consistently maintained (A. Freud, 1965). There is a period of instability before these more advanced functions attain autonomy. During this period it is the rule, given certain conditions, for a deterioration in functioning to appear with the emergence of manifestations appropriate to an earlier developmental phase. The most obvious effects of these "regressions in normal development" (A. Freud, 1965) involve the ego. There may be transient disturbances of speech, bladder and bowel control, motility, and control over drive and affect.

Accompanying this loss of advanced ego functioning (the secondary process) are phenomena attributable to the re-establishment of the primary process. Anna Freud (1965) describes two situations where the movement from secondary to primary process can be readily observed. The first is during the course of the psychoanalytical treatment of children. The child's thinking and speech no longer has primarily a communicative function, but increasingly becomes a means for the expression of drive derivatives. A similar temporary ego regression affects the young child at bedtime: "Here too, what impresses one especially is the growing disorder in the thought processes, the perseveration of single words or sentences, the general lability of affects shown in the almost instantaneous mood swings from hilarity to crying" (A. Freud, 1965, p. 101). These phenomena, which normally occur in the period immediately before sleep, also make their appearance when the young child is subject to stresses of different kinds, such as fatigue, physical illness, and separation from love objects. Sometimes the regression affecting the ego is also accompanied by a libidinal regression. The results of these regressions are usually reversed when the child is no longer tired, has recovered from his illness, or is restored to his love object; there is an immediate return to the previously achieved level of ego functioning. These regressions are temporary, serving an adaptive and a defensive role—defensive insofar as the regression helps to obviate awareness of all those external and internal stimuli that would provoke anxiety and mental distress. As Anna Freud (1965) points out, the activity of the defenses limits the impact of extraneous stimulation but, in so doing, leads to a less effective level of ego functioning. Denial and repression result in disturbances of memory; projection distorts judgment of self and others.

The consequences of regression, whether affecting the drives or the ego, may not be reversible. In particular, this can occur after traumatic experiences. The effect of these permanent regressions is to provide a predisposition for pathological developments in childhood or later, in adolescence and adulthood.

ABNORMALITIES OF OBJECT RELATIONS AND THE EGO IN EARLY CHILDHOOD

The clinical phenomena described and discussed here consist of neurotic syndromes, borderline states, and childhood psychoses. The data are drawn from cases reported in the literature. In these cases the symptoms commenced in early childhood and treatment was instituted by the age of three. The attitude of the children to their illnesses and treatments can be likened to that of the adult psychotic patient who does not acknowledge that he is ill and in need of help. Anna Freud (1965) has commented that the child, like the adult psychotic, feels threatened by analytical treatment. In both instances this is due to the limited strength of the ego vis-à-vis the drives and the pressures exerted by the environment. In neither case does the patient doubt the reality of his anxieties and fantasies. The cases described here have been chosen because of the similarity of their symptomatology to acute psychotic attacks in adults, where persecutory delusions play the leading part.

The first case is that of a two-and-a-half-year-old

female child, whose treatment was reported by Fraiberg (1952). This child was either in a state of constant anxiety or in a withdrawn condition, when contact with her was almost impossible. Anxiety was caused by noises, both real and imaginary, which, when experienced, led to terror. The child was constantly alert to the possibility of such noises occurring. She would scream out or hold herself in rigid positions. She was afraid to approach the front door of her house because she feared a man might come in. She was frightened of her father and her grandfather; she was frightened of hat pins. Loss of contact with reality was apparent in transient misidentifications, withdrawal from others, and a vagueness in manner. During the analysis there were periods when the anxiety and withdrawal were pronounced. The child was described during the early months of the treatment as passive, overwhelmed, and helpless in the face of omnipresent danger. Nevertheless, she was still capable of making violent attacks on her brother, who was born when she was 23 months old.

The analysis disclosed a series of events in the child's life, which culminated in witnessing her grandparents having sexual intercourse. Prior to the age of two she had been taken regularly to a pediatrician who included an inspection of the genitalia in his examination. When she was 23 months old, her brother was born. In the three months following her brother's birth — during which time she was intensely envious of his penis and jealous of his closeness to her mother — two significant events occurred. First, she discovered a used menstrual pad in the wastepaper basket. Second, she had sex play with an older boy. This aggravated the sadistic wishes aimed at the penis. At one point during the analysis she tried to bite her brother's penis. It was soon after the sexual experience with the older boy that she observed the grandparents having sexual relations. Some weeks later she had to have several injections for boils. This treatment was administered by the same pediatrician who had conducted the routine examination.

Fraiberg concluded that the sadistic wishes (the wish to bite off the penis), the discovery of the menstrual pad, and the seduction in conjunction with her mother's attempts to enlighten her on sex differences led to her interpreting coitus as a destructive attack that would be perpetrated on her. The outcome was the terror of noises and hat pins and the dread of the father, the grandfather, and the unknown man.

The second case, a female child of two years, was described by Sperling (1952). This child developed a paroxysmal tachycardia at the age of seven months. The attacks were accompanied by grunting sounds and the assumption of a crouching posture. She was hospitalized at the age of nine months for investigation of the tachycardia. At 19 months she was hospitalized again and had her tonsils removed. Following this last period in hospital, bladder and bowel control was lost, after having been acquired at about nine months. After discharge from the hospital, she was extremely withdrawn and would sit in a crouched position licking her tongue and grunting. She would remain like this for several hours, quite out of touch with reality.

Treatment began when she was 23 months old — the mother being seven months pregnant at the time. Shortly after her brother's birth she lost her appetite, refused to eat, and her sleep was very disturbed. She would waken in the night in a panic, shouting that a dog or cat was biting her finger. She was hallucinated in both the visual and tactile spheres. On one occasion she tried to brush fish from her face. The fear of being bitten by animals was present during the day as well. Even when playing a feeding game with a doll she was afraid to put her finger near the doll's mouth in case her finger was bitten.

On the basis of the analytical material, Sperling proposed that the anxiety was a reaction to her oral sadism. The tonsillectomy had interfered with the smooth development of the oral drives. It was the birth of the brother that activated the oral-sadistic wishes as a consequence of penis envy. The mother's premature attempt to complete toilet training, her overstimulation of the child, and the witnessing of primal scenes played a decisive part in leading to the symptoms.

The third case is that of a three-and-a-half-year-old girl, whose treatment was reported by Furman (1956). This child presented with many symptoms, including a severe feeding disorder, disturbances of motility, incoherent speech, and periods of complete withdrawal. She would engage in monotonous repetitive play. She would hold her body rigidly or rush about in an excited fashion. She attacked other children without cause and then appeared to be afraid of her victims, as if uncertain as to whether she had hurt them or whether they had hurt her. Masturbation was frequent. In contrast to the presenting symptoms, the child had developed normally until she was well over two years old. Walking had taken place at 13 months and by two and a half she had acquired a good vocabulary. Anxieties had commenced at about two and a half years, and these were accentuated when her mother had to take to her bed because of adverse reactions to a pregnancy.

The young patient responded well to the first four weeks of treatment. On this account the treatment was continued and it lasted for over three years with a good result. In the first months of the therapy it became apparent that the incomprehensible speech served a defensive purpose: she said, " 'If nobody knows what I'm saying, then nobody knows that I am angry' " (Furman, 1956, p. 316). At various periods during the analysis this defense was used to prevent the emergence of anxiety-provoking topics. The failure to distinguish herself from those she attacked was repeated during play activity in the treatment sessions — for example, she picked up a pair of scissors and ran to the other side of the room shouting, " 'You are going to hurt me' " (Furman, 1956, p. 317).

During this phase of the treatment she generalized (externalized) her aggression and her anxieties to external objects, both animate and inanimate. She was very frightened of bodily injury, of doctors, and of men in particular. She feared the effects of her aggression on her dolls and other inanimate objects. In play with dolls sexual themes were prominent and there was great excitement. She had the fantasy that a man had bitten off her penis. When dealing with these sexual ideas, her speech rapidly deteriorated and was impossible to understand. It became clear that she had frequently witnessed parental intercourse and had observed her mother practicing fellatio with her father. At a later period of the treatment, after much resistance expressed in nonsense speech and changes in identity (becoming mother, sister, teacher, etc.), her preoccupation with oral fantasies, as well as such symptoms as anorexia, nausea, etc., were traced to a seduction by her uncle who had not only stimulated her genitalia but had inserted his penis into

her mouth. She had bitten it and he had been very angry
with her.

In this later period of the therapy she no longer
uttered disconnected sentences describing the traumatic
experiences. These utterances were the automatic repetition of overheard speech, as for example: " 'Honey, I'm
going to tear off your clothes . . . I'm going to bite it
honey. I'm going to put it in' " (Furman, 1956, p. 319).
Memories began to emerge in the form of repetitive
traumatic dreams. When the traumatic memories approached consciousness there was some deterioration in
ego functioning. Self- and object representations were less
clearly differentiated. For example, when recalling a
dream in which a big dog sat on top of her and poked her
eyes and genitals, she began to play with a lipstick. She
wanted to push this into the analyst's mouth, "saying at a
pitch of excitement, 'You just open your mouth nicely,
honey. You'll be okay.' Upon interpretation of her active
defense, Carol pushed the lipstick into her own mouth,
gagged, and in panic gurgled, 'I can't talk, I can't talk' "
(Furman, 1956, p. 327).

This young patient showed all the phenomena found
in children regarded as suffering from borderline states.
Ekstein and Wallerstein (1954) have described as characteristic of borderline states in children the easy movement
from advanced levels of the ego and object relations to
primitive levels where the primary process dominates
cognition and drive control — from organized to disorganized states in the case of the ego and from object
constancy to primary forms of identification and need-
satisfying behavior in the case of object relations. On the
basis of their therapeutic experiences, Ekstein and Wallerstein propose that these regressions occur under three

separate conditions: when changes occur in the child's relationship with the therapist; when there are endogenous fluctuations in drive economics, independent of external events; and when affective responses follow changing identifications. The regressions of both the drives and the ego lead to psychotic phenomena. They are in part the result of defenses, which are quite different from those that operate in the neurotic phase of the illness — that is, when the ego is relatively intact.

The presenting symptoms and behavior in childhood psychoses do not differ significantly from those in borderline states. The "dominant cast of the relationship," to use a concept introduced by Ekstein and Wallerstein (1954), is predominantly autistic. The characteristics of this autism have been described by Mahler (1952), Weil (1953), Thomas and her colleagues (1966), and others. The underlying differences between borderline and psychotic cases only appear in the course of therapeutic endeavors. This was demonstrated in the borderline case treated by Furman (1956). Analytical treatment was possible because of the pre-existing libidinal cathexis of the mother. Object constancy was never abandoned. In psychotic children the arrest of libidinal and ego development prevents the establishment of a treatment relation. At best the external object becomes a means of drive control, rarely an object that can provide a stable identification. Most commonly the external object is looked to as a means of need satisfaction or regarded as a source of dread. This is the effect of the generalization of pregenital sadistic tendencies (Thomas et al., 1966). The absence of a stable object cathexis in psychotic children renders the external object vulnerable to attack whenever there is an increase of unpleasure due to need or frustration. It is at such times during treatment that whatever gains have been made are lost.

In the three cases described above, the developmental lines concerned with object relations, rational eating, bowel and bladder control, etc., were so affected that the most recently acquired functions were lost and there was no further forward movement. None of the children entirely lost the representation of the object or its cathexis; the potential for object constancy remained, although there were occasions when the external object was used in a need-satisfying manner. At such times there was a merging of self and object. Object cathexis was periodically withdrawn with a resultant hypercathexis of the self, leading to a state of inaccessibility. In all three children psychoanalytic treatment strengthened the capacity for object cathexis.

A striking feature in the three cases was the fear of being attacked by oral means. This fear arose from two interrelated sources—one external, the other internal. The former comprised actual experiences of physical assault (medical and surgical treatment, seduction, etc.). The latter consisted of destructive (pregenital) wishes whose intensity had been heightened as a result of the traumata to which they had been exposed. These pregenital wishes were generalized and located in the fantasied persecutor. Owing to the poorly developed state of the ego, the children were able to give free vent in thought, speech, and action to their destructive impulses, while simultaneously dreading the possible attacks of the fantasied objects. This easy externalization was a consequence of the ill-defined boundary between the self- and object representations. It also provided the basis for a limited defense against the destructive impulses.

The external events (traumata) that initiated the abnormal mental states can well be described as "developmental interferences" (Nagera, 1966). It was these interferences that brought about the heightening of the drive derivatives and provoked danger situations. The expression of these pregenital drives led to conflict with real external objects (the parents) if they were to find satisfaction. As Nagera (1966) suggests, developmental interferences result in external conflicts. Externalization employed as a defense against the drives only enhanced the fear of being attacked (punishment) or of loss of love (object loss). The result of the interferences was either an arrest or a regression of the ego and of object relations. Both followed from the prematurely intensified drive-state.

A DEVELOPMENTAL APPROACH TO THE SYMPTOMATOLOGY OF ADULT PSYCHOSES

In this section the phenomena characterizing adult psychoses are classified in accordance with their similarities to the manifestations of normal and abnormal mental development in early childhood. This approach is based on the hypothesis that the majority of phenomena occurring in adult psychoses result from regressions involving the ego and object relations. These regressions lead to a revival of modes of mental functioning appropriate to early phases of healthy mental life and to the re-emergence of ideational and affective manifestations arising from libidinal fixations in conjunction with abnormal ego states.

Similarities to Early Phases of Object Relations and the Ego

In adult psychoses of acute onset and in chronic schizophrenia (hebephrenia-catatonia) there is a dissolution of the last stages achieved by each developmental line. As is well known, the individual who succumbs to a psychosis did not, prior to the illness, reach the most advanced stages in all the developmental lines, as a consequence of arrests and fixations of the libido, on the one hand, and deficiencies and deficits in the ego, on the other. In the acute and chronic psychoses referred to here there is a return of early stages of developmental lines so that object relations, emotional self-reliance, and body independence have features almost identical to those found in infants and in young children (see also Chapter 2).

In the case of object relations the patient functions on the level of need satisfaction. The real object is poorly, if at all, represented in the mind. Attitudes to the object follow from an egocentrism little different from that obtaining in the young child. The frustration of needs and wishes leads to aggressive outbursts against the external object or to withdrawal. Self- and object representations and occasionally body boundaries are not clearly differentiated. Thinking proceeds in accordance with wish fulfillment and the pleasure principle.

Many instances have been described in the literature of the egocentrism of acute and chronic psychotic patients. Like young children, these patients judge the external object purely in terms of whether or not needs are satisfied or frustrated. As in the child, the differentiation of self and external object is dependent on subjective experiences of pleasure and unpleasure. The withdrawn, inattentive, chronic schizophrenic patient emerges from a state of self-object confusion to a clear awareness and recognition of the external object as distinct from himself and others when there is unpleasure arising from a bodily need or from the frustration of that need. When there is disappointment the patient is indifferent to the real causes for the frustration, which may lie in factors over which the external object (psychiatrist, nurse, etc.) has no control. The rage against the object converts him into a persecutor.

In psychoses of acute onset and in chronic schizophrenia, independent control of the body and its management is lost (see Chapter 3). These capacities disappear contemporaneously with the ability to engage in adult object relations. Care and responsibility for the body is now handed over to external objects. The situation is identical to that existing in early childhood. Whether or not a return of interest and concern will take place depends on the libidinal cathexis of an external object and on the kind of object relation that develops. In cases of chronic schizophrenia the patient may assume some responsibility for the management of his body as long as an object relation is maintained. Once this is lost there is a return to dependency on others. A comparison can be made with the young child whose capacity for self-feeding and bladder and bowel control is entirely dependent on the object relation. In cases of acute onset it is apparent that the loss of body independence takes place simultaneously with the dissolution of the identifications comprising the superego. As these representations become externalized due to the far-reaching regression,

responsibility for the body is passed over to the environment.

Accompanying these phenomena are others, which can be compared with later stages of infancy. Negativism and resistiveness are common in acute and chronic psychoses. In conjunction with this negativism are other manifestations closely associated with the anal phase of the libido. These are the various inappropriate attitudes to food and eating habits. Patients may refuse to eat; there may be delusions of being poisoned; and valueless articles are sometimes hoarded. Destructiveness and violence, an indifference for the feelings and standards of others, and a lack of concern for cleanliness reflect the absence of reaction formations against anal-sadistic and anal-erotic drives. These pregenital drive derivatives occasionally find an outlet in delusions, which have as content the idea that flatus or bowel movements can damage and destroy the object world. These delusions are little different from the anal-sadistic fantasies of healthy young children.

In many cases of psychosis object cathexis is retained to some degree. In others object constancy is transitorily or permanently achieved as a result of some form of psychotherapeutic intervention. When object constancy is present, the patient may regard the external object as a means of drive control and expect him to function in this respect. Many case reports have described this situation arising in the course of psychotherapy. The external object (psychiatrist, nurse, etc.) is sometimes taken as a model for identification in a manner no different from the way the child takes the parent to serve the same purpose. Cases of chronic schizophrenia have been described where the patient, over a number of years, gradually assumed the behavior and habits of a nurse with whom he had constantly been in contact. These identifications are stable and differ from the passing identifications occurring in acute and chronic psychoses, where the identification is based on a transient merging of self- and object representations — the patient functioning at the level of need satisfaction.

It is in patients in whom object constancy remains that the ego functions continue to operate in accordance with the secondary process. Wish fulfillment is less in evidence, as are direct expressions of the drive derivatives. In these cases delusional ideas occur that are reminiscent of drive attitudes and fantasies of the oedipal period (rescue fantasies, birth fantasies [see Chapter 6]). The content of these delusions is usually altered so that the patient does not recognize the significance of the positive or negative oedipal fantasies, as in the case of the patient who believed that his mother had murdered his father. A further series of delusions, akin to typical fantasies of the latency period, are the family romance fantasies, twin fantasies, and fantasies of the imaginary companion (Nagera, 1970).

The tendency for adult patients to act on their instinctual wishes leads to conflicts with objects in the environment in much the same way as with young children, while, at the level of need satisfaction and in the absence of a cathected object representation (object constancy), insistent demands for oral and genital satisfaction occur. Genital exhibitionism is commonly directed to both homosexual and heterosexual objects. Active and passive sexual wishes are freely expressed, again equally to homosexual and heterosexual objects.

All these manifestations of sexual activity are similar to those observed in the young child at different stages of sexual organization. As with the child, these forms of drive behavior result in external conflicts with ensuing aggression and anxiety.

Those who have treated chronic schizophrenic patients psychotherapeutically have commented that improvements in functioning may occur in object relations and in the ego (Freeman et al., 1958). In object relations there is progress to object (representation) cathexis with a corresponding diminution of egocentrism. The primary process recedes and the secondary process is re-established. These new developments are unstable; they may rapidly disappear, with the patient reverting to the previous level of mental functioning. The causes for this deterioration are similar to those described for borderline states in children by Ekstein and Wallerstein (1954). Disappointments in the therapist, separations from him, and frustration of needs are among the commonest causes for relapse. It would seem that the changes in ego function, whether progressive or retrogressive, depend on the state of the object cathexis.

Ego regression can also be indicated as the cause of the phenomena characterizing a group of mental illnesses where the patient gradually abandons contact with reality. Delusions and hallucinations do not appear. One ego function after another is given up. The patient takes to bed and is immobile, giving up all voluntary movement. Thinking and speech slow up until there is mutism. No attempt is made at self-feeding, and incontinence of urine may occur. Sometimes the patient passes into a state of stupor or semi-coma. After some weeks there is a gradual recovery to the previous healthy state. This tendency to spontaneous remission led to these states being designated "benign stupors" (Hoch, 1915). In two cases observed by the author the regression was initiated by object loss. In the first case a young girl had lost her boy friend; in the second a young pregnant woman had been abandoned by her husband. Similar transient, but severe, ego regressions appear in soldiers on the battlefield.

A comparison can be made between the phenomena appearing in chronic schizophrenia, other psychoses, and benign stupors and those occurring in healthy children as a result of a temporary ego regression (see Chapter 3). In both adult patients and in young children there is a falling back from an advanced to a lower level of ego functioning. In the young child the loss of speech or bladder control may follow illness, separation, or even fatigue. In the adult patients object loss, frustrations, etc., provide the immediate causes.

Reference has already been made to the changes occurring during the treatment of borderline and psychotic children. Ekstein and Wallerstein (1954) have described how logical and coherent speech with its effective and appropriate employment of concepts is replaced by verbal content that has, on the one hand, lost its communicative role and, on the other hand, become intimately connected with affectivity, bodily needs, and wishful fantasies. Even recall may be affected so that the memory of pleasurable experiences is replaced by hallucination in either the auditory, visual, or tactile modality. This transition from secondary to primary process is accompanied by a loss of restraint and control so that there is overactivity, with the carrying over of wishes into actions. When there is a change in the opposite direction (from primary to secondary process), the extent of the advance in ego functioning may be limited, as is the case in childhood psychoses and chronic schizophrenia.

Similarities to Childhood Disorders of Object Relations and the Ego

There are cases of psychosis beginning in early adult life where some of the most dramatic symptoms are almost identical to those recorded by Fraiberg (1952), Sperling (1952), and Furman (1956). Two young adult patients will be briefly referred to in order to illustrate the near identity of the clinical presentations. The first case was a young man of 19, who was terrified of being attacked in such a way as to lead to changes in his body. He believed that his body was developing female characteristics and that he was becoming a hermaphrodite. He thought himself surrounded by creatures of this kind, who were capable of injuring their victims by oral means. In this case oral-sadistic drives and aspects of his bodily representations (femininity) were externalized onto external objects including the author. The fact that object constancy was retained led to the patient's being fearful for the safety of those who were emotionally important to him.

In cases of this kind the anxiety reaches such an intensity that the patient, like the young child, clings to the parents to save him from the persecutors. He is too frightened to stay by himself, and at night insists on sleeping with one of his parents. This was the situation in the second case of an 18-year-old farmer, who suddenly feared that a particular cow was going to bite him. His fear may have been provoked by seeing blood on a calf's mouth. He came to dread being attacked by vampirish creatures who would suck his blood. He complained of weakness due to lack of blood. Prior to falling ill, this young man often indulged in the fantasy of being a vampire by manipulating a denture he wore. At a later stage of the illness he fought against conscious destructive impulses directed against his brother. These wishes had an oral component insofar as they were an expression of his greed and ambition to inherit all his father's property (see Chapter 5).

In their preoccupation with oral-sadistic ideas these two patients were similar to the children previously described. However, in the adult patients these oral-sadistic tendencies had a close connection with fantasies derived from the castration complex. The fears of being bitten and injured orally were akin to similar fears expressed by young children whose sexual curiosity is taken up with the anatomical differences between boys and girls. Such children explain the difference as due to the penis' having been bitten off in the case of the girl. It is more than likely that the delusions of these adult patients had such childhood fantasies as their precursors.

The adult patients also differed from the children described insofar as they were possessed by passive feminine wishes, which influenced the way in which they perceived their bodies. Delusions with this content, the fear of being turned into a woman, are very similar to fears boys express at a time when they have regressed from the phallic phase to the anal-sadistic phase of sexual organization under the impact of castration anxiety. In both young boys and adult patients the anxiety regarding changes in sexual characteristics can also be traced to feminine identifications (the mother) and to a preference for passive libidinal aims.

A further similarity between adult psychotic patients and children like those described by Fraiberg, Sperling, and Furman is their animistic and omnipotent thinking. In both child and adult patients every wish, emotion, percept, and sensation is associated with environmental events. At the same time, the object world is endowed with physical attributes as well as wishes, fantasies, and anxieties. This movement both inward and outward follows from the absence of a well-developed boundary between the self and the object world.

In psychoses of acute onset and in chronic schizophrenia the ego regression that is in part responsible for the magical and animistic thinking also leads to phenomena that closely resemble manifestations of borderline states in children. As in the case reported by Furman (1956), the adult psychotic patient cannot, at the height of the illness, intentionally and purposively describe traumatic events from the past. Instead the patient utters phrases and sentences that are disconnected and apparently meaningless, or he reports on hallucinatory voices. Like the child, the adult patient no longer feels these mental contents as memories — they have lost their "ego" quality and are regarded as something strange and foreign. Sometimes, as with Furman's patient, it is possible, with the recovery of the ego, for the adult patient to recall at will those memories that previously only had an alien, automatic form of expression.

Borderline and psychotic children frequently show similarities to adult patients with respect to disturbances of motility. All kinds of motility disorder have been reported. In all cases, whether adult or child, the motility disorder is associated with a regressed state of the ego. Children have been described who present signs indistinguishable from catatonic manifestations. Mittelman (1954), for example, has described a child who showed cataleptic signs following object loss.

Developmental Aspects of Symptom Formation

The similarities between adult psychotic patients and severe "neuroses," borderline states, and psychoses in young children support the hypothesis that the symptomatology of adult cases results from a regression of the libido (object relations and sexual organization) to fixation points and from the revival of pathological ego states. The evidence available from cases of adult psychoses that have been studied and treated intensively points to the likelihood that the libidinal fixations were the result of environmental interferences (Nagera, 1966). It is commonplace to find, in the history of psychotic patients, that during childhood they sustained separations, seductions, hospitalizations, parental deaths, and overstimulation in general. These occurrences must have had a traumatic effect. The delusional content in adult cases, in conjunction with the kinds of fantasies found in abnormal childhood mental states, supports the view that it is the libidinal fixations that provide much of the predisposition necessary for the development of a psychosis in adulthood (see Chapter 6). It is impossible in the adult case to determine exactly when and how the environmental interference made its impact — whether the fixation appeared directly or whether a latent period intervened before it emerged coincident with the anxieties of a new developmental stage.

As in the healthy or neurotic individual, the libidinal fixations were left behind with the advance of the libido. The external conflicts resulting from the environmental interferences were internalized. With their decathexis, the conflicts inherent in the fixations no longer had the capacity to sustain a danger situation as they had done previously. Only when regression of the libido occurred as a defense against an internal danger arising in early adult life were the fixations recathected. The outcome was a new danger situation, this time in relation to the fixated drive representations.

The mechanism of symptom formation in adult psychoses appears akin to that leading to adult neuroses insofar as the factors leading to the immediate conflicts (death wishes, object loss, etc.) do not find a solution on the developmental level on which they occur:

> . . . neither adult nor child neurotics deal with their problems on the developmental level on which they arise. Faced by losses, disappointments, frustrations or conflicts in his mature sex life, the adult neurotic abandons his genitality and returns, i.e., regresses to the polymorph, infantile sexual urges which have preceded it. The child, in similar quandaries, does likewise and returns from the oedipal-phallic level to its precursors. Both the adult and the child find themselves in the same situation. They are confronted with urges and phantasies which had been age adequate at the oral- or anal-sadistic level of development but which, re-cathected at this later stage, are

rejected by the personality as unacceptable and therefore rouse deep seated anxieties. The latter have to be defended against and their content compromised with [A. Freud, 1971].

In adult psychoses an additional factor operates to bring about the distinctive symptomatology over and above the regression of the libido as it affects sexual organization and object relations. The results of the ego regression are not limited to the disorganization of volition, self-awareness, conceptual thought, speech, memory, and perception and to the reappearance of animistic, magical, and concrete thinking, with cognition following closely in the path chosen by the drive representations. In addition, there are other phenomena that, in view of the evidence obtained from the treatment of adult and child patients, must be regarded as arising from pathological ego states (Federn, 1952) revived by the ego regression. These pathological ego states comprise forms of ego functioning that occurred in early childhood as a response to and a means of adaptation to external and internal stresses. This is well illustrated by the child treated by Furman (1956), in whom the ego functions were subject to serious deviation as a consequence of the intensification of the libidinal drives following a sexual trauma.

Object loss can also have a profound effect on ego functioning, as in the following instance. After separation from his mother a three-year-old child reacted by telling everyone that his mother would soon come for him, put on his coat and hat, and take him home (A. Freud, 1939-1945). This repeated statement was accompanied by a nodding of the head. During the ensuing days his head nodding became more pronounced and his claim that his mother would come increasingly repetitive. After being asked to stop, he gradually replaced the spoken words by lip movements and by gestures representing the putting on of his coat and hat. These stereotyped movements dominated his behavior, even interfering with dressing and eating. He would stand in a corner moving his lips and hands, quite isolated and apart from the other children. Such observations encourage the idea that many of the abnormalities of ego function occurring in psychoses — inattention, disorders of speech form, catalepsy and other motility disorders, etc. — have their origin in the response of an infantile ego to stimuli with which it was unable to deal. The dissolution of the adult ego as a result of the morbid process leads to the exposure of the pathological childhood ego state.

When the ego regression is rapid, as in psychoses of acute onset, and far-reaching, as in chronic schizophrenia, those defenses capable of permanently changing the aim and object of a drive are seriously deranged. Repression, reaction formation, and projection therefore play little part in the defense instituted to deal with the regressed drive derivatives. A conflict occurs between the drives and the defenses, but this conflict is entirely different in nature from that appearing in a neurosis. The difference is caused by the regression of the ego, which disturbs the distinction between self and object, with a resulting confusion between mental and environmental events and the real relation between them. The externalization of mental representations, on the one hand, and the assimilation of the object world, on the other hand, comes to be employed defensively whenever necessary during the normal development of the child. While defenses based on this process (externalization, primary forms of identification) cannot prevent the individual from becoming aware of the unwelcome derivative of the drive in question, it can be disowned by having its stimulus located in an external object. The result is that the conflict between the drive and the forces opposing it is no longer centered in the individual. An internalized conflict has been replaced by an external one.

Thus, the symptoms of a psychosis differ from those of a neurosis in that they are not compromise formations derived from an internalized conflict. In this respect, psychotic symptoms are akin to those appearing in young children prior to the differentiation of the ego and superego from the id. In both adult and child patients, many of the symptoms are directly related to external conflicts. Neurotic symptoms based on a compromise between the drive representations and the ego forces opposing them serve to prevent the repressed wishes from reaching consciousness. In psychoses of acute onset and in chronic schizophrenia the defense does not succeed in this respect; it only alters the source of origin of the drive or self-representation. In the adult and child patients described earlier, destructive impulses of an oral-sadistic nature found expression in consciousness and sometimes in action. At the same time, these patients were afraid of being attacked themselves. The destructive tendencies had been generalized to the object world. If the persecutory anxieties had been the result of projection, then there would have been no inclination or wish to attack the object. It is a fact of observation that projection is only to be found as a defense in those psychoses where the ego is almost wholly intact — that is, in the different varieties of paranoid psychosis (see Chapter 4).

The developmental approach to symptomatology avoids the danger of overestimating the significance of the form and content of the clinical phenomena. Identity among symptom presentations does not indicate identity of causes. As has already been mentioned, psychotic symptoms in adulthood can be likened to the "neurotic" symptoms of infancy and early childhood. The cause of a childhood phobia, for example, depends on the degree to which object relations and the ego had developed at the point in time when the phobia appeared. In the case of a psychotic symptom in an adult, its causes will depend on how far object relations and the ego have regressed from the highest level achieved prior to the illness. In other words, the descriptive approach to the symptomatology of psychoses must be superceded by the metapsychological one. This principle has already been postulated and employed by Anna Freud (1970) in her evaluation of the manifold forms of childhood symptomatology.

The persecutory symptom complex may be taken to illustrate how a group of symptoms with similar characteristics can have different causes. Persecutory ideas may arise because of the egocentric orientation brought about by the regression of the libidinal component in object relations. The patient complains that the object (psychiatrist, nurse, other patient, etc.) is responsible for unwanted thoughts, feelings, physical symptoms, etc. Here the accusations are found to be closely related to a failure on the object's part to reduce the level of unpleasure created in the patient by needs and wishes (see Profile II). Persecutory ideas may also follow from the externalization of unwanted drive derivatives with a resulting attribution of responsibility. As has already been mentioned, this defense is facilitated by the regressed state of the ego.

Again, persecutory ideas may result from the projection of libidinal wishes (see Profile III). A further cause of persecutory delusions is the externalization of the superego (see Profile I). In both of these last instances the ego organization retains much of its integrity. The defense is effective insofar as drive derivatives do not enter consciousness. Nevertheless the basic nature of the defense is such as to promote external conflicts in place of the internalized conflicts that existed prior to the illness.

CHAPTER 2

Manic-Depressive Psychosis and Childhood Psychopathology

In the last chapter attention was drawn to the similarities between adult psychoses and childhood borderline states and psychoses. In this chapter the phenomena that may appear in manic-depressive syndromes will be described and evaluated from the metapsychological viewpoint. This will be followed by a review of several cases of childhood mental disturbance drawn from the literature and from reports of the Hampstead Clinic. A comparison will be made between the adult and child cases.

MANIC-DEPRESSIVE PSYCHOSIS

The following case, illustrating the manic-depressive psychosis, demonstrates all the phenomena that may occur in the different manic-depressive syndromes. Only a small number of cases conform to the textbook types of mania and depression. The majority present, at some stage of the illness, one or more of the features observed in this particular case.

The patient, Mrs. A., a 40-year-old woman, was first admitted to mental hospital at the beginning of 1971. She had recently been divorced after 16 years of marriage. She had two children: a boy of seven and a girl of five, who was mentally retarded. A spontaneous abortion had occurred between the two pregnancies. After the second birth, Mrs. A. had developed a deep vein thrombosis, which had culminated in a pulmonary embolism. She had been seriously ill for some months.

Most of her married life had been spent in the United States, where she and her husband had emigrated from Northern Ireland. Her husband had had considerable success in a managerial position and this had led to their moving from time to time. Following the birth of her daughter, the patient had been easily upset. (At first admission in 1971 details of the child's serious failure to develop and its effect on Mrs. A. were not available.) After the daughter's birth the husband had been frequently away from home on business. This had been distressing to the patient, particularly when it became apparent that he was having an affair with his secretary. This had resulted in Mrs. A. leaving the United States, applying for a divorce, and returning alone to Northern Ireland, leaving the children in America. In the two-year period prior to her return to Northern Ireland in 1970, she had had two admissions to a psychiatric hospital in the United States. Details were not available regarding the clinical state on those occasions, but it seemed likely that she had been acutely distressed and possibly overactive.

The patient was the eldest of five children — there being four younger brothers. The youngest brother had suffered from nervous symptoms and there was some question of his being a homosexual. Her father, a quiet, reserved man, had died in 1968. Mrs. A. had returned to Northern Ireland for the funeral. She had been very upset as she had been very attached to him. No data were available regarding the effect of the father's death on Mrs. A. and its possible relation to her mental breakdown. Her mother was still alive. The patient claimed that she and her mother had always got on well together.

The Manic Phases

At the first admission in January 1971, Mrs. A. presented an extreme degree of psychomotor overactivity. She talked at speed, and it was impossible to hold her attention. She was elated in mood and expressed omnipotent ideas: "I am God," she said. She was easily distracted; the slightest stimulus of any kind drew her attention. She talked as if her divorce had not occurred: "My husband loves me.... I can get my children back any time." The content of her talk was limited to her grandiose ideas and to her husband and children. The distractibility was influenced by this thought content. When the telephone rang, she abandoned the topic with which she was preoccupied saying, "That's my husband, to tell me he's here." Typical of her utterances are the following: "My husband would have been a homosexual but for me"; "My husband does not know who he is and I don't know who I am"; "My husband never had an affair, he loves me"; "My husband is God." Denial and grandiosity alternated with depression of mood and tearfulness — "I divorced him on November 11, 1970, and that is the day I died." While still in tears she continued, "I only wanted to help." Interspersed between remarks about her husband were references to her being God and, on one occasion, quite inappropriately: "My mother never knew her children."

A week after admission the overactivity subsided and

was replaced by a condition in which she was unresponsive, negativistic, and cataleptic. She rarely spoke but on one occasion said, "My mother has put a tape over my mouth and forbade me to speak." This withdrawn state passed after a few days, during which she made such remarks as: "I'll talk if it doesn't hurt anyone"; "I'll die before my mother"; "My mother and brother are to be killed"; "I don't know who I am"; "If I die the whole world crashes"; "I've destroyed my mother."

In the ensuing weeks the overactivity returned. Mrs. A. misidentified the attending psychiatrist as her son, saying that he was now grown up and a doctor. She wanted to kiss the doctor and showed signs of sexual excitement — "I would do anything for you in bed . . . kiss your arse . . . yes, I would kiss you anywhere . . . I would have made a good prostitute . . . I want to enjoy myself . . . I am going to do whatever I like . . . I'm having a burning pain . . . I'm going to have a baby." In succeeding sessions she continually returned to the themes of prostitution and pregnancy. Usually there was genital arousal with expressions of the wish to have coitus with her husband. Mixed with the sexual wishes were references to her divinity. The disorder of thinking frequently affected the manner in which the delusional ideas were expressed — "I am God . . . G.O.D. — D.O.G." and "I am a vain God . . . I don't have veins in my body" (denial of the thrombosis). Apart from the elation of mood, there were periods of anxiety and depression. With regard to the latter she said, "I can't relax because my mother is in the building . . . she's going to stab me." She feared the nurses were going to poison her and shouted, "I don't want to die." Sometimes she wept saying, "I want my family back."

Five weeks after admission to the hospital she once again developed a deep vein thrombosis and was seriously ill for a month. As she recovered, the psychomotor over-activity reappeared with the addition of incontinence of urine. This lasted for three weeks. During this time she claimed she was God, President of the United States, Elizabeth Taylor, etc. There was a direct expression of sexual wishes, as before, and she was frequently violent. The following illustrates how her preoccupation with her husband's lover (named Pamela) influenced the content of her talk:

> What the hell are you doing, Pamela? [misidentifying a nurse to whom she was talking as Pamela] . . . shut that fucking window . . . I'm getting cold . . . Oh God, I am pregnant again and so are you Pamela. . . . How do you think I look, Pamela? [after changing her pajamas] . . . You lousy bitch, Pamela.

A male nurse passed by at this point, which led to the following:

> He gives you contraceptive pills, Pamela . . . I can smell them on you . . . I knew that's why I didn't like you . . . he didn't want you to get pregnant . . . Pamela, you took my Don. Let me see the engagement ring he brought you back from America. He's mine anyway.

During the ensuing weeks a rational note began to appear in her speech. Mrs. A. described how she had become anxious and depressed while in the United States and how her husband had been away for long periods leaving her alone with the children. She had found the retarded daughter difficult to manage. The child had been overactive and could not control her bowel or bladder.

> I'll tell you what made me ill. I was too frustrated. I had to look after two children and my husband was traveling all the time. I had no one to turn to and I couldn't trust anyone . . . she [the daughter] weighed two pounds at birth and was in an incubator like a rat but she survived. She's not mentally retarded she's a genius . . . I was tired and fed up . . . I wanted to get away from the children. I wasn't able to sleep properly for months because my daughter cried all the time. I was fed up and completely exhausted. I went to hospital voluntarily to get some rest. I was depressed . . . there is no such thing as depression . . . that bloody doctor told me I was a schizophrenic and they wanted to send me into an asylum.

At this point the psychosis irrupted in a more forceful fashion, and she continued as follows:

> I'm fed up . . . I'm the Lord . . . I'm Jesus Christ . . . I'm tired of chasing you. . . . Why are you scared of me? . . . Will you marry me? . . . I have to live a new life . . . I know I'm pregnant . . . I haven't had a man for six months . . . I love you . . . my husband married a bloody bitch . . . I'm the Lord . . . I wrote the bloody Bible.

Gradually the psychomotor overactivity abated and she was discharged from the hospital on June 11, 1971. In the weeks prior to discharge no fresh data emerged. Mrs. A. came to recognize that she had been ill and could recall all her grandiose ideas. She wanted to leave the hospital and get work. She succeeded in this respect, working initially in a tea shop. At the end of June 1971, she was seen at an out-patient clinic and appeared to be in reasonable health.

No more was heard of Mrs. A. until July 1972, when her mother contacted the author to say that her daughter, who had returned to the United States at Easter in 1972, was now ill again. During the winter of 1971-1972 Mrs. A. had worked in the canteen of the Army barracks near her home and had saved enough money for her fare to the United States. In the late spring of 1972 her health had broken down and she had been admitted to a mental hospital in the United States. She had been brought back to Northern Ireland by her mother and was readmitted to hospital on July 25, 1972. At the time of this admission she was reasonably calm but her speech was rapid and there was a mild elation of mood.

Mrs. A. gave a good account of all that had happened since leaving hospital in July 1971. She had missed her children and so had decided to get a job in the United States as near to them as possible. She had obtained a position as housekeeper to a man whose wife had committed suicide. There were two children for whom she had been responsible. After working for two months she had arranged a birthday outing for one of the children. While at a shop, she had decided to buy the children whatever they wanted. Her behavior must have appeared unusual and attracted the attention of customers. The manager had been called and she had been escorted home. Later that day she had been hospitalized.

Although less disturbed than at the first admission in 1971, the extent of her disorder was reflected in such questions as "Is that woman really my mother?" (pointing to her mother) and the ease with which omnipotent ideas emerged. She claimed she was perfectly well and was ready for discharge, notwithstanding such statements as: "Christ is back on earth. . . . He is about 62 years old; I know him; he's a genius"; "America is only 12 miles away, that's why it takes such a short time to get there." Shortly after admission she became involved with a male patient, but fortunately this relation did not have any serious consequences. Although not physically overactive, she claimed she was about to initiate important business deals and make a fortune. This state of affairs continued for two months. During this time it was impossible to distract her from her wishful fantasies or to dissipate her denial of the loss of her husband and children. As on the first admission, there was a gradual disappearance of manic symptoms and she was allowed to leave the hospital in October 1972.

The "Depressive" Phase

Mrs. A. was readmitted to hospital on November 5, 1972. The material now to be described emerged during the period from November 1972 to June 1973. At this admission there were signs of a severe depressive illness. She said, "I want to crawl into a hole . . . I do nothing right! . . . I feel scared . . . I want to get away from everything." Her speech consisted of self-reproaches — "I've taken too much out of my mother." She asked, "Have I harmed someone?" She was retarded in both speech and action and this affected her body care; she was unkempt. During a physical examination it was noted that her bladder was distended. On questioning she said she could not be bothered to pass urine. During interviews she had little to say and sometimes seemed on the point of tears —

"You can do nothing for me," she said. Later she expressed shame about the earlier incontinence of urine and embarrassment over the grandiose ideas.

Then abruptly her mood changed. She was angry. In a demanding voice she said, "Do what you have to do. . . . I've been selfish . . . prosecute me." Otherwise she refused to speak — "I can't speak to you." This attitude continued for a few days and then she began to speak more freely. She said she had never been carefree as a child, she was always nervous and frightened of being alone. Her mother had been the dominant parent and was a capable person. Interspersed with these statements were further self-criticisms — "I've disrupted the hospital. . . . I've never done anything right."

Quite suddenly the retardation, which had lessened in intensity, disappeared entirely and was replaced by over-activity and elation. This lasted for one day. The next day she was depressed and then the following day elated once more. During her brief phases of overactivity, prostitution fantasies reappeared along with eroticism. There were also omnipotent ideas — "I've made the world, let them look after it." The elation of mood was accompanied by denials — "My daughter only pretends she's defective." The only unusual event, which occurred on the day the overactivity reappeared, was a visit of a male nurse to the patient's ward. This man had attended the patient during her first attacks of illness, and she had been attracted to him.

The day after the transitory phases of elation and overactivity it was observed that, while Mrs. A. talked at speed and length, her mood was one of depression. There were self-reproaches and tears. She recalled a miscarriage a year after her first child was born. At the time she had been glad because her parents were due to visit and she had not wanted to be pregnant. Nevertheless she had felt guilty. Her theme then changed. She wanted to be a prostitute to get money for her children. There was no justice. Her parents had been poor. They had had to work hard and had little from life. She recalled wishing, as a child, to have lots of children when she married. This brought memories of her mother's last pregnancy when Mrs. A. had been about seven years old.

The depression and self-reproach disappeared. The overactivity, elation, and denials recurred. This time they persisted for about two weeks. Mrs. A. claimed she had established world peace and provided food for everyone. Her daughter was a genius. Toward the end of this phase she seemed to recognize the irrational nature of her thinking, but this was not easily sustained — "I'm at a level where I am not sure what I can do . . . last week I thought I could accomplish anything . . . but I can't help believing I'm Jesus Christ . . . I still feel I am here for a purpose . . . I've been coming back and back and the world is still the same." Some days later her insight seemed better when she said, "What scares me is that I get so high."

Gradually the depressed mood reasserted itself. She was preoccupied with the widespread destructiveness in the world. She wept, "Why can they [men] not change? There is no peace . . . I can't understand it . . . my brother is driving a car with poor brakes. . . . Why can we not make things that are safe? . . . they make things to destroy children . . . like fireworks." Over the ensuing days her speech became slower and her movements limited. Typical of her speech content at this time was the following: "I hate myself because I've never learnt anything. I need to be punished; I was a bad mother and a bad wife." She ran away from the hospital and presented herself at the police station, saying she was a criminal. She became so retarded in speech and action that she had to be fed, washed, and taken to the bathroom (see Chapter 3).

For the first time the psychomotor retardation was accompanied by intense anxiety—"I'm going to be crippled . . . I will never see my family again . . . I am to be blinded because I didn't want any children." She sat with her head bowed and her hands over her eyes—"I've destroyed my mother. . . . The world is coming to an end. . . . I've committed the crime of jealousy . . . my brothers are to be castrated and blinded . . . I wanted to be the only one . . . I only wanted money . . . I didn't love my husband . . . I didn't want children." Occasionally the thought content was disjointed and inappropriate. She began to have difficulty in identifying others correctly; they appeared changed: the author looked different, a nurse was mistaken for her daughter. Her mother and father were dead; they had not been her real parents.

The retardation, which had been constantly present for six weeks, resolved itself. Mrs. A. no longer had to be fed or taken to the bathroom. She said her mother was dead and she was her mother reincarnated. She did not know who the author was—"Years ago you were not a free man, you were a slave . . . you are someone else . . . each time you come in you're someone else." A note of grandiosity appeared—"This ward was booked for me . . . I'm expecting a baby." This mood was immediately replaced by frightening thoughts—"My father was buried alive . . . someone is going to come and blind me and burn my mother's house." Despite Mrs. A.'s depressed mood, her speech was fluent although the content was disordered — "This was built as an Old People's Home . . . the Chinese venerate their elders." Denial of unpleasant realities dominated her thinking — "There is no such thing as cancer . . . there is no unemployment . . . there are no mental defectives." This was quickly followed by anxious thoughts — "I won't be here tomorrow, I'm to be tarred and thrown in a ditch . . . I'm to be burned in a well . . . my family will have no home." One of her many remarks about the author illustrated the disorder of her thinking. Commenting on the fact that he had injured his finger while trying to close a window, she said, "Was it the window sash? Christ wore a robe with a sash."

The combination of wish-fulfilling ideas, self-reproaches, and anxieties continued for a further week, as illustrated by the following: "Mongoloid children are very clever . . . there are no divorces . . . only remarriages . . . people can travel the whole world over . . . they can go and see their grandchildren . . . the slums are all to be cleared . . . there is enough oil in the world to fill all the heaters." Concurrently she accused herself of killing her mother, eating everyone else's food, and injuring the other patients.

During the ensuing days her anxiety increased in intensity. The following exemplifies her speech content: "I'm to be tortured and burnt alive"; "They're going to make me eat shit"; "I'm to be cut to pieces." At this time she was acutely distressed and agitated — "I'm a monster; they've rats and cats in a sewer under the ward; they're collecting vomit and shit . . . they're going to bomb the churches." During one of these periods she suddenly shouted out, "I claw, scratch, and bite . . . I'm dangerous to people . . . my husband is dead . . . they're giving

children poison; they're making treacle with rat poison."
From time to time she expressed fears for the author's
health — "Are you going to die from a heart attack? It's
my fault ... you're tired ... don't stay with me ...
death follows wherever I go." At a subsequent session she
said, "I'm not washing myself, I'm stinking inside and out
... they're collecting urine, dog shit, and making candy
out of it and selling it to the children."

Throughout these weeks she was completely unresponsive to anything the author said. When told that he
would be away for three days, she continued with the
theme of children being poisoned and mutilated. There
was a repetition of the fear of her destructiveness — "I'm a
deadly weapon ... I'm going down the sewer with the
rats." The predominant affect throughout this time was
anxiety — "It's a nightmare ... what's going to happen?"

Three days before the short interruption in the sessions Mrs. A. became calmer and was less of a management problem for the nursing staff. She was depressed in
mood. The self-reproaches reappeared but were less
dramatic and intense. The anxiety had receded. She
began to question the author about his personal life: How
many children did he have? Where did he live? How long
would he stay at the hospital? She said, "I never did
anything deliberately to hurt people." She expressed a
wish to return home, because as long as she remained in
the hospital the patients would suffer. This calm period
lasted for about two weeks. Her speech, although limited,
was coherent and comprehensible. During one session she
wept, blaming herself for having destroyed her children.
She constantly asked to be discharged from the hospital.
On other occasions she spontaneously referred to childhood, saying she had been a solitary child, always

daydreaming. She wished to return to her early childhood and start again. During another session she referred to things that had happened in her early life and yet could never have happened. Prevailed upon to explain what she meant, she said she remembered being left with her aunt. She had not been allowed out but recalled wearing woolen stockings. Then she said, "That must have happened to someone else." Occasionally there were denials similar in content to those described earlier. She prophesied difficult times for everyone. There were self-reproaches — "I suppose I wanted to be an only child and have everything for myself."

Immediately prior to the end of this calm phase Mrs. A. appeared brighter and more cheerful. There were no self-criticisms. She talked more freely and frequently made comments about the author — "You were transferred here when my father died." Later in the same session — "You're thinking of retiring." This followed the author's saying, not for the first time, that she feared he would leave. She seemed to agree because later she said, "You'll be transferred." However, it was reported that during the subsequent weekend Mrs. A. had been restless and generally disturbed. When seen, she was extremely agitated and frightened — "Don't spend time with me . . . I haven't kept my pact with the Jews." She claimed that money left for her on trust had been stolen. In the course of an interview later in the day she was incontinent of urine. She was afraid the author would be injured. It is possible that Mrs. A.'s disturbed state may have been provoked by the extreme restlessness of another patient.

Mrs. A. was reported by the nursing staff as being very aggressive. She attacked another patient and bit a nurse. There was overactivity and pressure of talk. The following illustrates her speech content:

> I'm hurting you ... I'm hurting children ... they'll have their toes cut off ... find a safe place to go ... they say it's treatment day; a new doctor comes and the price goes up and my children are not cared for ... you are going to get poorer and poorer ... they're going to tar and feather you.... What do the Jews wear when they go to church?... You are going to be thrown in the well and burn in hell and suffer.... Did you ever read Jesus Christ?... You are my second coming.

The next day she struck another patient. To the author she said, "I make you work day and night ... I didn't give you anything to hit back with ... prices are going up and you are working for nothing." Her speech was disconnected—"these children I maimed ... oh, God ... you will never be free again."

The overactivity subsided. During one session she sat at the desk, picked up a pen, and said, "I can't prescribe anything for you ... go away from me ... I'm making you ill ... I won't do anything to myself because I'll kill someone else ... we're sitting on a gold mine ... there's a sewage tank under this building." Gradually she became silent; then she said, "I don't understand ... how do you make a baby?"

On the first session of a new week she was restless again and frightened. She said, "I'm going to burn you ... scoop out your eyes ... you're getting weaker and weaker ... I'm scared of everything ... I shit on everything I have ever seen ... I'll scare you too ... I'll hit you over the head . . . go away . . . I'll kill you." Interspersed with these utterances was the statement, "I promised everyone I'd be their God." At times her speech content was determined by the sound rather than the meaning of a word—"Everytime I waken I hear the birds . . . lady-birds . . . Johnson birds." During these sessions she was inclined, when silent, to imitate the author's movements. "I want everyone to suffer like me," she said and then picked up a cloth and tried to put it over the author's face. She walked up and down the room saying, "You're my father . . . I don't remember you . . . I was born millions of years ago." Suddenly she began to shout, "Get out of here . . . I am going to whip you to death." In this and following sessions she made several efforts to touch the author's face.

As this disturbed period came to an end, Mrs. A. was told that there would be a break in the sessions for 10 days. There was no reaction to this information. She had now become calmer but was mostly silent. When she did speak, it was to repeat that she was confused and did not know how to do anything. She was not even sure when she needed to pass urine. She gradually became frightened again, especially fearing that she had harmed the author. "I have destroyed you . . . I have given you too many patients . . . you never enjoy yourself . . . no one looks after you . . . you are uncomfortable." The self-reproaches were accompanied by the belief that she was unclean and dirty. She was uncertain as to whether it was herself or the author who was to be killed.

On resuming the meetings after the 10-day break Mrs. A. was found to be withdrawn and retarded. During the previous seven days she had been incontinent of urine. When asked about this, she exclaimed in a startled voice, "It's a fire ... the world is in flames—they're burning babies." She was silent for a while and then shouted out, "I've eaten everyone's food." The next day she announced, "I've eaten the world, the world has come to an end." She refused to sit down and would either walk about the room or stand motionless for long periods. The following weekend she was found to be incontinent of feces as well as of urine. She was mute. The nursing staff reported that she had suddenly attacked a nurse during the weekend. During the period of the break and immediately afterward Mrs. A. had to be fed and taken to the lavatory. Control of her bowel movements was gradually re-established but not control of her bladder function. On two successive days she urinated in the ward in front of other patients and visitors. As before, she was unable to give an explanation for this behavior. However, at the session following an episode of incontinence of urine, she shouted, "I did it again ... I caused an explosion ... I'm a monster ... I put out people's eyes ... I burn children." During the sessions she continued to stand motionless, her lips moving without audible speech. She attacked another nurse with such violence and persistence that a male nurse had to be called to detach her from her victim.

Her speech continued to be limited in quantity with the content as before—"I've killed you ... my hands are for scratching ... I've made a monkey out of you ... I've demanded everything." Later in the same session she said, "Today was to be my wedding day ... I went to the pictures with my father ... I was raped." It was impossible to get her to enlarge on these associations. The only response was — "You're a lazy bugger." At this point she rushed out of the room to go to the bathroom to pass urine.

Two weeks elapsed from the time of the break in the session until urinary control completely returned. Questions as to why she had been incontinent were ignored. When her mother came to visit, Mrs. A. ignored her, saying she was not her mother. The mother told the author that her daughter had told her he was dead. At a later session Mrs. A. expressed this idea: "You're dead . . . I killed you . . . I put your eyes out with scissors . . I did it again . . . I killed you . . . I ate you all up . . . I made you too fat but I couldn't deliver a baby . . . I tortured you . . . I cut your hands off."

Metapsychological Assessment

Prior to the onset of the psychosis Mrs. A. had achieved a reasonable level of psychosocial and psychosexual adjustment. The loss of her family acted as the immediate cause of the illness. The ensuing dissolution of adult object relations was accompanied by the symptoms of the manic attack. During the attack there was a generalized loss of psychic structure. Secondary-process functioning was replaced by the primary process, as evidenced in the free expression of drive derivatives, the predominance of wish fulfillment, and the impact of condensations and displacements on cognitive processes. With the dissolution of the secondary process, the cathexis of real external object representations was lost, but not those of husband and children. This facilitated the predominance of wish fulfillment over reality judgments. While the attack continued, self- and object representations were subject to a merging process, as were different object representations. With regard to the former, Mrs. A. merged self and husband, self and nurse, and self and author. Nurse and husband's lover, doctor and son were condensed in the case of the latter.

In the course of the manic attack, pregenital wishes appeared as well as a series of fantasies, some of which were typical of the oedipal period. A rescue fantasy (see Chapter 6) could be discerned in her claim that she had saved her husband from homosexuality. Prostitution and pregnancy fantasies were also present. The sexual wishes followed active aims and this, in conjunction with the rescue fantasy, suggested that, in the course of childhood development, fixations of the libido had occurred at the phallic level with the mother as its object. The masculine orientation of the libido (see Chapter 4) was also revealed in the redeemer fantasies and in the delusion that she was President of the United States.

In the manic state internalized conflicts were in abeyance due to the dissolution of the ego. Nevertheless the free expression of needs and wishes periodically gave rise to anxiety, during which Mrs. A. feared being stabbed by her mother and poisoned by the nurses. These fears were in keeping with earlier expressed hostility to the mother and to the nurses condensed with her husband's lover. At no time during the manic phase did she express homosexual interests, indicating that the homosexual wishes were weakly cathected in contrast to the heterosexual drives. This is of interest as Mrs. A.'s belief in her husband's homosexuality probably resulted from the externalization of such an unconscious tendency within herself.

The post-manic period began with depressive manifestations, but these were soon supplemented and re-placed by other phenomena. At the onset of this "depres-sive" phase, psychic structure had been regained, as indicated by the return of secondary-process functioning and the restoration of the superego. A sense of guilt and self-criticism were the leading clinical manifestations. Real object representations had regained their cathexis, as had the destructive fantasies for which she held herself responsible. In this limited sphere reality testing was lost. It appeared as if the overt aggression of the manic phase had been introjected into the superego.

This depressed state was followed by a gradual dis-solution of ego and superego. Concurrently there was a loss of reality as a result of the withdrawal of cathexis from real external object representations. Mrs. A. no longer identified real persons correctly. She said her parents had not been her real parents and believed the world had come to an end. Anxiety was the predominant affect—she feared punishments of different kinds and described herself as destructive and dangerous—"I claw, scratch and bite."

For a short period these manifestations subsided and the reintegration of psychic structures seemed to have taken place. She returned to self-blame, indicating the renewed activity of the superego. There was a recathexis of real objects with concern for the author, nurses, and other patients. However, this was only a passing phase and soon she returned to that state where primary-process activity and anxiety led to the leading clinical manifesta-tions. Destructive wishes were no longer confined to thought but extended to action. She attacked and bit nurses and other patients. As previously, the action of the primary process resulted in her believing in the truth of her destructive wishes. Thinking and perception were influenced by condensations and displacements.

The destructive fantasies had an oral and anal content, and this pregenital sadism was associated with the incontinence of both urine and feces. The sadistic fantasies were paralleled by a dread of bodily injury and mutilation. It can safely be surmised that such fears were a consequence of the externalization of the pregenital sadistic wishes. In support of such a hypothesis is the absence of an effective ego and superego and the predominance of the primary process. Under such circumstances the fears could not spring from a compromise between internal conflicting forces or from the action of projection.

When the manic phases are compared with these latter forms of the depressive phase, similarities and differences immediately emerge. In both the primary process was operative with the loss of reality and oral wishes played a prominent part — in one the libidinal, in the other the destructive. Anal-sadistic wishes were prominent in the depressive but not in the manic phase. Taken together the data point to fixations present at the pregenital and phallic levels of the libido. In the manic phase phallic wishes with active aims predominated, which, once lost, were replaced by the sadistic wishes of the depressive phase. During both psychotic periods material emerged that pointed to the kinds of internalized conflict that must have been present when the patient was mentally healthy. These conflicts revolved around the mother, the siblings, and penis envy.

In Mrs. A.'s case the manic attack precipitated by

object loss was followed by depression — a not infrequent occurrence. In other cases object loss leads to a circular illness in which depression is followed by mania. These instances provide an excellent opportunity to observe that the identification with the lost object that characterizes the depressed state continues into the manic phase (Freeman, 1971). In mania, whether subsequent or prior to depression, object cathexis (object constancy) still gives precedence to identification. Such object cathexes as appear operate under the primary process as evidenced by the predominance of wishful thinking and acts based on this. Two possible courses may follow. Recovery may occur if the libidinal cathexis withdraws from the representation of the lost object merged with the self and, adopting secondary-process characteristics, invests real external objects, new and old. Alternatively, and as in Mrs. A.'s case, object cathexis may give way entirely to identification with the ambivalently regarded object, leading to depression.

Clinical observation indicates that in those manic states precipitated by frustrations and disappointments there is little sign of the typical "merging" (identification) found where the manic depression follows object loss. These and other considerations suggest that the movement of libido from object to self in the face of object loss — object cathexis to identification — is characteristic of only one particular category of the conditions described by the term "mania." Such a hypothesis is consistent with the idea that the psychomotor element is the feature common to all manic states and that the other phenomena are dependent on the presence of constellations specific for the individual case.

THE ADULT PSYCHOSIS AND
CHILDHOOD PSYCHOPATHOLOGY

It is well known that the symptoms and signs of manic and depressive psychoses vary between patients and even within one patient. This was true in the case described. The classical symptoms — the alteration in psychomotility to overactivity or retardation, the change in affect to elation or depression, and the disorder of thought content, either grandiose or self-depreciatory — do not always appear together, nor is the movement of the phenomena in the same direction. Overactivity is not necessarily accompanied by elation. Depression of mood is not always associated with psychomotor retardation. Anxiety resulting in restlessness and agitation (a form of psychomotor overactivity) may appear alongside depression of mood. Again, psychomotor retardation may be associated with grandiose ideas rather than with self-criticism. It is also true that overactivity may be confined to action with a virtual absence of speech. Delusional self-reproaches may occur with psychomotor overactivity.

In order to reconcile these different clinical presentations with the ideal types of mania and depression, Kraepelin (1904) introduced the category of intermediate forms or mixed manic-depressive psychoses. He described an "anxious or depressive mania," an "excited depression," an "unproductive mania," a "manic stupor," a "depression with flight of ideas," and an "inhibited mania." This concept of disease entities presenting a mixture of manic and depressive phenomena was criticized in detail by MacCurdy (1925). He proposed that the different phenomena appearing in the course of manic-depressive illness are reactions to intrapsychic complexes.

When all the phenomena, which together constitute the manic-depressive psychosis, are regarded as reactions to intrapsychic changes rather than as expressions of cerebral disease entities, their comparison with certain kinds of childhood psychopathology becomes feasible. The syndromes of manic-depressive psychosis consist of manifestations that are loosely connected together. Alterations in internal or external circumstances can lead to symptomatic changes and thus to different syndromes. It is important to add that persecutory ideas are by no means uncommon during the course of a manic-depressive illness. Such ideas were pronounced in the case of Mrs. A. These anxieties range from the fear of being observed to fears of injury, bodily mutilation, and death. The persecutory fears, like the other abnormalities of thought content (self-depreciation, self-aggrandizement) and the disorders of mood, rarely persist throughout the illness.

This fluidity of symptoms characterizing the adult case is even more pronounced in childhood mental disorders. It is this that precludes the emergence of syndromes that can be regarded as equivalent to those of the adult psychoses. From this standpoint it follows that there is no qualitative difference between the phenomena occurring in adult and child patients other than that the two categories have a different developmental status.

MANIC-DEPRESSIVE-LIKE PHENOMENA IN CHILDHOOD

In adult patients the disturbances of mood, guilt feelings, and ideas of omnipotence are ephemeral when compared with the disorder of psychomotility. They are not only the most prominent but also the most persistent signs of the illness. They frequently initiate the psychosis, the patient presenting with restless overactivity affecting movement and speech or with varying degrees of retardation of the same functions, so giving an impression of bewilderment and confusion. It is only because the disorders of mood (elation, depression) and thought content (grandiosity, self-depreciation, persecutory fears) periodically come into association with the psychomotor disturbances that these conditions (manic depressions) can be set apart from the other forms of psychotic illness.

The study of manic-depressive-like phenomena in children can start with the disturbances of psychomotility. Hyperactivity is frequent in children regarded as suffering from severe "neuroses," borderline states, and psychoses. This hyperactivity makes itself manifest during therapy and is often accompanied by sexual manifestations of different kinds. At other times the hyperactivity is replaced by a symptom complex of withdrawal, which includes a kind of psychomotor retardation. The question is: what kinds of phenomena appear concurrently with the hyperactivity and with the withdrawal, and how far do they resemble the signs and symptoms of adult manic depressions? In order to answer this question, several cases of childhood mental disorder will be cited from the literature and from case reports of the Hampstead Clinic.

Rochlin (1959) has described a syndrome of hyperactivity in boys aged between two and five years. This hyperactivity was reported by the parents as continuous over days, weeks, and months. It was usually associated with destructiveness and with self-critical and self-punitive thought and action. Rochlin concluded that, although "There were . . . individual variations between one child and another, as a group the similarity was striking. The relationship to objects was characteristically destructive and sadistic, aggressive without any respite, and the same impulses were directed toward the self, which was typically devalued, denigrated and pronounced worthless" (1959, p. 307).

In an earlier paper Rochlin (1953) described the case of a four-year-old boy, who was referred for treatment because he could not settle in or conform to a school group and because he appeared withdrawn and self-preoccupied. He was only at peace when he was able to sit in a cupboard with a fur coat, belonging to his mother, which he rubbed against his cheek. He was impulsive, restless, and unpredictable. At home he was overactive and destructive; he threw things about, tore the wallpaper, and destroyed any article he was not interested in. Sometimes he soiled his bed or defecated on the floor. He was indifferent to his mother's attempts to comfort him; instead he would go to the cupboard where the fur coat was kept.

At the first consultation the child's hyperactivity was revealed in the way he clambered over his mother and in her anxiety lest he damage the contents of the room during his aimless wandering. The first attempts to gain the child's attention were fruitless. Eventually Rochlin sat with him in a dark cupboard. After some weeks he was willing to emerge and never again expressed a wish to return to the cupboard. In the consulting room he threw objects about and was generally destructive. Sometimes he remained silent for several sessions and, when he did speak, it was only to utter a phrase without completing the sentence.

After a period of time an imaginary game developed in which he was to be thrown into the grate, down the stairs, or out of the window. He continued to be destructive, and whatever he did or said was rushed through at speed. At one point he took to beating himself; this notably occurred at the height of his destructive attacks on toys or other articles. At home he was observed to bite his toys and his mother as well. He talked of eating her. In play during treatment, he chewed the heads of dolls representing his mother, his sister, himself, and the therapist. Later in the treatment he violently attacked the mother doll. He was overactive, hurrying in speech from one item to the next. This caused him to become breathless and hoarse. At times he was quite frenzied: shouting, squirming, clutching his penis, and smearing his face with saliva. At home, during this time, he masturbated frequently and ostentatiously. He was either considerate to his mother or attacked her. He said he was bad and wanted to be punished. He asked his mother to cut off his finger and actually cut his hair and beat himself.

Wolfenstein (1955) treated a boy, aged five years, who not only showed hyperactivity but also laughed incessantly. The boy was brought to a child guidance clinic because he was quite unmanageable. His mother, who had been abandoned by the father, constantly threatened to have him placed in a foster home. Even when reassured by the therapist that she would not send him away, he was still provocative, destructive, and overactive. At nursery school he was frightened of the other children but aggressive toward the teachers. Later he seemed to develop an attachment to one teacher but still could not remain in the nursery school if he thought his mother had left to go home. He would run wildly into the street, oblivious to the dangers of the traffic.

It was during therapy that Wolfenstein first heard the little boy's laughter. The laughing was initially expressed in the context of a game intended to overcome separation fears. In the game the boy became the one who left. Wolfenstein suggested the laughter was a substitute for his tears when left by his mother at school. During the ensuing months the laughter increased in intensity and assumed a crazy or mad quality. This "mad laughter" began in connection with the word "odor." It transpired that the boy was in conflict with his mother over cleanliness. This was reflected in his need to mess his own house and the consulting room. During therapy he would ask the therapist to scold his toy pig. The pig was to be told it was bad and to clean up the mess. He shouted, "Odor," and this was followed by laughter. There were attacks on the mother.

He was destructive both at home and in the treatment room. He would spill the tobacco torn from cigarettes onto the floor, shout, " 'It's duty on the floor,' " pick it up, and throw it over the therapist's dress. Then he said he wanted to go into the room where his mother was and " 'giggle' " over the floor. This development culminated in his suddenly exposing his penis and urinating over the therapist. He ran to get water to clean things up but spilled some on the floor. He said a Pinocchio doll had spilled it and the therapist should scold the doll.

Wolfenstein proposed that the "giggling" and the laughter allowed the release of genital, hostile, and excretory wishes as well as being a defense against the fear of object loss. The boy, it should be added, had been subject to much sexual overstimulation by his mother.

The withdrawal, self-criticism, and wish for punishment reported by Rochlin in his cases has also been described by Bornstein (1935) in a child of two and a half years of age. This child presented with intense anxiety, which was most pronounced at bedtime. She could not be induced to lie down and would stand fearfully in her cot. Quite soon after the treatment began it was noticed that she blamed herself for all kinds of trivial mishaps. She said, in her childish way, that she had hurt her mother. Then she added that the cook and her father were also hurt. When the treatment had proceeded some distance and her fear of having hurt her genitalia had been discussed, it was possible to discern a fear that her grandfather might take her mother away. After this had been raised, the child's behavior changed. She was no longer willing to work with her mother. She became hostile, trying to kick and bite her. Constipation appeared and she soiled her bed with feces. Up to this time she had been clean at night. The incontinence and the anxiety pointed to a conflict over cleanliness and bowel control. The child feared giving way to her anal wishes for fear of losing her mother.

The last two cases to be described are taken from the records of the Hampstead Clinic. The first is the child Nettie treated by Elkan (1973) and the second the child Basil treated by Kennedy (1964). Hyperactivity was a prominent manifestation in both cases. Nettie was nine and a half years old when referred by her school because of her attitude to learning and her erratic and unpredictable behavior. Hyperactivity and a profuse flow of fantasies appeared right from the start of treatment. The fantasies were expressed in stories, games, and acting. Usually the fantasies' content consisted of situations in which she was in danger or was undertaking a rescue. At the time of referral Nettie had an imaginary friend Mr. Collettie, who was blamed for causing her various upsets — for example, " 'He stops me from hearing' " — and on whom responsibility was placed for her own misdemeanors. According to the mother, Nettie was frequently withdrawn and self-preoccupied.

During the treatment the young patient seemed to be in no doubt as to what constituted fantasy and what reality. She expressed grandiose-like ideas — " 'I'm marvelous; I'm ruler of the world.' " She was inclined to overvalue herself and at such times reality testing may have been breached. One day, when working with a knife and balsa wood, she exclaimed, " 'Look at me, look at my marvelous craftsmanship.' " Her overactivity was accompanied by aggressiveness and sexual excitement. Right from the start of therapy she wanted close physical contact. This was followed by bodily exhibitionism and by masturbation in which she wanted to involve the therapist. The sexual feelings often arose from excitement generated by sadistic fantasies of torturing and beating. On one occasion the excitement led to urinary incontinence.

Another prominent feature was a tendency to see herself as bad and naughty. This was expressed, sometimes directly, at other times indirectly, in play with dolls. She was afraid of being bad and damaged. On one occasion, prior to a holiday, she said she deserved to be tortured because she was so wicked. When she expressed such thoughts, there was depression of mood, anxiety, and despair. In general, aggressive and destructive wishes were easily moved from real and fantasy objects to herself. This was seen vividly when, after trying to cut the therapist's hair with scissors, she cut her own instead. Anxiety was ever prominent; it either appeared directly or in fantasies played or lived out. It was reflected in sadistic fantasies about doctors, hospitals, treatments, dentists, mental hospitals, electrical treatment, bodily disease, and mental deficiency.

The last case to be described is the boy Basil treated by Kennedy and reported by Thomas and her colleagues (1966). This boy was admitted to a children's psychiatric hospital at the age of seven. He was transferred there from residential care because he was unmanageable. He was overactive and restless with little awareness of dangers to his bodily integrity. He was withdrawn from other children but liable to impulsive outbursts of anger and destructiveness. He was dirty in his habits, given to touching his feces and urine. In the hospital he sought body contact with one staff member and comfort and support from another; with others he was provocative and tormenting.

At the start of treatment at the Hampstead Clinic he was restless and hyperactive. He walked around the treatment room, picking up toys, sucking and chewing them. He ate glue and chewed paper and plastic. He made constant demands of the therapist, asking for sweets, drinks, and gifts — "he brought wishful phantasies of owning a sweet shop which would enable him to eat sweets all day long" (Kennedy, 1964). Wishful thinking led to various "delusional-like" ideas. He said he was the most popular boy in the children's hospital and everyone looked at him admiringly. In addition to demands for satisfaction of one kind or another, he was very concerned about his body contents. He retained feces because he feared passing them signified the loss of body parts. The necessity to control his body contents was accompanied by a fear of being unable to control his needs and affects—"he felt threatened by a primitive, explosive body excitation that would blow him to pieces. He first referred to this as 'being in a hurry' and later likened it to a dangerous electric charge" (Kennedy, 1964).

DESCRIPTIVE, DEVELOPMENTAL, AND METAPSYCHOLOGICAL COMPARISONS

The descriptions given of the children reveal all the different signs and symptoms found in manic-depressive syndromes in adults. The childhood symptoms comprised hyperactivity; rapid speech and thinking; free expression of genitality; soiling with feces and urine; aggressive and libidinal manifestations of orality; wishful fantasies and magical thinking; affects of elation, depression, and anxiety; withdrawal; retardation of speech and movement; self-criticism; physical assaults on the self; and fears of being criticized, punished, and unjustifiably attacked.

Developmental Status

Before proceeding to a metapsychological evaluation and comparison of adult and child cases, their different developmental capacities, achievements, deficiencies, and losses must be defined. Only with this as a background can the descriptive data be properly assessed in terms of the dynamic, economic, and structural aspects. Differences in developmental status existed between the children as well as between the children and the adult patient Mrs. A. The most striking contrast was between

Mrs. A. when depressed, self-critical but cognitively intact and the child patients. This difference receded almost entirely when she was in a manic phase and in the other state of psychic dissolution. At such times some of the clinical phenomena approximated those resulting from regression or arrested development found in young children. Then, considerations of reality were subordinate to the impact created by body needs, wishes, and affects. This was less so in the case treated by Elkan (1973).

The children, with the possible exception of Basil at the outset of his treatment, and Mrs. A., at certain stages of her illness, cathected an object representation in a constant manner, but the object relations had essentially need-satisfying characteristics. In the case of the children, the object, whether mother or therapist, was also looked to as a means of drive control. As the dissolution of psychic structures advanced, Mrs. A. no longer maintained object constancy. This was accompanied by the merging of self- and object representations and by the predominance of the primary process. Such a continuing loss of object cathexis, based on the failure of object constancy, did not occur in the children, although in Basil's case, at the time of referral, there was an inability to initiate or sustain an object relation.

In accordance with their developmental status, the children's thinking was characterized by wish fulfillment. Over and above this, however, there was drive activity that was not age- or phase-appropriate, as illustrated by the oral and anal phenomena. At such times, the developing ego was overwhelmed by the action of the primary process. Similarly, wishful thinking and pregenital and genital drive activity occurred in Mrs. A.'s case during the manic and other phases of dissolution. The effects of the primary process were also seen in her thinking and perception. Consistent with the modes of functioning observable in the children and Mrs. A. were phenomena resulting from externalization. Wishes, thoughts, and affects were generalized to others. This can be regarded as a consequence of the lack of complete differentiation between self- and object representations. The frequency of phenomena due to externalization could be attributed to the fluctuations affecting the state of the self-object boundary.

Prominent Symptoms

In the child cases cited the psychoanalytic therapy disclosed that the developmental conflicts naturally arising during the first years of life (A. Freud, 1965) were intensified by reality events — withdrawal of interest on the mother's part (Rochlin, 1953), threats of abandonment and overstimulation (Wolfenstein, 1955), premature toilet training and changes in the caring object (Bornstein, 1935), separations (Kennedy, 1964), and overstimulation (Elkan, 1973). These "environmental interferences" (Nagera, 1966) had the effect of confronting the child with danger situations resulting in separation anxiety, fear of loss of love, and fear of object loss. The interplay between external and internal events resulted in the reinstitution of earlier modes of mental functioning as well as the obstruction of further growth of the ego and the drives. The outcome was the appearance of oral and anal sadism (biting and fecal incontinence) and various forms of aggressive behavior (attacks on the mother and therapist and destructiveness). This drive expression must be considered a major force behind the hyperactivity — heightened by the effect of the sexual overstimulation to which some of the children were exposed. The tendency to actively repeat traumatic experiences made manifest and enhanced the hyperactivity.

Anxiety, withdrawal, self-criticism, and physical attacks on the self were prominent symptoms. The anxiety, comprising fears of being attacked and injured, can be understood as resulting from an externalization (generalization) to real objects of conscious pregenital sadism and aggression. This externalization heightened the fears of object loss and punishment. The withdrawal from external objects was part of the attempt to lessen the danger situation. This withdrawal, part of the general regressive process, acted in the service of defense by reducing the "excitation" evoked by the frustration of wishes and needs. A consequence of the withdrawal of cathexis was the turning in on the self of aggressive and destructive drives. This provided the basis for the self-reproaches and physical attacks on the self. The self-reproaches were an active repetition of criticisms expressed by the love object against the child.

Rochlin (1959) believes that a clinical withdrawal from external objects is a uniform occurrence in children who are under the threat of object loss or who actually sustain object loss. In his view, the withdrawal alternates with primary-process phenomena and with destructive (pregenital) attacks on the object. He also suggests that there is a concurrent disturbance in the steady growth of ego identifications (see Chapter 6). The self-criticisms can be attributed to this disturbance. According to Rochlin, the self-criticisms result from a premature identification with the lost love object. The self-criticism is therefore a result of a process of restitution whereby the child regains the lost object.

When the children's self-criticisms are compared with those uttered by Mrs. A., some light can be thrown on a fundamental difference between them. Mrs. A. blamed herself and was guilty while psychic structures remained intact. The conflict over her husband (death wishes) was dealt with by identification and introjection. With the withdrawal of object cathexis and the dissolution of the ego and superego, the self-reproaches diminished in frequency, eventually disappearing. The withdrawn state was periodically interrupted by aggressive outbursts or by fears that she had injured or damaged someone, as in the outburst, "I've eaten everyone's food." Utterances of this kind were accompanied by anxiety as great as that associated with her fears of being destroyed. The "self-criticisms" expressed by the children were of the same kind. They too were gripped by the fear of the consequences of their aggression and sadism. The "self-reproaches" in both cases arose from anxiety. Genuine self-reproach arising from guilt only occurred in the case of Mrs. A. when psychic structures were reconstituted.

The hyperactivity in the children and in Mrs. A. had a similar aim — namely, the discharge of drive cathexis heightened either by the frustrations imposed by object loss or by excessive sexual stimulation. On occasions this hyperactivity, sometimes accompanied by elation, replaced a state of withdrawal. A prior condition for the hyperactivity was the dissolution of the ego organization in the adult patient or its absence due to regression or failure to develop in the children. It was characteristic of the hyperactivity, both in the children treated by Rochlin, Wolfenstein, and Elkan and Mrs. A., that it gradually abated to be replaced by withdrawal, depression, and anxiety. At such times it seemed as if the hyperactivity was exploited as a defense against a danger situation of great magnitude.

MANIC-DEPRESSIVE SYNDROMES IN LIGHT OF CHILDHOOD PSYCHOPATHOLOGY

The purpose of this chapter has been to inquire into whether an examination of certain aspects of childhood psychopathology can throw any light on the nature of manic-depressive syndromes in adult life. A survey of these syndromes showed that a wide variety of signs and symptoms may be encountered and that only a small number of cases conform strictly to the manic or depressive type. The majority are transitional forms, the manifestations of which bear a close similarity to the phenomena observable in childhood mental disorders. Further similarities were found when the adult and childhood cases were compared from the metapsychological viewpoint. This was particularly so in the case of the hyperactivity and the phenomena associated with it. In both children and adults the hyperactivity was found to spring primarily from a breakthrough of instinctual drive derivatives with libidinal (pregenital) and aggressive wishes finding various forms of outlet. In some cases the hyperactivity was directly related to a premature enhancement of the libido by overstimulation of one kind or another.

Descriptive similarities exist between children and adults in the sphere of the "depressive" manifestations. The situation here is confused because children do not complain of depression of mood as such, yet they present many of the typical symptoms of a depressive syndrome. The withdrawal symptom complex includes not only a turning from others to the self but also lack of interest, loss of spontaneity in speech and movement (a kind of psychomotor retardation), lack of appetite, and sleep disturbance. Anxiety may also be present, as is so common in adult depressive states (agitated depression). However, child cases lack one essential element, which is pathognomonic of the adult syndrome — namely, guilt and genuine self-reproach. This is because in the child the ego is far from maturity and only the forerunners of the superego have appeared. In both adult and child patients the withdrawal symptom complex results from the decathexis of the representations of current external objects. The aim of the decathexis is economic in that it is directed to a reduction of the level of the stimulation provoked by perceptual, sensory, and kinesthetic experience.

Hyperactivity is a common manifestation of childhood psychosis where the signs and symptoms are the outcome of arrests in ego and drive development. This results in a serious defect in object relations, one feature of which is a preference for inanimate over animate objects (Thomas et al., 1966). However, in the children cited here the hyperactivity and associated symptoms occurred against a background of regression from levels of ego functioning already achieved. Equally important was that these children were capable of object relations even though the latter had characteristics of early developmental phases. It was this capacity for relating that allowed treatment to proceed even under considerable difficulties.

The same considerations apply to the symptom

complex of withdrawal. The withdrawal, again in contrast to similar phenomena in psychotic children, was not maintained indefinitely. It was replaced either by hyperactivity or by the expression of fears of punishment or abandonment, or by self-criticisms and physical attacks on the self. All these manifestations indicated that object representations were strongly cathected.

A somewhat similar situation exists in adult psychoses. In manic attacks, in contrast to the hyperactivity of other psychotic states, there is object cathexis, but the object relation has need-satisfying characteristics (Freeman, 1971). There may be anxiety that is hardly perceptible or it may be pronounced. This may lead to passing fears of being attacked or to attributing responsibility for a destructive or sexual wish or act to another person. Where there is withdrawal and retardation in adult cases, this can be distinguished from the negativistic withdrawal and inattention of the schizophrenic psychoses. In the manic-depressive syndrome the withdrawal and retardation does not entirely abolish or preclude contact with external objects. All the evidence suggests that, while the representation of current external objects may have lost much or all of their cathexis, this does not apply to the object representations of parents, spouses, siblings, etc. These theoretical inferences can be related to the observation that in the majority of these states the trend is toward the remission of symptoms with the patient reaching the premorbid level of personality functioning.

That the events precipitating manic-depressive syndromes are so often similar to those leading to psychopathology in children prompts the thought that the sensitivity of adult patients to object loss, to the threat of object loss, and to loss of self-esteem must result from a vulnerability already established in the ego and in the capacity of the drive representations to resist regression. In the children whose cases have been cited, environmental interferences disturbed the growth of the ego or brought about a regression in its function. These adverse consequences were mediated through disturbances affecting the instinctual drives and induced by deprivation (object loss, etc.) or by overstimulation (seduction, etc.). The effect was interference with the conditions necessary for the smooth emergence of the ego as an organization of functions. In addition, the instability of object cathexis upset the processes of internalization, rendering the identifications prone to dissolution under the appropriate psychical stress (see Chapter 6).

Similarly, the psychotic attack in the adult can be envisaged as resulting from an upset in the drive economy, which secondarily involves the ego. The drive representations, being predominantly pregenital in nature, evoke a defensive reaction whose characteristics depend on the state of ego organization. In mania and the mixed states the ego is subject to varying degrees of regression with resultant drive expression and signs of primary-process activity. The defenses are of an elementary kind. In the depressive type of manic-depressive psychosis the ego appears to retain much of its integrity vis-à-vis the primary process.

Is it possible that those destined to succumb to one or another of the manic-depressive syndromes experience in childhood a disturbance of drive development akin to that discovered in childhood cases? If so, is the result an ego deviation, the exact nature of which must depend on constitutional factors as well as on the final outcome of drive development, hindered as it has been by fixations of the libido? These deviations of the ego, in conjunction with the drive state finally achieved, might then determine in adult life the form the object relations will assume as well as specifying their vulnerability. Given the necessary conditions for the arousal of the regressed drive derivatives, the ego deviation might either facilitate dissolution or heighten resistance against the drive activity; one or another manic-depressive syndrome would be the result.

The case of Mrs. A. can be used to illustrate the way in which childhood experiences combining with innate disposition might create a specific vulnerability for the later occurrence of a psychotic illness. The clinical phenomena and the information gathered about the patient's early childhood provide sufficient material with which to attempt the reconstruction of periods of psychical disturbance which, if they indeed occurred, could have provided the predisposition for the illness of adult life. Mrs. A.'s failure to acknowledge her mother as her mother, the nonrecognition of the mother and the belief she was dead, when taken in conjunction with the childhood memory of a family romance fantasy, points to a grave disillusionment with the parents. Mrs. A. described herself as a solitary child given to daydreaming, while her mother reported her as cheerful and active. Mrs. A. recalled wishing to be an only child, and, when she was acutely disturbed, she gave vent to the death wishes she harbored against her brothers.

In early childhood the sadness and depression that must have followed the arrival of each new brother may well have been contained by activity and cheerfulness, followed by withdrawal and bouts of apathy. The mother's preoccupation with the new child may have created the kinds of oral- and anal-sadistic ideas so prominent during the psychotic attack. The anxieties Mrs. A. recalled from her childhood may indeed have been a reaction to these destructive wishes against mother and child. Thus, the denial and reversal of instinctual aim (passive into active), which so characterized Mrs. A. during the manic attacks, may well have come into operation in early childhood as a means of dissipating the unwelcome drive derivatives engendered by the "loss" of the mother. This reconstruction of the childhood defensive ego is even more convincing if one considers that there are children who react to the threat of object loss or to real object loss with hyperactivity and elation of mood (Rochlin, 1953; Wolfenstein, 1955; Schiff, 1974). When Mrs. A. lost her family, her instinctual reactions were responded to by an ego whose defensive operations were governed by the processes of denial and reversal.

CHAPTER 3

Neglect of the Body in Psychotic Illness

In almost all forms of psychotic illness the patient appears to lose interest in his body or foregoes responsibility for its functions and management. The extent of the ensuing neglect and misuse varies with the severity of the clinical state. The manifestations reflecting this loss of concern and interest in the body are of a different order from the phenomena constituting the symptom complex of a particular mental disorder. Loss of function is the predominant feature of the former, while derangement of function typifies the latter. For example, lack of attention to body hygiene results from the loss of an acquired ability, while a delusion is the outcome of a derangement of intellectual functioning. In order to understand the causes of body neglect in psychosis, one must consider that the special function that guarantees an individual's capacity to care for his body has a developmental history. This leaves the mature function with an inbuilt vulnerability to dissolution. When body neglect is studied from this standpoint, an additional path opens for the scrutiny of the psychopathological processes underlying psychotic states.

DEVELOPMENT OF INDEPENDENT BODY CARE

The concept of the developmental line (A. Freud, 1965) provides a focus around which observational data can be ordered. It accommodates and gives recognition to the different factors that together promote intra-familial and social adjustment. In the sphere of body care the developmental lines, commencing in infancy and running through into adolescence, describe the continuing processes of modification and elaboration of the innate psychobiological endowment. Each stage of a developmental line results from an interaction between the instinctual drives, the external object (the mother or her substitute), the maturing neuropsychological functions, and the emergent ego organization. The initial manifestations comprising the first stage of a line are due solely to the interaction between the drives and the external object. Later stages are the product of those other factors to which reference has just been made. Not the least in this respect is the increasing differentiation of self-representations and the concomitant shifts in libidinal distribution between self and objects.

Progress to independent body management can be followed along three developmental lines (A. Freud, 1965). They are so intimately interconnected that a failure in one is reflected in deviations of the other two.

> [These] lines — always contributed to from the side of both id and ego development — lead, for example, from the infant's suckling and weaning experiences to the adult's rational rather than emotional attitude to food intake; from cleanliness training enforced on the child by environmental pressure to the adult's more or

less ingrained and unshakable bladder and bowel control; from the child's sharing possession of his body with his mother to the adolescent's claim for independence and self-determination in body management ... [A. Freud, 1965, pp. 63-64].

The three lines discerned are: first, "from suckling to rational eating"; second, "from wetting and soiling to bladder control"; and third, "from irresponsibility to responsibility in body management." The following description of the lines is based on observation of healthy children and mentally abnormal children studied or treated by the psychoanalytic method.

The first stage of the line to responsibility in body management is placed at the period when the infant's body is conceived of as having obtained a libidinal cathexis and when the pain barrier has been established. At this time the infant does not distinguish his body as separate from that of the mother and, insofar as this is so, his body belongs to the mother as part of her. Hoffer (1952) proposes that the libidinization of the body finds its first expression in an "oral primacy," which results from the mother's care and the infant's need for food. He draws attention to the fact that the body is the first object in which and through which an instinct seeks gratification.

The second stage on the line is marked by the emergence of the ego functions of thinking, perception, memory, and control of motility. At this period the influence of the primary process on these rudimentary functions is pronounced. It is this that leads to the unpredictable behavior in young children — "At one moment, therefore, the infant acts impulsively, unrelated to reality dangers and a moment later, uninfluenced by them, he attacks a loved person or destroys a toy and a moment later, expects to find them unharmed, as objects of his positive feelings . . ." (A. Freud and Dann, 1951a, p. 152). Between 18 and 24 months the secondary processes gain in strength and progressively the ego functions become resistant to the impact of the primary process.

Once the major ego functions have established themselves the third stage of the line may be said to have been reached. The ego is still limited in its powers, and thus it is easily moved to action by wishes and needs. As the ego has not yet acquired the functions of judgment, reflection, and reality testing, the body is intentionally used to bring about the satisfaction of needs. The impression given is that responsibility for the body belongs to the mother (A. Freud, 1952b). The child's indifference to the fate of his body in the course of the satisfaction of wishes can lead to real danger. This recklessness is often used as a weapon in conflicts with the mother (A. Freud, 1952b). Ultimately it is the libidinal cathexis of the mother and the internalization of her attitudes to body care that counteract the risks of injury. It is conceivable that those who, in adult life, expose themselves to real dangers do so on the basis of an identification with an omnipotent, caring parental figure or by creating such a figure out of the leader of an occupational or sporting activity. The internalization in childhood of the parental attitudes to body care comes to provide another facet of superego functioning. In adult life, then, the attention and interest given to the body springs as much from the superego as it does from narcissism.

As with the development of independent body care, a

balanced attitude to eating and the achievement of bowel and bladder control are only acquired after a long period of interaction between the child and the mother. During this time the mother's attitude to the expression of the child's oral and anal wishes is fundamental in determining the rate at which the new capacities are acquired and the quality of their function.

In the development "from suckling to rational eating" the fundamental change that has to take place is a movement away from eating based on attitudes to the mother and on fantasies about the food itself. When this movement has occurred, eating will be established on reality-based considerations. The developmental line that has been sketched out shows that the equation food equals mother persists throughout the first year of childhood. The infant's inability to perceive food apart from his feelings for his mother is but another aspect of the process whereby he experiences his body and his mother's body as a unity. Progress along the line to rational eating depends on how the infant reacts to the emergence of anal instincts and to the destructive tendencies that are part of pregenital sexuality. Pleasure in messing with food alternates with distaste and a sense of disgust. Similarly oral-sadistic fantasies may, if intense enough, result in disturbance of appetite. Entry into the oedipal phase brings new attitudes to food, which are dependent on the fantasies imposed on it.

Control of bowel and bladder requires that pleasure in the free expression of anal and urethral wishes be given up. Four stages have been described for the developmental line to bowel and bladder control (A. Freud, 1965). The first stage is during the oral phase, when the child retains his freedom to wet and soil at will. This comes to an end when the mother decides to begin toilet training. The second stage is initiated with the advance to the anal stage. Here serious conflict with educators commences. A compliant or rebellious attitude to the mother can now find an outlet through the channels of excretion — "Since in this phase the body products are highly cathected with libido, they are precious to the child and are treated as 'gifts' which are surrendered to the mother as a sign of love; since they are cathected also with aggression, they are weapons by means of which rage, anger, disappointment, can be discharged within the object relationship" (A. Freud, 1965, p. 73). The acceptance and assimilation of the mother's standards with regard to excretory products depend once again on the extent to which she is a satisfactory object for libidinal cathexis. This will be less so where there is an excess of conflict and she becomes a focus of aggression and anxiety. Under optimal conditions, the object cathexis leads to identification with the mother's standards and a consequent expansion of the ego. For some time the new achievements have a precarious existence. Their vulnerability can be attributed to the fact that the new identifications are still responsive to fluctuations in the object cathexis. Complete control of bowel and bladder occurs at the fourth stage of the line, where the functions are entirely disconnected from the parental object.

The description of these developmental lines highlights the continuing interaction between the libidinal cathexis of the infant by the mother and of the mother by the infant. The former leads to the libidinization of the infant's body and stimulates the child's growing capacity for object cathexis. This is the primary factor leading to the acquisition of new abilities. Concurrently, the mother's capacity to cathect the emerging functions enhances the speed of their growth and their future stability.

DISTURBANCES IN THE DEVELOPMENT OF INDEPENDENT BODY CARE

Failure to progress satisfactorily along a given developmental line or a falling back to an earlier stage has been consistently shown to follow the appearance of some kind of "environmental interference" (Nagera, 1966). Disorders of eating and of excreting are among the most common disturbances of early childhood. They may be mild or severe in their expression and found alone or in combination with other clinical manifestations (neurotic or psychotic phenomena). The factors leading to these disorders of intake and elimination may be simple, as in infants, or complex, as in older children. These disorders are prominent in children who have been separated from their mothers in early life. Some of the manifest reactions to separations, particularly withdrawal, lack of appetite, and refusal of food, closely resemble equivalent symptoms in adults whose psychosis followed object loss.

Infants who are temporarily or permanently separated from their mothers during the first year of life lose appetite and refuse to eat (Spitz, 1945). When there is a prolonged separation with repeated change of mother substitute, a loss of enjoyment in food and disturbances of appetite occur (A. Freud and Dann, 1951b). Loss of the mother in the first year of life has other adverse consequences. Spitz (1946) has described how such deprived children indulge in thumb sucking and push their hands, toys, or bedclothes into their mouths. He has also reported that these children are found playing with their feces. Autoerotic activities may further interfere with the wish to eat. Freud and Dann (1951b) describe the case of a boy of three and a half years, one of a group of children who had suffered from repeated separations, who was given to bouts of compulsive masturbation. Preoccupation with masturbation stopped him from eating and he could not be persuaded to resume his meal. The boy's attitude to food was such that for many months he would only eat carbohydrate foods and then unreliably. This lack of interest in food was common to all the children; they were "reluctant to chew, and unwilling to try new tastes and dishes" (A. Freud and Dann, 1951b, p. 201).

Lack of a stable mother relationship during the first years leads to a failure to progress along the line to independent bowel and bladder control. In the group of six young children, who from infancy had been cared for by a series of adults (A. Freud and Dann, 1951b), toilet training had been successfully accomplished during their stay in the children's ward of a concentration camp. When they arrived at their new home in England, however, four of the children had partially or completely lost the capacity to control bowels and bladder. This loss was unrelated to the degree of the child's emotional disturbance. In one case, wetting was a means of expressing aggression and defiance.

The young child who is separated from his mother does not immediately hand over the care of his body to an adult as with his mother — "motherless children proceed to care for their own bodies in an unexpected manner" (A. Freud, 1952b, p. 277). Instances of children expressing concern for their health, the duration of their sleep, and the adequacy of their diet have been described — "The child actually deprived of a mother's care adopts the mother's role in health matters, thus playing 'mother and child' with his own body" (A. Freud, 1952b, p. 278). Loss of an adult to whom a motherless child has become attached can lead to a different kind of reaction. Freud and Dann (1951b) describe how a four-year-old boy became depressed 12 days after the departure of a young woman to whom he had become attached. He was reluctant to dress himself and, when asked if he wanted to be dressed, began to cry, calling out the girl's name. Later that day he arranged his hair in the way she had occasionally done for him in the past. The following day he struck trees, flowers, and children with a stick. This aggressiveness continued over the next few weeks.

Neglect of the body and disregard for its safety can occur in older children as part of a severe emotional disturbance. In these cases such capacity for body care as has been acquired is lost and behavior appropriate to an earlier period of life takes its place. Machlup (1974) reports the case of a seven-year-old boy who, following his father's remarriage, became hyperactive, destroyed his clothes and toys, and showed a complete disregard for the safety of his body. He had poor eating habits and was enuretic and encopretic. All this contrasted with his behavior prior to his father's remarriage, when he was described by his nursery school teachers as a "good" and "nice" boy.

The immediate effects of separation can be classified according to metapsychological criteria (A. Freud, 1960). First there are the psychosomatic conditions that arise in infancy, where somatic and psychological processes have yet to be differentiated. Feeding troubles, digestive upsets, and constipation are prominent symptoms. Second are the phenomena attributable to regression of the libidinal and aggressive drives. The quality of object relations deteriorates as a result of the activity of the oral and anal drives, and behavior is periodically characterized by aggression and destructiveness. Third are the phenomena resulting from regression in ego development. Loss of speech and of bowel and bladder control are some of the principal consequences. Fourth are the phenomena due to changes in libido distribution. Hypochondria, enhanced self-love, beliefs in omnipotence, self-preoccupation, inattention, and disinterest may all be found.

An alteration in libido distribution between self and object is postulated as the basis for the most significant adult psychotic phenomena. However, in the case of a child separated from his mother, the immediate libidinal response consists of attempts to maintain the libidinal cathexis of the object (A. Freud, 1960). The subsequent phase of withdrawal described by Spitz (1945) and others is caused by a decathexis of the object representation. The period between the cathectic withdrawal and the cathexis of a new object is one where the child is most liable to develop a vulnerability for later psychopathology. It is while the child is denied a real object that the libidinal cathexis invests the body, a self-representation, or fantasies of a primitive kind (A. Freud, 1960).

The outcome of a separation, from the pathological standpoint, depends on the developmental status of the child prior to his loss. Different consequences ensue, depending on whether the child is still at the stage of need satisfaction or whether he has proceeded some way to the establishment of object constancy. In the latter case, object cathexis is maintained for a longer period, even in the absence of the real object, and the withdrawal of cathexis is correspondingly delayed. That the age of the child at separation from the mother determines the extent to which ego and instinctual regression will occur suggests once again that the decisive influence is exerted by the capacity to maintain object cathexis. It was found possible at the Hampstead Nurseries to limit the impact of regression in children aged from three to four years upward by avoiding a sudden separation from the mother. Such preventive measures were of no avail with children between the ages of one and a half and two and a half years—infants of that age could weather sudden changes and separations of a day without any visible effect. Whenever it was more than that, however, they tended to lose their emotional ties, revert in their instinctual pursuits and regress in their behavior (A. Freud, 1939-1945).

There are psychotic illnesses initiated by object loss. In these cases the leading phenomena result from the redistribution of libido, with the cathexis investing some feature of the bodily or mental self. There are disturbances of eating, of bowel and bladder control, and of body care. Sometimes the patient is inaccessible and stuporose or negativistic, refusing to eat or drink. Retention or incontinence of urine and feces occur. Neglect for the body follows from overactivity or from disinterest. These phenomena are descriptively similar to those described by Spitz (1946) and others in very young children who have sustained a long separation. Older children who sustain the impact of loss by attempting to care for themselves do so by virtue of their already having achieved and maintained object constancy.

Neglect of the body and its functions also occurs in psychoses initiated by circumstances other than object loss. Fear of object loss, death wishes, disappointments, fears of heterosexuality and homosexuality are some of the common precipitants. There is reason to believe that in many of these psychoses, "process" schizophrenia excepted, body neglect is minimal and the break with reality less complete, with the patient still retaining contact with others, even if only through the medium of his delusional ideas.

BODY NEGLECT IN ADULTS

Limited Psychic Dissolution

The less extreme forms of body neglect are to be found in patients suffering from those forms of manic-depressive psychosis where the illness is of the depressive type, either retarded or agitated, and where the dissolution of psychic structures is limited. In these cases the patient may be withdrawn but the withdrawal is not so great as to preclude relating to others. Reality testing is only breached with respect to the self-reproaches so prominent in depressive psychoses.

The following case illustrates the way in which the capacity to care for the body is disturbed when the dissolution of mental life is limited in degree. The patient Mrs. O. was a married woman of 48 years of age whose illness had been present almost continuously for five years, i.e. from 1968. When seen in the summer of 1970, she was restless in her appearance. Her unkempt state reflected her disinterest in her appearance. Her anxiety reached the proportions of panic. Speech was rapid and under pressure, with its content comprising the endless repetition of accounts of her great distress. She said she was bad and evil, not trying hard enough to get better. She blamed herself for neglecting her husband and her child. Her husband must die because of the strain she imposed on him. She was fearful of the boy becoming ill. What would happen to him if her husband died and she did not recover? Her sleep was broken in the night and she would become terror-stricken by such thoughts.

In the morning Mrs. O. felt sick and would retch and vomit. Her only wish was to stay in bed with the curtains drawn. She was unwilling to wash or dress. She did not want to eat and when she did there was an absence of pleasure. If she ate, she stuffed food into her mouth in a crude fashion. She was uncertain whether or not she wanted to urinate, not being sure whether her bladder was full or empty. She dreaded wetting the bed. She wanted her physical needs to be attended to and to be comforted. When not in bed, she followed her husband around the house, asking him to reassure her that she would get well. If the husband was out, she would behave in the same way with the live-in help. In states of panic she would run into the neighbors' houses and ask for help.

The illness began in 1968 following a surgical operation. Soon after the operation Mrs. O. became depressed in mood and was unable to attend to her domestic tasks. Between 1968 and 1970 she had several admissions to a mental hospital. Such treatment as she received did not lead to lasting remission. In the summer of 1970 she fell ill once again. She was admitted to hospital and remained until October 1970. There was an improvement. Once the symptoms disappeared she became bright, cheerful, and overactive. While concerned to find help when anxious and depressed, she was reluctant to pursue therapy once the symptoms had disappeared.

When, after discharge, she continued the psychotherapeutic sessions started in hospital in the summer of 1970, she would not stay for more than 10 to 15 minutes, saying that she was quite well and had nothing to say.

At Christmas of 1970 she relapsed into the original state of illness. She had to return to the hospital, where she remained until the end of January 1971. There was relief from symptoms but later in 1971 she relapsed again and had to be readmitted to hospital. A further two months in hospital led to an improvement and she was at home from May to August 1971. Another bout of illness beginning in August again required hospitalization, which continued until November 1971. A brief spell of freedom from symptoms was followed by a readmission in December 1971. This lasted until March 1972, when she was discharged. A further relapse took place in May 1972 and lasted until June 1972. Two months after her discharge in June a further relapse occurred in September 1972.

Once Mrs. O. became anxious, sleepless, and agitated there was a progressive increase in the intensity of the symptoms until hospitalization was essential. During the periods between hospitalizations Mrs. O. would attend psychotherapeutic sessions once or twice a week, but neither a therapeutic alliance nor a working transference materialized. It was only during bouts of illness that she was able to describe her thoughts, feelings, and memories, although these comprised only a fraction of her communications, which consisted principally of a recitation of her discomforts and demands for reassurance. She wanted to know was she evil, was she really ill, would she become a drug addict, etc. Mrs. O. tortured her husband by running after him demanding his attention and reassurance, but then she would both fear his anger, believing that he was fed up with her, and fear he would fall ill. This behavior and thought activity was displaced to the author. She wanted him to reassure her and answer all her questions, but she would fear his getting angry with her. She was frightened something might happen to him. Interpretations directed to making her aware of how her aggression made love objects hostile and liable to have accidents or fall ill were without effect.

Mrs. O. was an only child. She remembered her father saying they had to take her everywhere. Later she recalled that she was terrified of being left alone. During her early years her mother had suffered from a depressive illness. The result was that the family had moved to live with the patient's grandmother. The mother had been unable to look after the patient and so her upbringing had been left entirely to the father. The significance of separation experiences, with their accompanying reactions of anger and rage, in providing a danger situation for Mrs. O. was reflected in the circumstances attendant on some of the relapses into illness. These bouts of illness occurred at Christmas, Easter, and at holiday times when the patient's live-in help would go on holiday, leaving Mrs. O. alone in the house.

Mrs. O. was very impatient. She could not tolerate waiting for anything. Whatever had to be done had to be done immediately. This impatience was seen in her manner of eating—the food being eaten as quickly as possible. The impatience was accompanied by psychomotor activity. During two years of psychotherapy the patient was never able to get beyond a dependent, demanding, controlling kind of transference behavior. It was impossible to resolve this transference resistance because of her constant preoccupation with anxieties. Interpretations of both transference and nontransference kind were wholly ineffective.

Extensive Psychic Dissolution

Body neglect is extreme in patients whose manic-depressive psychosis is characterized by an extensive psychic dissolution. In these cases (and Mrs. A., described in Chapter 2, is typical), there is a profound withdrawal from reality. This may render the patient wholly inaccessible, although he may express sufficient ideas to reveal something of the way in which he feels about those around him. The ability to manage his body is lost with the result that he is no longer able to feed himself or attend to his hygiene.

In the case of Mrs. A. the withdrawal alternated with outbursts of anger and violence, particularly if she was expected to cooperate with the nursing staff in her body care. She attacked the nurses by kicking and biting them. During one phase of the psychosis she picked at her face continuously, with the result that she developed a series of boils on her forehead and chin. She was given to pulling the lobe of her ear, so that in time a skin infection occurred. She did not wash her body or hair and, as a result, appeared dirty and unkempt.

When manic-depressive patients reach that mental state where the capacity for independent body management is lost, their utterances, few as they are, reveal that they can no longer differentiate adequately between self- and object representations. Mrs. A., for example, attributed her own sense of disturbance, her thoughts, feelings, and experiences to the author. Concurrently she assimilated aspects of his appearance, behavior, spoken words, identity, and occupation. Nonrecognition of persons well-known to Mrs. A. was frequent, and the slightest change in an individual's appearance led to misidentifications. When the author brought his briefcase to the ward consulting room, she asked, "Have you come to witness a signature?... Are you a customs officer?"

Mrs. A. first became incontinent of urine and feces following a break in the daily meetings with the author. This suggested that there was a connection between separation and the loss of bowel and bladder control. Subsequent bouts of incontinence did not confirm such an association. Instead the incontinence appeared to be either an aggressive reaction or the consequence of inattention. It was impossible to obtain information from Mrs. A. as to why the incontinence occurred. She refused to admit it had happened, and the only reference to it was the following remark: "I left you sitting in dirt."

Mrs. A.'s behavior was little different from that observed in very young children who have suddenly lost their mother (A. Freud, 1939-1945). As the withdrawal from reality proceeds, both in the adult and child, there is a concomitant deterioration in the level of ego functioning, with the appearance of various forms of instinctual activities. Negativism, stereotyped movement, nonrecognition of external objects, autoerotic behavior, incontinence, destructiveness, and aggression are some of the phenomena common to the child and adult in whom psychic dissolution has followed object loss. It was object loss that led to the manic-depressive illness of Mrs. A.

Mania

The effect of a sudden and widespread dissolution of psychic structure on the capacity for independent body care is to be seen in mania. Lack of concern for the body and its safety are outstanding features of the acute attack. The overactivity that occurs results in the patient paying little or no attention to his body. Delusional beliefs in the integrity, strength, and capacities of the body intensify this tendency. The patient may believe he can safely submit himself to physical dangers and acts accordingly. In this respect he is like a small child who, in enjoying the pleasures of physical activities, easily endangers himself.

During the manic attack the patient loses the ability to eat in a rational manner and concurrently abandons all restraints regarding his excretory functions. He is greedy for food, and when he eats he does so voraciously, without any consideration for those about him. Frustrated, he becomes angry and often violent. Again, like the small child, he cannot control his pleasure in eating and this leads to digestive disorders. He is not only oblivious to the feelings of others regarding his feeding and excretory habits, but uses urination and defecation as a means of expressing aggression. These manifestations occur against a background of relating where persons are not consistently recognized and misidentifications are common. Another characteristic is a merging of self with those objects toward whom the patient has strong positive feelings. While in the acute attack, the patient is inaccessible to suggestions to modify his habits or to pay more attention to body care.

Object loss frequently precedes the onset of a psychotic attack. This is true in mania, where the lost love object figures prominently in the delusional content. Other persons are believed to be the love object and, as a result, denial of the loss can be maintained. Object loss initiates other forms of psychotic illness, and its effect is to be seen dramatically in cases of schizophrenia where the patient, having passed through one or more acute phases of illness, has remained for some time in a state of partial remission (defect state). The following is a case in point.

Schizophrenia

The patient Miss E. was an unmarried woman of 55 years of age, who was admitted to the mental hospital in October 1970, because she was found wandering in the street in her underwear. When admitted to hospital, she was unresponsive and withdrawn. She resisted all attempts at physical examination. Her body was dirty, her hair unkempt, and she was dehydrated. She rejected all offers of food and drink. Most of her utterances were incomprehensible, but there was a recurring reference to fire and being burned. During the day she was found to be incontinent of urine. Her physical state was such that she had to be treated medically to restore her body fluids and re-establish her kidney function.

The following history was obtained from the patient's sister: Miss E. developed schizophrenia at the age of 21. This took the form of a religious preoccupation, which led to an outburst of shouting while at church. She was admitted to mental hospital, where she remained for some months. No details are available of this attack, the manifestations, or the treatment. The second bout of illness occurred at the age of 30 and required readmission to hospital. Again, at the age of 34 she had to be readmitted to hospital. This time she was found to be dull and depressed. Her speech and actions were slow and she expressed anxieties, the details of which were not recorded. She was eventually discharged. A further admission to hospital was necessary when she reached the age of 40, at which time she complained that she was being shunned, treated like a "doormat" by the people in church. She cursed people in the street and criticized them. During the night she believed the neighbors were talking about her. A period of hospitalization led to the disappearance of these symptoms, and she was discharged after two months. However, she was readmitted again two months later in an excited state. She remained in a noisy, resentful state for a period of five to six months. Her speech was usually incoherent and her manner suspicious and aggressive. She eventually improved sufficiently to be discharged. The improvement was short and she had to be readmitted to hospital one month later in May 1957. It was reported that she was found standing in the street, preaching to all that came by, condemning their behavior. When admitted to hospital, she was abusive and aggressive. She remained in the hospital until March 1959, when she was discharged.

During the whole period of her illness until coming to hospital in October 1970, she lived in the family house. The patient was one of six children; two died in childhood. Her father died at the age of 88. The date of his death was not available. Prior to 1955, the patient worked as a nursing orderly in three different hospitals, but after her discharge from hospital in 1959, she remained at home with her mother. According to the sister, the mother undertook Miss E.'s care completely and entirely — that is, from 1959 to 1970.

Unless forced to rise from bed, Miss E. would remain there for the rest of the day. Similarly, she would remain unwashed unless the mother prompted her to attend to her hygiene. The mother cooked all the meals and supervised the medications, which had been prescribed at the hospital. Miss E.'s mother was an active, energetic woman who took the patient for walks—evidently the patient and the mother were well known in the district and were frequently observed walking hand in hand. For five years prior to 1970, a man friend regularly visited Miss E. He wanted to marry her, but she would not leave her mother. Miss E. was always apprehensive if separated, however briefly, from her mother. As far as could be ascertained, Miss E. was quiet and manageable throughout the years 1959-1970 but showed little initiative or interest except in religion.

In 1969 the mother fell ill; she died in 1970 at the age of 88. During the illness Miss E. was able to look after her mother and demonstrate an activity previously foreign to her. Following the mother's death she began to neglect herself and the house. She spent a great deal of time in bed, and her sister could not get access to the house when she called. Miss E. took to wearing her mother's clothes, even though she had plenty of her own. She even visited her sister on one occasion, wearing her mother's clothes. After her mother's funeral she stopped visiting relatives. She also broke off her relation with her man friend. It was the sister's opinion that Miss E. had gradually stopped eating after her mother's death. Eventually she had taken to her bed, remained there, and, in a sense, behaved as the mother had done in the last weeks of her life. Some time prior to the patient's admission to hospital, the sister arranged for her to go on holiday, but she returned to the house after a few days.

During her stay in hospital, which lasted from October 1970 until August 1971, she gradually regained contact with those about her. She was quiet but not withdrawn. She ate and drank in a normal fashion and attended to her personal needs. This time she did not express irrational ideas. She left the hospital in August and returned to her own house. Arrangements were made for a home help to come each day and cook the patient's meals. A social worker also kept close watch on Miss E., visiting her at least once a week. Unfortunately Miss E. was unable to manage at home and in September 1971 she had to be readmitted to hospital. Her condition was much the same as at the end of 1970, with the difference that she was somewhat more responsive and less negativistic. On this occasion she was not incontinent but suffered instead from retention of urine.

In this case the patient lost her residual capacity for independent body care once her mother died. Only gradually, with the development of a relationship with the sister of her ward, did this capacity return in some degree. The greatest degree of body neglect is certainly found in cases of chronic schizophrenia. In addition to neglect of the body, there are serious disorders of eating and excretion. Poor appetite and refusal of food alternate with gluttony. Food is held in the mouth for long periods, and the patient appears to have difficulty in swallowing. Incontinence is common. Patients are oblivious to the state of their bodies, and their clothing is always untidy and dirty. Washing, dressing, and attention to other aspects of hygiene are neglected unless the patients are encouraged or pressed to undertake these tasks. Frequently such attempts to help are met with hostility and resistance.

At some point during the acute and chronic phases of schizophrenia the patient becomes estranged from some part of his body. This leads to active neglect or to an attack being made on the part of the body in question. A young male patient, who had bitten his mother on more than one occasion, attempted to remove his incisors. In hospital he continually asked for them to be removed, stating that their presence was driving him mad. In pre-neuroleptic therapy days it was not uncommon in mental hospitals to find patients who had mutilated their genitalia or other parts of their bodies. The author had occasion to observe a chronic patient who over the years had, by his own efforts, removed the majority of his own teeth.

Those who have worked with chronic hospitalized schizophrenic patients have reported that beneficial changes, particularly in the sphere of body care, occur in the context of a close relation with a member of the nursing staff. It has been observed that patients regain some interest in their appearance, their diet, and their general hygiene. Eating habits improve and episodes of incontinence diminish. At the same time, relapse into the former state of indifference, with loss of appetite and refusal of food, occurs when a favorite nurse goes on holiday or when there has been a disappointment (Freeman et al., 1958).

As far as adult patients suffering either from manic-depressive psychosis or schizophrenia are concerned, the capacity for independent body care correlates directly with the condition of their interpersonal relations. Withdrawal from others is always accompanied by some deterioration in body care. In the more severe psychoses neglect of the body is one of the first indications of a break with reality. The gradual appearance of signs of body neglect in incipient schizophrenia contrasts with their sudden emergence in patients whose psychosis is initiated by the trauma of object loss.

METAPSYCHOLOGICAL CONSIDERATIONS

From the descriptive standpoint many similarities exist between the manifestations resulting from faulty development of independent body care in children and the signs of body neglect in adult psychotic patients. In some children the phenomena follow from the dissolution of functions already acquired, but many disturbances arise from an arrest at some point of the developmental line. In adult patients body neglect is always due to the dissolution of acquired capacities. A comparison between adult and child patients that goes beyond description must consist of an assessment of the signs of body neglect in terms of the disorders that have affected the drive derivatives, ego, and superego.

Assessment of Drives, Ego, and Superego

Certain aspects of body neglect in adults result from drive regression. This may occur alone, with objects still retaining some degree of cathexis, or it may be combined with an alteration in the distribution of libido between self and objects. In the depressive psychoses represented by the case of Mrs. O., drive regression from the phallic-genital to the oral- and anal-sadistic levels accounted for some of the changes in attitude to body care. Oral wishes were expressed in greed for food and impatience. The constant need for her husband's presence and her torturing demands reflected the activity of anal-sadistic impulses. At times the dangers created by the oral needs led to the fear that she would become a drug addict. Then she would lose her appetite and refuse food. Her unwillingness to keep herself clean derived from the negativism of anal sexuality and from a wish to have her body cared for.

In contrast to Mrs. O., whose ego defenses were strong enough to prevent the expression of the regressed drives, Mrs. A. gave free vent to her destructive (anal-sadistic) drives, with an outlet in fecal incontinence. Oral-sadistic wishes were expressed verbally and in action. Soon after such aggressive behavior she became frightened in case other patients might be harmed, not by herself, but by some unknown agency.

Chronic schizophrenia affords a good opportunity to observe the expression of regressed drive activity. This alternates with manifestations arising from attempts to curtail the action of the oral and anal drives, as in the instance of the man who bit his mother and later wanted his teeth removed. In other cases bulimia alternates with anorexia. Genital masturbation has a regressed expression in urinary incontinence. This and other autoerotic activities so frequent in chronic schizophrenia sometimes lead to skin infections and other injuries. As with the child cited by Freud and Dann (1951b), autoerotic activity so preoccupies the patient that he cannot be distracted from it.

The neglect and misuse of the body occurring in psychoses are contributed to by the changes that have affected the ego organization. Two aspects must be taken into account. First, there are the phenomena resulting from the regression of certain ego functions and, second, there are the consequences of the general instability of the ego. This instability affects the secondary autonomous functions (Hartmann, 1952). In the less severe forms of depressive psychosis the primary functions of the ego remain intact except insofar as they may be subject to retardation. However, the patient's indifference to his appearance indicates that there is a weakening of the secondary autonomous functions. Mrs. O., for example, was indifferent to her lack of body cleanliness and to the manner in which she ate during phases of acute disturbance. When this subsided, self-reproach was prominent on account of these lapses.

Where the primary functions are themselves disorganized, as in severe psychotic illnesses, there is a concomitant disintegration of secondary autonomy. In cases like that of Mrs. A., as also in acute psychotic attacks and chronic schizophrenia, motility is disorganized in both its voluntary and automatic aspects. Incontinence and other disorders of voluntary movement occur — for example, perseverations and catalepsy. Voluntary movement becomes the focus of conscious conflict — ambitendency — so that the patient cannot decide whether to eat or not to eat, to urinate or not to urinate, etc. Such phenomena reveal how the ego functions can be drawn into conflicts and become a means for their representation in thought or action. Furthermore, those traits of personality that ensure the state of the body does not give offense to others, as well as to the self, are inoperative in severe psychotic states. There is a dissolution of the reaction formations that provide much of the basis of the secondary autonomy of the ego. This is replaced by destructive and libidinal tendencies, the expression of which is similar to the instinctual behavior of very young children.

In acute psychotic attacks it is the rule to find that instinctual regression rarely takes place alone. There is always an accompanying regression of the ego. In this respect the adult patient is similar to the child who sustains a regression in his instinctual development. When this occurs, ego development is also affected — "When under the influence of traumatic experience, such as separation anxiety, or any of the anxieties and conflicts of early childhood, an infant regresses from a later to an earlier level of instinctual development, this backward move is accompanied almost invariably by some undoing of ego achievements" (A. Freud, 1952a, pp. 242-243). In both children and adults the result is the loss of some aspect of the capacity for independent body care.

Independent management of the body is to a great extent dependent on superego functioning. When the superego is subject to dissolution, the patient is no longer motivated from within to attend to his body. Once dissolution has taken place, the degree of attention the patient pays to his body depends on whether there is the potential for object relations, and, if a relation is established, on whatever libidinal level, on the progress of that relation. The chronic schizophrenic patient and the very young child are similar in this latter respect.

An alternative reaction by chronic schizophrenic patients to the dissolution of the superego occurs when instructions regarding body care are externalized onto a real or fantasy figure. The identifications necessary for the maintenance of body management have been replaced by an object relation of a hallucinatory kind. The hallucinated voice may be resented or accepted and acted on. Both positive and negative attitudes were observed in a 28-year-old unmarried woman suffering from chronic schizophrenia. This woman maintained, in fantasy, a relation with her general practitioner, a woman, whom she had not actually seen for five or six years. According to the patient, she was in daily contact with her doctor (Dr. H.) through the radio and television. The doctor told her when to bathe, when to wash her hair, when and how to attend to her menstruation, when to defecate, what to eat, and so on. The patient complied with all these instructions. One day she was found shouting at the television, "I use my own sense, Dr. H." — clearly resenting a hallucinated command. The immediate stimulus for this outburst was her sister, who had visited the evening before and suggested to the nurse that the patient should have her hair washed. The tendency for chronic psychotic patients to regulate body care in accordance with hallucinated instructions is not at all uncommon.

In depressive psychoses neglect of the body is accompanied by self-criticism arising from increased activity of the superego. The patient, as exemplified by the case of Mrs. O., blames himself for the neglect. Quite apart from the role that the regressed drives play in leading to neglect of the body, superego pressure leads to a loss of interest in the body and to a situation where it no longer provides sources of pleasure. Body neglect in depressed states differs from that occurring in other forms of psychotic illness in that the superego remains internalized in the former, maintaining the sense of guilt, while it is subject to varying degrees of dissolution in the latter.

In acute psychotic attacks and in chronic schizophrenia object representations are depleted of libido. Insofar as the body is an object, there is a decathexis of its representation. The autoerotic activities so common in chronic psychoses indicate that the erogenous zones periodically regain their cathexis. In the case of Miss E., neglect followed the decathexis of the body. This was part of the general libidinal withdrawal, the aim of which was to avoid the pain of object loss. During the period immediately following the mother's death there was an attempt to maintain the object cathexis. This attempt to cling to the object took the form of an identification, as manifested in her wearing of her mother's clothes and her imitation of her mother's behavior during the days prior to her death. However, this libidinal movement could not be sustained and gradually, but progressively, a withdrawal of cathexis from the object representation took place.

Similarities to the Developmental Line to Independent Body Care

The neglect of the body found in psychotic patients results from a fall in the level of functioning of the drive derivatives, ego, and superego. Insofar as this is so, it is reasonable to assume that these changes reconstitute states descriptively akin to the stages of the developmental line to independent body care.

In those cases of psychosis where ego-id differentiation largely disappears and where self and object are no longer adequately discriminated, body care becomes the responsibility of external objects. This state differs, metapsychologically, from the earliest stages of the developmental line to independent body care in that the former is characterized by reactions resulting from a withdrawal of cathexis and the action of the primary process (leading to loss of object constancy), while the latter presents all the signs of a developing object constancy and an increasing capacity for object cathexis. Only in infants who have suffered from severe deprivation (Spitz, 1946) is there a failure to maintain object cathexis and, as a result, libidinal cathexes are directed to the self. Then there is clinical withdrawal, autoerotic activity, and negativism. There is a failure to develop along the line to independent body care. Development will be restored if a new object becomes available in time to attract the libidinal cathexis. This reversibility can be compared with the restoration of object cathexis and the capacity for independent body care that takes place in some psychoses, on the one hand, and the irreversibility of the pathological libidinal distribution that occurs in cases of chronic schizophrenia, on the other hand.

The phenomena of neglect are similar to the manifestations of stages in the developmental line in that they are the outcome of an interaction between the drives and the ego. This results in certain kinds of object relations and attitudes to the body. In severe psychosis and in healthy young children, responsibility for body care is the task of an external object. This need diminishes in the child once he has reached the final stages of the developmental line, but, even when it is still in evidence, there is an absence of that indifference to the body characterizing the patient suffering from a serious psychotic illness.

The extent to which responsibility for body care is retained, once it has been achieved, depends on the ego and drive state. The changes in this relation can be observed in certain adult and childhood conditions. In moderately severe depressive states, precipitated by object loss, some degree of ego autonomy is retained, but this is constantly under pressure of the regressed drive derivatives and the superego. The patient, as in the case of Mrs. O., wishes to transfer responsibility for body care but is guilty on this account. Sometimes the former predominates, at other times the latter.

Although Mrs. O's depressive illness did not follow on object loss, it is this event that in adult life may lead to a depressive state where there are self-reproaches and manifestations arising from an identification with the lost object. Similar reactions have been described in latency-age children who have lost a parent through death (Furman, 1974). In these depressed children and adults the representation of the lost object is hypercathected and, until some decathexis of the object representation takes place, the mourning process cannot be said to have terminated. However, some of the adult patients reported on in this chapter and others described in the literature (MacCurdy, 1925) reacted to object loss not by depression but in a manner similar to that found in younger children. Here the dissolution of psychic structure in the adult and the ensuing body neglect occurred simultaneously with the loss of object cathexis. The object representation as well as the libidinal cathexis became subject to the primary process.

It is the integrity of the object representation and the maintenance of its cathexis that enables the depressed adult patient to preserve a limited degree of concern and care for the body in spite of the depletion of its libidinal cathexis and the self-directed aggression. It is as if the hypercathexis of the representation of the lost object stands in the way of a full scale regression of the instincts and the ego. When the cathexis of the object is abandoned, as in the case of Mrs. A., dissolution and signs of serious body neglect make their appearance.

The theory that it is the stability of the object representation and its cathexis that constitutes the decisive factor determining the nature of the reaction of an adult to object loss finds considerable support in the observations made on young children who have been subject to separation (A. Freud, 1939-1945). Where there are only the rudiments of the object representation (the mother), as in children aged between one and a half and two and a half years of age, the reaction to separation is the loss of whatever has been acquired in the way of independent feeding and excretion. The failure to recognize the mother some short while after the separation reveals the extent to which the object representation has been damaged. Such observations suggest that when object loss leads to psychic dissolution in adults the object representation and its cathexis must have been characterized by a vulnerability in the period prior to the loss and thus are liable to a disintegration no different from that occurring in the young child. A similar vulnerability of the object representation and its cathexis must be postulated for all those other psychotic states provoked by dangers other than object loss.

CHAPTER 4

The Metapsychology of
Persecutory Ideas

A wide range of persecutory ideas is to be found in psychotic illnesses. These include not only delusions whose content is both consistent and logical but also those ideas that are disconnected and ephemeral in nature. Persecutory ideas occur in married as well as in unmarried patients, and the delusions may emerge in early adult life or at a later period. The content of the delusions bears no relation either to the marital status or to the age of onset of the illness. The purpose of this chapter is to examine the different kinds of persecutory ideas in order to assess how far dynamic, economic, and developmental factors contribute to the formation of these manifestations. The clinical phenomena are drawn from the cases of three female patients, each presenting a distinctive delusional content. The data is systematically described and classified in metapsychological and developmental terms in accordance with a profile schema previously described (Freeman, 1973).

When the symptoms of psychoses are evaluated from the metapsychological viewpoint, the phenomena can be understood as resulting from several, if not all, of the following changes: alterations in libido distribution between self- and object representations, inability to sustain awareness of the physical boundaries of the self, failure to discriminate fantasy from reality, and failure of repression. The loss of repression results in the emergence in consciousness of drive derivatives, which may or may not find their way to expression in action.

Many of the intrapsychic changes can be attributed to regression that has affected the libido, ego, and superego. The activity of regression is hypothesized on the observation that in most cases the patient has abandoned modes of thinking and acting (secondary processes) that enabled him to make a satisfactory psychosocial adjustment. With the disorganization of psychic structure during the acute psychotic attack, the patient's mental life approximates that of a young child prior to the differentiation of ego and id and self and object. The emergence of persecutory ideas in the adult does not depend on a uniform dissolution of psychic structure. Persecutory phenomena appear as frequently in cases where the dissolution is limited as where it is extensive. Ego-id differentiation and the secondary process are operative in those psychotic states where the leading manifestations comprise the delusion of being observed, spied on, followed, criticized, or tested or of thoughts being read and adverse comments made on past thoughts or behavior. Externalization of the superego may be inferred in these cases.

The preservation of psychic structure and function is largely retained in a further category of paranoid psychosis where the patient believes he is the victim of a systematic persecution by a known or unknown person. In these cases mental and physical powers are no longer at the patient's disposal. He is conscious of an inability to concentrate, think, or remember. He complains of weakness, bodily pains, alterations in sensation. He believes attempts are being made to change his personal and sexual identity. Daily experiences are endowed with a special significance relating to the persecution. The patient insists that the persecutor intends to drive him into insanity. The patient also complains that thoughts, affects, and action are set in motion without his wish ("made" ideas and "passivity" experiences). What is experienced is a source of distress. Everything is the result of influences brought to bear on him by a persecutor; the patient disclaims all responsibility. In both sexes there may be consciousness of a change in physical and sexual identity.

When such manifestations appear, the ego state is such that the defense against the intrusion into consciousness of unwanted drive derivatives is defective. Under the pressure of unwelcome affects the patient may generalize them to others (externalization). He believes that those with whom he is in contact are having identical experiences. He may claim that he is only experiencing secondarily what others have previously undergone. Sometimes he may declare that another person, the persecutor or his agent, has insinuated himself into his body so that it is not his voice that speaks or his limbs that move.

Acute psychotic attacks present yet another category of persecutory phenomena, where anxiety reaches the proportions of panic. Then, persecutory ideas occur against the background of an extensive dissolution of the ego and superego. The content of the persecutory ideas comprises fears of bodily injury, of the body being changed, and of sexual assault. At the height of the attack the persecutory ideas are accompanied by omnipotent and omniscient delusions and by a merging of self- and object representations (transitivism). The patient dreads attack by a real or fantasy person while, at the same time, expressing grandiose ideas and seeking out the gratification of wishes of all kinds. In these acute psychotic attacks ego-id differentiation is lost with the result that drive representations, as well as pleasurable wish-fulfilling ideas, reach awareness, while the primary process influences thinking, perception, and memory. In consequence, the patient is no longer correctly oriented for time, place, or person. Object and self-representations are no longer distinguished from each other, and this loss of discrimination may also affect the body boundaries. These phenomena are best seen in the context of the doctor-patient or nurse-patient relation.

A further series of persecutory ideas that must be described are those appearing during the course of the psychotherapy of psychotic states. The patient comes to accuse the therapist of being responsible for unwanted thoughts, feelings, body sensations, and even actions. These persecutory ideas are often found to spring from a failure on the part of the psychotherapist to reduce the level of frustration caused by needs and wishes on the patient's part. Persecutory ideas frequently arise in cases of chronic schizophrenia where an extensive dissolution has affected the ego. They also occur in cases of paranoid psychosis where drive derivatives, reactivated by the therapy, lead to regression and to a dissolution of the ego.

PROFILE I

The data on which this profile is based were obtained from the patient Mrs. B., a married woman of 32, over a period of 10 months between February and December 1972. The patient spent most of this time in hospital and, while there, she was seen several times a week by the author and by a colleague. The material described in the first four sections of the profile did not emerge until the later stages of the patient's stay in the hospital.

1. REASON FOR REFERRAL

Mrs. B. was referred to the out-patient clinic in February 1972 because she complained of being depressed in mood and irritable. However, when asked why she felt as she did, she immediately responded by saying it was because of a bad relation with a woman at work. She explained she worked with a middle-aged woman, Mrs. Y., who was about 20 years older than herself, and had done so for the past six months. At first they had got on very well together, but in the previous eight or 10 weeks Mrs. Y. had become very critical of her, particularly of her sexual morality. Mrs. Y., according to the patient, began to spread rumors to the effect that she (Mrs. B.) was promiscuous. Mrs. Y. alleged that Mrs. B. wanted to have coitus with a particular manager at the factory where they worked. Mrs. B. explained that this man, Mr. X., was very friendly and was in the habit of talking with her, but she insisted that at no time had she had sexual feeling for him.

Mrs. B. said she had not been feeling very well since the summer of 1971. During the previous two years she had been working full time on the domestic staff of a local school. She noted that she was easily tired and that she was irritable and bad-tempered. During the summer of 1971 she had also suffered from frequency of micturition and a burning sensation in her genitals. A bacteriological examination of the urine had not revealed any organisms, and therefore an infective cause for the symptoms had been excluded. Mrs. B. decided to give up her post at the school because of her various symptoms. However, after being away from work for two or three months, she became lonely and bored. On this account she found her present position and started work there in September 1971.

The discord at work, which had started before Christmas 1971, increased in intensity during the following weeks. Mrs. B. found it difficult to concentrate because she was constantly preoccupied with the idea that Mrs. Y. was telling everyone at the factory she was a "bad" woman. It was an ordeal to get to work. She told her husband and he went to see her immediate superiors. Reassurance and explanation by the latter and by her husband had no effect. Mrs. B. remained nervous, ill at ease, began to be sleepless, and lost her appetite. It was therefore decided that she stop work and seek medical advice.

2. DESCRIPTION OF THE PATIENT

When seen at first Mrs. B. appeared frightened, agitated, and depressed. She was untidily dressed and was clearly paying little attention to her appearance. She was completely preoccupied with her thoughts about Mrs. Y. but was reluctant to say much about this beyond what has already been described. At the time of the first interview, Mrs. B.'s symptoms were confined to the falsification of her relation with Mrs. Y. and there were no signs of her misinterpreting her immediate external experiences or suffering from hallucinations. There was also no sign of self-criticism. If anything, she felt resentful not only of Mrs. Y. but also of her husband and the management at work for not stopping what she considered to be a persecution.

During the first few interviews she was willing to answer questions about her home life and about her childhood, but the answers were limited in extent. At no time did Mrs. B. find it easy to talk about herself or to fully reveal the nature of her thoughts. It was only after her admission to hospital that the extent of her illness revealed itself. The details of this are described below under the appropriate profile headings.

3. FAMILY BACKGROUND AND PERSONAL HISTORY

The following data emerged gradually during the period of hospitalization. Mrs. B. said she was the eldest of a family of six, there being four brothers and one sister. She claimed her childhood had been happy until her mother became ill when Mrs. B. was nine years old. Her mother was ill for one year and then died. The cause of death was a newgrowth of the lung. During that year Mrs. B. had to look after the younger children and help her mother as much as she could. She had virtually no memories of her mother. When her mother died, the family split up. The brothers remained with the father, but Mrs. B. and her sister were sent to an aunt in England. Shortly afterward the sister was adopted by an older cousin and the patient was left with the aunt.

Mrs. B. was very unhappy with her aunt and uncle, partly because the aunt made it perfectly clear that the patient was a burden and an additional responsibility. The aunt and uncle took little interest in Mrs. B. and did not allow her presence to interfere with their lives. As a result, Mrs. B. was frequently left alone in the house when the aunt and uncle went out. In her younger years Mrs. B. would be locked up alone in the house while the uncle and aunt were out to prevent her from running away. According to Mrs. B., the aunt and uncle were often drunk and this frightened her. As she got older she was able to tolerate being left alone, but she was never without anxiety. She recalled that she suffered from nightmares and was frightened of the dark. Her work at school was poor, and she attributed this to her unhappiness at home. A further contribution to her difficulties with her aunt was that when she was about 12 or 13 years of age she had been seduced by the uncle. Mrs. B. believed her aunt knew about this sexual activity — taking as evidence the fact that the aunt was disinclined to leave her alone with her husband.

When she was 15 years of age, Mrs. B. was sent back to the North of Ireland. A year earlier her uncle had died and her aunt said she was no longer able to undertake responsibility for Mrs. B.'s upbringing. During that year the aunt was reluctant to allow Mrs. B. to go out alone and Mrs. B. resented what she regarded as a continuing criticism of her behavior. On return to the North of Ireland, Mrs. B. obtained a residential post as a domestic servant. She had two such positions prior to marrying at the age of 18. Mrs. B. remembered that at about the age of 15 she had passed through what she described as a religious period, which had lasted for about one to two years.

She met her husband when she was 17 years old. He was not her only boy friend, and for a period she was having coitus both with her husband to be and another young man. She became pregnant and this led to the marriage. The first child, a boy, was born some six months after the marriage. A girl was born a year later. When the children were three to four years of age Mrs. B. began part-time work, and when the children started school Mrs. B. took up full-time employment. When asked to describe the kind of person she thought she was,

she said she believed herself to be shy, retiring by nature, and rather nervous. She rarely expressed anger or dissatisfaction, although she sometimes felt her marriage left much to be desired from her point of view. She said that, although conscientious and considerate, her husband did not seem to understand that she liked to go out rather than stay at home all the time. Mrs. B. found this boring and unsatisfactory. Her husband was quiet and not given to talking a great deal. At times she felt he was not really interested in her.

In 1968, when Mrs. B. was 28 years of age, she found herself easily fatigued; she attributed this to a menstrual disturbance. During treatment for this condition it was discovered that she suffered from pulmonary tuberculosis. She was treated in hospital for four months. Chest x-rays one month prior to admission to the mental hospital in 1972 did not show any signs of disease. Finally a reference to Mrs. B.'s father — following his wife's death he took alcohol to excess with the result that he had several admissions to a mental hospital. One brother suffered in adulthood from nervous symptoms, but the other siblings appear to have managed quite well.

4. POSSIBLY SIGNIFICANT ENVIRONMENTAL CIRCUMSTANCES

(a) *In Adult Life:* Some weight must be given to the attack of pulmonary tuberculosis in 1968 as a predisposing factor for the subsequent mental illness. Of greater and perhaps decisive importance was the presence of frustrated genital needs arising from the practice of coitus interruptus. This method of contraception started in 1970. Also of note was the arousal of heterosexual libido in the work situation (the daily contact with a man attractive to the patient).

(b) *In Childhood:* The mother's illness, her death,

and the separation of the family must be regarded as of great significance in promoting the predisposition to mental ill health. Further adverse influences were the unhappy relation with the uncle and aunt and the seductions.

5. ASSESSMENT OF THE DRIVES

A. *The Libido*

(1) *Problems of Libido Distribution*

(a) *Cathexis of the Self:* Certain aspects of the bodily representations of the self were subject to a hyper-cathexis. This was reflected in a burning sensation present all over the body surface. It was particularly intense at the genito-urinary area and was associated with frequency of micturition. The hypercathexis especially affected the mental representations of the self, leading to a preoccupation with mental contents and a form of ego-centrism that led the patient to believe she was the focus of an unwelcome interest. This hypercathexis of mental life had the effect of causing a neglect of personal appearance.

(b) *Cathexis of Objects:*

i. Cathexis of real persons (current relations)

(i) Author: There was a limited cathexis of this representation, as was the case with all heterosexual objects. In part this limited cathexis had a defensive function in that it restricted the impact of the perception of the external object (see Ego reactions to danger situations and Defense). The effect of this minimal cathexis was to limit the expression of conscious mental contents.

(ii) Nurses and other patients: While the representations of these external objects were also cathected with

libido with secondary-process characteristics, their behavior and speech were subject to misinterpretation (see
below).

(iii) Husband: The representation of the husband
was adequately cathected. The relation, as has been
described, was unsatisfying to the patient. For example,
she said, "R. and I don't get on very well.... I don't
really understand him.... He doesn't talk much; he
keeps quiet most of the time.... He's not the sort of
person you could discuss anything with ... it is as if he
didn't care.... He doesn't want to know anything if it
doesn't interest him."

(iv) Children: In contrast to her reaction to the
husband, the patient expressed great concern for the
children, indicating a strong cathexis of their representations. In particular, she feared for the daughter; this
fear had its basis in the fantasy that the girl would
succumb to sexual temptation or be seduced.

ii. Cathexis of representations of real and fantasy objects

The most important object cathexis in this category
was that of the older woman, Mrs. Y. The initially
friendly relation was replaced by one where the patient
felt victimized — "At first everything was all right. I took
her into my confidence.... She was a widow.... She
would criticize me when I was serving at the counter....
The least little thing I would say she would broadcast all
over the place." Mrs. B. said one of her employers
realized that she was being unfairly treated and a senior
official (Mr. X.) had said to Mrs. Y., "Stop getting on like
that." The older woman had denied that she was criticiz-
ing the patient in any way.

Mrs. B. described the circumstances leading to the intensification of the persecution as follows:

> One day Mr. X. came down to help me improve my confidence ... I was in the room alone.... He came in.... I had been crying and he asked me to look at him when he was speaking to me in order to gain my confidence ... I did look him up and down and then looked at him to let him know I liked him. Later that day I was in the canteen standing in the queue for lunch. Mr. X. said, "She nearly stripped me." ... I thought he was joking.... They must have thought I touched him ... different ones in the place said to me, "You are not like that." I didn't ask them what they were talking about but I should have. After that Mrs. Y. became very objectionable. She would say to all the men, "You like her because she is like that." I did not tell my husband what Mr. X. had said because I knew I hadn't done anything wrong.... My husband might have made a fuss. Later I did tell my husband because I was so upset and could not work. [Mrs. B. explained that she then began to experience a burning sensation in her throat and felt sick.] I got muddled up and was unsure as to whether my husband believed me or not.... I think he didn't believe me about the carry on at work, but he just thought I was carrying on. I heard him saying, "I know it was that."

Other external objects — the neighbors, the mailman, the television and radio announcers — became cathected in the same manner as Mrs. Y:

> I heard the news announcer on the television say,

"We know it was that," and then another voice would say, "We know it was not that." I thought he was referring to what was going on at work. One night I thought I heard the television announcer mention something about contraception when you are 16 and there's a girl of 19 or something like that. I thought he was talking about when I got married. I was worried in case my son heard this. . . . I hadn't told him that I was pregnant before I got married. . . . One night I was so upset with the television that I ran out of the house.

She described the kind of phrases she heard people say when she was out shopping or when the mailman came to the door: "I know it was that"; "I know it wasn't that"; "because they thought it was"; "do you know what this is all about"; "it's about that." The phrases were repeated all day. This delusional form of object cathexis continued in the hospital with respect to both patients and nurses. Mrs. B. said, "There is definitely someone here trying to needle me . . . all this carry on on the television and wireless even in here and in the ward . . . as if I am a criminal. . . . I want to know what it is that I've done." She believed the patients were friends of the people at work. Everyone in the ward knew her thoughts including the nurses and the author.

Not only did external objects know her thoughts, but she heard her thoughts coming from outside herself (thought echoing). She only revealed a few of the ideas that frightened her and that she believed others knew. These were either genital or sadistic in nature. Thoughts of the penis or of harming someone would enter her head. She spoke as follows:

These awful thoughts keep coming back ... sexual thoughts.... They are too embarrassing ... I don't want to talk about them.... Everyone knows about them.... I was never like that.... Surely it's abnormal to have these thoughts ... sometimes they are about my husband and sometimes about someone else.... When I see a man I think he has an erection and it is the same with women. [By this she meant that she thought about their genitalia.]

(2) *Libidinal Position*

There is sufficient evidence to indicate that during the psychosis the phallic and anal-sadistic levels of the libido were recathected.

(a) *Phallic Organization:* From the onset of the illness the phallic orientation was reflected in the symptom of frequency of micturation — a masturbatory substitute. The patient's genitality had active aims. This was shown in her fear of having touched Mr. X. A further manifestation of the active wishes was a thought that by its nature points to the sadistic component of her sexuality: she said that while sitting talking to a woman doctor she had the fantasy of sticking a knife into her. This fantasy was accompanied by excitement and by what she described as "a vicious feeling." A further characteristic of her thought content was the lack of control over the ideas that entered her mind. In this respect her thinking was another kind of masturbatory substitute. She said, "They just go on and on and I can't seem to control them. I'm annoying people. They hear me whatever I'm thinking and I can't control whatever comes into my mind. I can't stop after saying something once. I must say it six times or more."

(b) *Anal-sadistic Organization:* Apart from the sadistic thought content (e.g., fear of injuring a baby who accompanied his mother to the hospital), she was also preoccupied with cleanliness. She emphasized her concern to keep her hands clean and her children well cared for. Any reference to dirt caused her embarrassment and shame.

B. *Aggression*

The principal object of aggression during the illness was the delusional object, Mrs. Y. Mrs. B. expressed feelings of hate against her. Some aggression was also directed against her husband in the form of the criticisms already described. She believed Mrs. Y. hated her, and the content of many of her delusional ideas indicated that she believed herself to be the object of criticism and hatred. At no time was aggression expressed through action. The principal defense against aggression was reaction formation — the patient generally being regarded as a person to whom violence was repugnant. The mechanism of isolation was also operative and could be discerned in thought content consisting of destructive ideas divorced from affect. There is some evidence of aggression being directed against the self, although not in action.

Recollections from childhood and adolescence revealed that Mrs. B. had hated her aunt. This hatred sprang from the belief that she was unwanted. As with Mrs. Y., the delusional object, Mrs. B. believed her aunt hated her. There is some evidence to suggest that the mother's death was interpreted as a betrayal and this provoked hatred.

6. ASSESSMENT OF EGO AND SUPEREGO

(1) *Ego Functions*

These were not materially affected during the illness except insofar as auditory percepts were misinterpreted in terms of the delusional beliefs.

(2) *Ego Reactions to Danger Situations*

(a) The initial danger was provided by heterosexual libido which, denied adequate outlets (the effect of coitus interruptus), took Mr. X. as an object. This danger evoked superego anxiety.

(b) The second danger, subsequent to a defensive maneuver (see State of Defense Organization), was provided by homosexual libido directed toward Mrs. Y. The consequence was a fear of loss of love (for example, the patient's wish to be loved and well thought of).

(3) *State of Defense Organization*

(a) *Prepsychotic Period:* In the months before the open expression of the psychosis, Mrs. B. suffered from a number of symptoms, outstanding among which was frequency of micturition, for which there was no physical cause. She also complained of being unduly irritable and depressed in mood. The frequency of micturition was associated with a burning sensation at the urethrovaginal area. Both manifestations, the frequency of micturition and the burning sensation, must be regarded as psychogenic in nature, reflecting the presence of conflict held in repression. This conflict consisted of a clash between the "unsatisfied" phallic libido and an ego under the influence of both fear of loss of love and the superego. The frequency of micturition resulted from repressed masturbatory wishes, which found expression through an intensified urethral erotism.

(b) *During the Psychosis:* At the onset of the psychosis repression was successful in dispelling from consciousness recognition of the demands of the heterosexual phallic libido. This was achieved by a decathexis of both the drive representations and the representation of the sexual object (Mr. X.). This decathexis was matched by a hypercathexis of the self as manifested in the sensation of burning felt all over the body. The profound alteration in the libido distribution led to faulty reality testing. The withdrawal of object cathexis resulted in the hypercathexis of the representations of Mrs. Y. (the persecutor) and her forerunners, the aunt and the mother. This hypercathexis initially had a defensive aim yet simultaneously provided a means of restitution. A homosexual object substituted for a heterosexual object.

The alteration in the libidinal distribution led to a homosexual object choice, which had to be removed from consciousness. The intense ambivalence to the aunt and the mother facilitated this repression by promoting hatred, which in turn deprived the libidinal (homosexual) tendencies from access to consciousness. These alterations (changes in origin and direction), which affected the homosexual libido, can also be described in terms of projection. Reference has already been made to the employment of the defenses of isolation and reaction formation.

(4) *Affects*

Apart from the affect associated with aggression (e.g., hatred of the persecutor), the only other significant emotion, consciously experienced, was jealousy. Mrs. B.

did not elaborate on the circumstances leading to jealousy or why this emotion disturbed her as much as it did. The presence of jealousy is not surprising in the case of a woman who was the eldest of a family of six and who had to carry much of the burden of the family during her mother's terminal illness. There is some justification for suspecting that Mrs. B. believed her aunt was jealous of her and that this suspicion was also present with regard to Mrs. Y., the persecutor. The externalization of jealous feeling followed from the patient's need to dispel the affect from awareness.

(5) *Superego*

In the immediate prepsychotic period the symptomatology can be understood in part as emanating from superego pressure. During the psychosis the superego was externalized, with Mrs. B. believing that everyone knew her thoughts. The hatred that had been activated accentuated Mrs. B.'s belief that she was not only under surveillance and criticized, but was also regarded as a criminal. The superego pressure accentuated the hatred arising from the ambivalence to the original love object (the mother). It is necessary to add that in adolescence Mrs. B. felt guilty following the sexual experience with her uncle. Guilt as well as fear prevented her from disclosing the event to her aunt.

7. ASSESSMENT OF REGRESSIONS AND POSSIBLE FIXATIONS

(a) *Regression in Object Relations:* Regression from heterosexual object choice led to the re-institution of a homosexual (mother) relation with characteristics of the pre-oedipal phase. The aim of the regression was to reconstitute a relation where the love object (the mother) would act as an auxiliary ego in the control of the feared heterosexual wishes. However, the re-emergence of the relation carried with it an ambivalence. The content of the ensuing conflicts will be referred to below (see Assessment of Conflicts).

(b) *Regression of Sexual Organization:* The regression in object relations was paralleled by a regression in the sexual organization. The phallic organization was recathected with the result that sexual aims with a homosexual object (the mother and her substitutes) were activated. Anal-sadistic formations were also recathected and they, in turn, led to defenses to which reference has already been made.

(c) *Regression of Ego Functions:* There was no significant regression of the ego functions apart from the failure of reality testing.

(d) *Regression of Superego:* During the psychosis the superego was externalized and replaced by its precursors. The patient no longer feared the voice of conscience but instead dreaded loss of love. Aggression invested in the superego prior to the psychosis intensified the patient's belief that she was hated and despised.

(e) *Fixations:* All the clinical phenomena point to the likelihood that during childhood development the libido became fixated at both the anal-sadistic and phallic phases of the sexual organization. The anal-sadistic tendencies influenced the nature of the phallic drives, imparting to them a destructive component — for example, the fantasy of sticking a knife into the female psychiatrist (a regressed homosexual wish).

8. RESULTS OF DRIVE AND EGO DISORGANIZATION

Such data as might be classified under this heading

are more adequately dealt with under the other headings of the profile.

9. ASSESSMENT OF CONFLICTS

(a) *External Conflicts:* Mrs. B. was in conflict with external objects, for example with the persecutor. However, these conflicts were in fact externalizations of internalized conflicts present in the prepsychotic period.

(b) *Internalized Conflicts:* These were to be discerned in the prepsychotic period and have already been referred to. The conflict occurred between the demands of the heterosexual libido and the pressure exerted on the ego by the superego. At the outset of the psychosis, regression led to a new set of conflicts. Active phallic (homosexual) wishes, on the one hand, and death wishes (arising from rivalry and jealousy) directed to the mother (homosexual), on the other hand, conflicted with the fear of loss of love. These conflicts were externalized and appeared in relation to the persecutor.

(c) *Internal Conflicts:* In this case homosexual wishes conflicted with heterosexual wishes, as did libidinal tendencies with death wishes.

10. THE PREPSYCHOTIC PERSONALITY

This assessment of the prepsychotic personality excludes the period immediately prior to the onset of the psychosis (the prepsychotic period).

Mrs. B. had apparently achieved an advanced level of object relation capacity during adult life, and there was nothing to indicate the presence of serious arrests in drive or ego development. That she succumbed to a psychotic attack suggests, however, that the object cathexis was not soundly based (see Chapter 6) and was vulnerable to a dissolution. From adolescence onward Mrs. B. was able to make heterosexual object choices and give expression to her genital needs. She was able to make a permanent object choice after a period of indecision and a shift of object cathexis. Because of the limited material available, nothing can be said about the nature of the object choice—whether it had a narcissistic or anaclitic basis.

The expression of genital needs in adolescence and in early adult life generated anxiety and guilt. Some of this guilt, as has been mentioned, was connected with aggression arising from the need to inflict on others the disappointment that was part of her mother relation. This active tendency can be associated with the phallic drives already referred to. The permitted seduction by the uncle and the betrayal of her fiancé are illustrative of her need to disappoint and abandon the love object. There is good reason to believe that the conflict, which such a repetitive trend promoted, was present during Mrs. B.'s marriage but only became cathected to a critical point when she began to work in the company of men whom she found attractive.

11. ASSESSMENT OF SOME GENERAL CHARACTERISTICS, ETC.

Mrs. B. retained some attachment to her love object during the psychosis. However, she did not have available object cathexis with which to form a treatment relation (therapeutic alliance) or develop a transference. This was reflected in her disinterest in the author and other doctors and in her preoccupation with her delusional ideas. It is of some interest that a female psychiatrist had no more success with Mrs. B. than the author, suggesting that during the psychosis homosexual objects could no more attract cathexis than heterosexual ones.

From the therapeutic viewpoint, these adverse factors were supplemented by the presence of personality traits that offered a resistance to the emergence of that thought and affect which offers success for a psychotherapeutic undertaking. Isolation and reaction formations were of significance in this respect. Shame as well as anxiety prevented Mrs. B. from describing fully the content of her misinterpretations and hallucinatory experiences. With the reduction of the intensity of subjective discomforts, resistance to treatment heightened, precluding further contact with the patient.

PROFILE II

1. REASON FOR REFERRAL

Miss M. first fell ill at the age of 18. At this time she was working as a temporary Civil Servant in London. She had started this work in order to fill in time until the university term started in the fall of 1963. The illness had an acute onset — she stopped eating, would not leave her bed, and became mute and stuporose. She was admitted to a mental hospital where she remained in the same state. She was treated with electroshock therapy and chlorpromazine. After a few weeks she was transferred to another mental hospital nearer to her home.

When Miss M. arrived at this hospital, she was unable to give a clear account of her mental state prior to her earlier admission. She recalled, however, that for a month or so beforehand she had found it difficult to concentrate, felt her thinking was slow, was in low spirits, and could not sleep easily. She could not account, though, for her illness and made no connection to the fact that her mother had died of cancer a few months before. Her mother had been ill for some months and the patient knew the cause of the illness. The patient had returned home just prior to the mother's death. She had no recollection of her admission to the first mental hospital. It was noted that she was restless and fidgety. However, she cooperated well, spoke easily, and volunteered information. She showed no delusional or hallucinatory phenomena. A diagnosis of depressive illness was made. As her symptoms subsided, she was discharged after 14 days.

Thirteen months later, when she was 19 years of age, Miss M. had to be readmitted to hospital. According to her father, she had become withdrawn over the previous weeks. After leaving hospital she had commenced a degree course in social science at the university. She had remained well but had failed most of her examinations at the end of the year. However, she managed to pass the majority of these subjects in the autumn. The second attack began just after she had started her second year at the university. The father reported that his daughter appeared to be very frightened — she would not go to bed and told him she would feel safer outside. Eventually she became so distraught and frightened that he sent for the general practitioner, who arranged for her admission to hospital.

When Miss M. was seen on this occasion, she was anxious and agitated. She said she was afraid of her father. She had difficulty in expressing herself and was unable to complete what she started out to say. Further interviews found her more relaxed and communicative. She said she had been reading a book called *Psychology of Sex* and this had upset her very much. She was preoccupied with the subject of homosexuality and had become obsessed with the idea that her father had become a homosexual since her mother's death. She began to fear that she might be odd sexually — perhaps she was a homosexual. She explained that on the night she was admitted to the hospital she had believed her father might assault her sexually. She had wanted to get a lock fitted onto her bedroom door but had not liked to raise this matter with her father. She also revealed that she was experiencing sensations at the mouth of the vagina and had the impression that the vagina was closing up.

Miss M. remained in hospital for about two months. During this time she came to recognize that her preoccupations about her father were irrational and that her anxiety about homosexuality was inappropriate. On this admission the question of a schizophrenic illness was raised, but the rapid resolution of the mental disturbance and the absence of symptoms of schizophrenia was in favor of the original diagnosis of depressive illness.

Four months after discharge Miss M. fell ill again. This coincided with the second anniversary of her mother's death. According to the father, the patient did not settle down well after leaving hospital. She showed little interest in her studies or friendships. She wept a good deal, but in the week or so prior to admission this disappeared and a preoccupation with cancer took its place. She became withdrawn and found great difficulty in communicating. This alternated with bouts of excitement and elation of mood. She could not explain why she was feeling as she was. This excited behavior made her unable to attend to her work and caused her father to consult the general practitioner. As with the previous admission to hospital, this breakdown occurred at the beginning of the university term.

Miss M. was observed to be distractible and unable to concentrate. She did not answer questions directly and would mutter to herself. She made free use of gesture. When asked if she felt depressed, she pulled a sad face, let her head fall on her chest, and bent her body forward; suddenly she sat up and roared with laughter. During the first weeks in hospital she neglected her appearance — her hair remained uncombed and her clothing untidy. The elated mood that had been present disappeared. She was reluctant to express her thoughts and quickly withdrew into herself. About a month after admission the elated mood returned, associated with extreme excitement. She sang, shouted, and rushed about the ward. Gradually this state passed, but she complained of being disturbed by noises and sudden movements. She remained in hospital for five months. At no time during this period did she express any further irrational ideas nor was there any evidence of hallucinatory phenomena. Toward the end of her stay in hospital she was able to explain some of her earlier behavior. She said she had felt very happy because she thought she had discovered the cure for cancer. She also believed she would live forever and, thus, there would be no more death. She recognized the unrealistic nature of these beliefs and understood that she had been ill. Miss M. returned home with the intention of abandoning her university studies and finding employment.

Unfortunately she only remained free of symptoms for about two to three months. On the third anniversary of her mother's death she was in hospital once more. She had remained at home looking after the house for the first three months after discharge from hospital. Then she obtained employment in a butcher's shop, but she became increasingly disturbed while in this shop. On this account she was discharged by the manager. After a consultation with a psychiatrist at an out-patient clinic, she was readmitted to hospital. She said, "It was the men . . . it was sex . . . I was attracted to women, the customers." She thought people in the street were talking about her, particularly one neighbor who called her a homosexual. She added, "I masturbate and she knows it." At the time of admission to hospital she appeared apathetic and disinterested in the interview and was easily distracted by noises. She was reluctant to speak but would answer questions, if somewhat aggressively at times. She made constant references to what she described as her sexual frustration and to the fact that neighbors talked about her masturbation.

During the next month her condition appeared to deteriorate. She was overactive and excited and then withdrawn and inaccessible. Often she would refuse to discuss her mental state. The acute phase of the psychosis passed after five months. She paid little attention to her appearance. She was indifferent to the author and made it clear to him that she had no time for doctors, as she thought they were too inquisitive and only wanted to pry into her affairs. She was neither anxious nor depressed and, apart from occasional outbursts of laughter, showed no affective phenomena. When she did decide to express her thoughts, she spoke rationally and clearly. During the whole of this phase she did not express delusional ideas or show any evidence of hallucinatory experiences. She seemed able to concentrate on what was being discussed, and there was no sign of the distractibility that had characterized her state at previous admissions.

2. DESCRIPTION OF THE PATIENT

When first seen by the author at the fourth admission to hospital, Miss M. was restless and talkative. She said she heard a man talking outside the door of the consulting room. She could hear his voice. He was saying, "Look sleepy"; "she masturbates." She started to giggle. "I didn't want to come to hospital ... I've done something wrong." Then she launched into an account of her masturbation problem. She was afraid it was the cause of her menstrual irregularity. While speaking, she announced she was hearing a voice saying, "Fits." Over all her speech was logical and coherent even if under some pressure. She was cheerful, at times humorous in manner. Her general appearance suggested carelessness and neglect.

3. FAMILY BACKGROUND (PAST AND PRESENT) AND PERSONAL HISTORY

The patient's father, aged 60, was an inspector in an engineering works. An intelligent man of working class origins, he was self-educated. He was ambitious for his daughter, as he was for himself. He had never suffered from a mental illness and had always been regarded as a stable individual. The patient's mother died in 1963 of lung cancer at the age of 57. The patient was an only child. There were no other pregnancies. There was no family history of mental illness.

The patient walked and talked at the correct times and was in every way regarded as a healthy child. As she got older she was rather shy with strangers but did not manifest any major disturbances of development. She did not suffer from enuresis. The parents remained in good health throughout the patient's childhood. There were no periods of separation. The patient was never hospitalized during these years. As far as could be ascertained, the parents got on well together and home life was settled and happy. It was impossible to obtain any detailed information about the patient's attitude to her parents in early childhood.

Miss M. attended school from five to 17. She was a good pupil, passing all the exams necessary for university entrance. She had only one close friend at school but had several acquaintances. Her father described her as extremely conscientious. She worked diligently and rarely went out, except perhaps on a Saturday or Sunday. Her menses commenced at the age of 12. No information was available about her reaction to the onset of menstruation. The menses had always been irregular — there were times when eight to 10 weeks elapsed between menstruation. Miss M. was always very shy and embarrassed with boys. At no time prior to the onset of the illness did she have a regular boy friend. She occasionally was taken out to a dance or the cinema. As a rule she was energetic and cheerful, but there were a few occasions when she felt in low spirits. Her bouts of depression of mood never lasted long.

4. POSSIBLY SIGNIFICANT ENVIRONMENTAL CIRCUMSTANCES

The death of the mother was the outstanding environmental stress to which this young woman was subjected, and it must be considered as the principal precipitating factor of the illness. Factors to be considered in relation to the recurrence of the illness are: living alone with the father, the anniversaries of the mother's death, and amenorrhea. The attack described in this profile was provoked by the consequences of the loss of a man friend.

5. ASSESSMENT OF THE DRIVES

A. *The Libido*

 (1) *Problems of Libido Distribution*

  (a) *Cathexis of the Self:* There was a hypercathexis of both the bodily and mental self. Miss M. was both preoccupied with her body and believed that she had extraordinary powers. She was afraid she might have cancer and was concerned about her menstrual irregularity. Prior to this admission to hospital, there had been a period of amenorrhea and she wondered if she was pregnant. She was aware of her genitalia, the clitoris and the mouth of the vagina. She frequently asked to leave the consulting room during sessions to urinate. This frequency of micturition expressed her phallic sexuality.

The hypercathexis of her mental self was reflected in the following: she influenced actors on the television — "I affect their actions, you only have to watch them." Looking at others induced sexual feeling in them. This was particularly worrying in the case of children because it might start them masturbating. She could hypnotize anyone. When the author happened to shut his eyes, she said she had hypnotized him. The hypnotic power was simultaneously attributed to the author (see Cathexis of real persons).

The hypercathexis of mental and bodily representations alternated with decathexis. She neglected her appearance. She was untidy and frequently unwashed. The decathexis of the self-representations was seen in her belief that her inability to think was due to the television announcers cutting thoughts out of her mind.

(b) *Cathexis of Objects:*

i. *Cathexis of real persons (current relations)*

The drive cathexes followed the primary process. While objects existed in their own right, frustration of needs led to a temporary withdrawal of cathexis. A conscious sexualization of the relation with her father was clear from the start. She asked the author whether he thought it a good thing for an unmarried man and woman to live in the same house. She was sure she embarrassed her father living alone with him. Then she said that a few minutes before she heard a voice saying, "Dirty old man." This was a hallucination as no sound had occurred outside the consulting room. She had not wanted to tell the author about this in case he should be embarrassed. She said she was conscious of sexual feelings for her father and they frightened her. Mixed up with this were fears that he might commit suicide or that he might get into trouble for being a communist. Sometimes she thought she was too easily influenced by her father and adopted his views and opinions. She was also afraid of homosexual feelings. (Further details of these will be given later.)

Sexual curiosity and sexual impulses toward the author initially made their appearance by displacement to the father. Did her father masturbate, how did he cope with his sexual feelings, etc. One of the first indications of her conscious sexualization was her joking about the door of the consulting room being locked — "I didn't use to trust you, you know." Then she thought she was being hypnotized by the author. This was followed a few days later by a declaration of her sexual interest in him. She said, "I'm attracted to you a bit. . . . Are you a lecturer? . . . lecherer . . . I can see it in your eyes." At this moment she hallucinated a voice, which said, "He's married." She laughed, continuing, "I'm sexually frustrated . . . I shouldn't have E.C.T." (She had had this treatment only once at the very beginning of her illness). "It's made me lecherous."

At a later interview she spoke as follows: "You don't love me, you hate me . . . you are hurting me . . . you are frustrating me . . . hurting my head." She complained that the author's eyes made her head sore. She was not always able to describe the sexual feelings that occurred during the meetings with the author. Very often she asked to leave to go to the bathroom or refused to speak. Sometimes she said she was afraid; what frightened her was the feeling of frustration. Smoking relieved these feelings. A period was reached when she was smoking one cigarette after another. She wanted to know how did men control themselves — really the author. She knew he had been attracted to her even if he no longer was. While speaking in this way, she suddenly said, "You're attracted now." When asked how she knew this, she replied, "Do you hear the vacuum cleaner [it had been switched on in the hall outside the consulting room]? It's the cleaning woman's movements causing it . . . she's a lover."

During many of the interviews the patient was actively hallucinated. Usually these auditory hallucinations had a sexual content. She heard young men talking about masturbation or women saying she was a virgin. More often than not she was unwilling to reveal the nature of the hallucinations, but their presence was usually revealed by laughter for which there was no apparent reason. On a number of occasions she expressed a wish for her mother. She wondered if her mother had died of a broken heart. She felt that if her mother had been alive she could have helped her to control her sexual feelings. This wish for an external agency to help control her sexuality will be referred to again later.

She was very sensitive to the other female patients. The following is an instance of her reaction to them: "The other women are testing me because I am not married — I know from the way they speak. They give me a headache." She was particularly irritated by a married fellow patient of her own age. During one meeting Miss M. mooed like a cow. When I asked her why she was doing this, she said she could hear this other patient passing outside the door — "She's jealous; she should share her husband . . . I was attracted to him . . . in fact to any man." Then she added, "I don't like talking about sex . . . stop talking about it . . . you think I'm mad because my mother is dead."

ii. Cathexis of representations of real and fantasy objects

The psychotic reality comprised auditory misperceptions and hallucinations. The phenomena reflected the expression of both heterosexual and homosexual object cathexes. The content of these phenomena was directly instinctual, as instanced in the interviews when she heard young men talking about masturbation or women saying she was a virgin. A further category of hallucinatory experience had a persecutory content. Announcers on the television interfered with her thinking.

(2) Libidinal Position

Sexuality found its principal expression at this stage of the illness through masturbation. This phallic sexuality had active aims and was as easily directed to homosexual as heterosexual objects. Miss M. exhibited her genitalia, and the frequency of micturition, so pronounced during the interviews, must be regarded as a masturbatory equivalent. Her pursuit of active aims was also seen in her considerable sexual curiosity. Mention has already been made of her query about her father's masturbating. She asked the author what sexual intercourse was like. She wanted to know if men were attracted to one another. "Do married people find themselves attracted to others?" she asked. At other times her curiosity was about pregnancy and, in particular, her own birth—"If parents are immature sexually [she meant her parents], does that affect the children?"

Anxiety and guilt about masturbation had been present long before the illness began—"It always made me feel I was odd. It started when I was seven, at the cinema. It stopped at 14 and did not start again until I was in hospital. I once told my mother about it and she said it was wrong to do it. I wish I had no feelings." The fear of her inability to control her masturbatory urges found expression in her oft repeated wish that she needed someone to help control herself—this applied equally to smoking—"I smoke too much, is morality behind it? . . . Is education behind it? The more educated you are, the more moral you are. I have indigestion from smoking too much . . . I am smoking more than 20 a day." When the author reminded her that she had smoked five cigarettes while with him the previous day, she said, "It's because of the stress here, that's why I smoke so much in here." When asked what the stress was, she replied, "Sexual feelings . . . I feel about any man." Attention has already been drawn to her fear that she might make children masturbate. The sense of lack of control included masturbation, smoking, urination, as well as her behavior with men and women.

B. *Aggression*

This patient did not strike out or attack others, nor was there any history of such occurrences in the past.

During remissions she had difficulty in expressing any kind of criticism. When ill, she expressed her angry feelings without difficulty, as illustrated by the following: "I have nothing to say to you . . . I have worked it all out for myself . . . I don't trust you." When she was really angry, she would curse and swear. These fits of temper would arise if she was refused a cigarette, if there was no response to her complaint of being frustrated, or if no one was willing to discuss the particular ideas occupying her mind at the time. These outbursts were generally directed at other patients rather than doctors or nurses. The aggression appeared to be associated with the oral and phallic sexual organizations. Frustration of these drives led to anger.

6. ASSESSMENT OF EGO AND SUPEREGO

(1) *Ego Functions*

The patient's speech was not seriously disordered in its form. There was never any evidence of blocking of thought and only occasionally were words or phrases connecting sentences omitted. At times there was some pressure and at other times a diminution in the volume of speech. The sound of words occasionally led to a new word, or a train of thought was due to an inner preoccupation. It was the patient's preoccupation with genital sexuality that led to the changes in speech content and thus to inappropriate responses. For example, she asked the author, "Is there any sense in mythology . . . who was the character with one eye?" When the author asked her if she meant Cyclops in the tale of Ulysses, she responded, "Do you think it will be banned? . . . It's very sexy." She went on to talk about the film of the book *Ulysses* by

James Joyce. "Lecturer" and "lecherer" is another example of the choice of a word being determined by a preconscious interest. The tendency to jump from one word to another, with which it was apparently unconnected, was expressed in her going from the subject of milk to cancer. The connecting word was breast.

At times she was distractible, as when in a giggly overactive state. She would interrupt whatever she was saying when the slightest sound occurred outside the consulting room. Then it was difficult to know whether she misinterpreted overheard speech or whether she was experiencing auditory hallucinations. The outstanding perceptual disturbance was the occurrence of auditory hallucinations. Examples have been given of these hallucinations, which appeared in the course of the interviews. Other hallucinatory phenomena may have been misperceptions of what was heard, as when she believed that television announcers were saying she was a lesbian. Details of a tactile hallucination will be described in the next section. Her memory function was quite intact. Only one feature is worthy of note: she said she often felt a penis pressing against her lower abdomen. This hallucination was a memory of love making with her former boy friend.

(2) Ego Reactions to Danger Situations

The clinical data show that it was libidinal drive arousal that provoked danger. In particular, homosexual wishes led to anxiety and this was reflected in her wish to stop masturbating. Active phallic sexuality was prominent even in her heterosexuality. However, oedipal wishes led to a danger situation in that they might have passive aims. Throughout the acute attack there was no evidence to suggest that danger situations were created by fears of object loss or loss of love.

(3) *State of Defense Organization*

During the attack repression had failed, resulting in the free expression of both heterosexual and homosexual drive activity. Anxiety arising from the danger situations referred to above led to two forms of defensive activity — both being forms of externalization of drive representations. Heterosexual and homosexual wishes were occasionally externalized with a defensive aim. In these instances Miss M. was quite conscious of the wish that was generalized to another person. Attributing responsibility resulted in her blaming persecutors for changes in her intellectual functions and in her emotions — for example, she blamed the author for causing her to feel sexually frustrated. It is worth adding that she also generalized this feeling in a nondefensive way. Aggression was also generalized, but here there was a defensive purpose.

Projection did not play a part in the defense organization. She was always conscious of the wish, affect, or idea that was externalized. Some note should be made of the hallucinatory voices within the framework of the defense organization. While these voices have a superego aspect, they must also be seen as the outcome of a defensive process whereby a drive representation — for example, a highly cathected homosexual wish seeking an outlet through masturbation — was experienced as an auditory percept. The young men's voices talking about masturbation represented her warded-off masculine (phallic-homosexual) wishes.

(4) *Affects*

Elation, depression of mood, anxiety, envy, and jealousy were affects expressed during the attack. Again externalization led the patient to believe that other women were envious or jealous of her.

(5) *Superego*

The superego was externalized during the attack. The result was the belief that she was criticized by other women for masturbating and that references to her homosexuality were made on the television. There was no guilt feeling at any time.

7. ASSESSMENT OF REGRESSIONS AND POSSIBLE FIXATION

(a) *Regression in Object Relations:* During the psychosis Miss M. behaved in a manner akin to that of a child in the pre-oedipal phase insofar as she could not tolerate the frustration of an instinctual need. Object cathexis was maintained, but the object, like the mother in childhood, was looked to as an auxiliary ego for the purpose of assisting drive control. Again, as with the young child, self-object discrimination was indefinite, permitting generalization of wishes, thoughts, and affects. The patient's homosexual wishes indicated that the regression had also recathected that libidinal phase when the female child has active phallic wishes directed to the mother.

(b) *Regression of Sexual Organization:* The patient's sexual behavior while in the psychotic attack and the limited knowledge of her psychosexuality prior to the illness made it difficult to decide whether or not her phallic sexuality was the result of regression or was the highest point in her sexual development. Scopophilic wishes were much in evidence (looking, sexual curiosity), suggesting a fixation having affected these instinctual drives. Sexuality also found expression through oral and urethral channels.

(c) *Regression of Ego Functions:* The data already described show that speech, thinking, and perception were influenced by the primary process. Libidinal wishes and anxiety on account of them directed the manner in which these ego functions found expression.

(d) *Regression of Superego:* The superego regression led to its externalization.

(e) *Fixations:* The clinical data leave no doubt that a fixation of the libido had occurred at the phallic phase, possibly resulting from a seduction in childhood (homosexual?). There was also evidence to favor a fixation at the oral level.

8. RESULTS OF DRIVE AND EGO DISORGANIZATION

(a) The disorder of drive activity that was observed can be understood in terms of regression.

(b) Ego functions were disorganized. This was reflected not only in the alterations in the flow of speech but also in the tendency for there to be an externalization of some of these functions, e.g., memory. The patient became aware of memories through her being hallucinated. When she saw a man she knew, a voice said, "He's married." While a defensive purpose can be discerned in this, the hallucinatory mechanism points to the disorganization of the ego.

9. ASSESSMENT OF CONFLICTS

(a) *External Conflicts:* Continuous external conflict occurred. This followed from Miss M.'s angry feelings when disappointed. She accused the external objects of causing this.

(b) *Internalized Conflicts:* The internalized conflicts present in the period of partial remission antedating the acute attack were externalized. This was seen in her tendency to attribute responsibility as well as to generalize wishes and affects to external objects.

(c) *Internal Conflicts:* The basic internal conflicts occurred between heterosexuality and homosexuality on the genital level and between activity and passivity on the pregenital level.

10. THE PREPSYCHOTIC PERSONALITY

This account of the prepsychotic personality also includes a statement regarding the patient's intrapsychic situation in the period immediately prior to the onset of the acute attack (prepsychotic phase).

(a) *Prepsychotic Phase:* In the months prior to the psychotic attack Miss M. struck up a relation with a married man who said that he had left his wife. He had served a jail sentence and was known to be most unreliable. It was only a matter of weeks before she announced that she was going to marry her man friend. This led to discord with her father, but she explained to him and to the author that she was confident she could change her "fiancé's" way of life. During this period she revealed herself to be in a state of conflict, which found expression in memories about disagreements with her mother. These arguments usually centered around her wish to be independent and her mother's objection to this. The underlying anxiety over her heterosexual wishes was quite apparent, and she looked to the author, in a transference role, as someone who should play the mother's part.

At this stage her libidinal drives were phallic with active aims. In her belief that she could save her man friend from himself she was living out a rescue fantasy. In this regard her attitude was more masculine than feminine (see Dynamic and Economic Aspects, this chapter). This raises the possibility that her urgent need for a heterosexual object was in part a flight from masturbatory activity with homosexual aims. This theory receives support from numerous statements made early in the remission to the effect that, if she could marry, then she would be free of the danger of being attracted sexually to women.

While in the stage of partial remission (see Chapter 5), the homosexual wishes remained in repression but her lack of energy, sense of inferiority, and pronounced sensitivity reflected the economic consequences of this defense. It was only when she realized that her man friend was a deceiver and had no intention of giving up his wife that a further psychotic attack ensued. This in itself suggests that the man not only served as a protection against the homosexuality but also represented her own wished-for masculinity.

(b) *Prepsychotic Personality:* In retrospect it is easy to assume that Miss M.'s object ties were weak and that their instability permitted the loss of object cathexis when her mother died. The mother is represented throughout by the patient more as an auxiliary ego than as a superego figure. The available data make it difficult to know whether a stable superego was ever established. At the same time, some of what the patient said, as well as her behavior, suggest that the nature of the libidinal cathexes of the parental objects was such as to obstruct their displacement to new objects. She said she had never met a young man who interested her sufficiently or to whom she could form a deep attachment. In this regard, account must also be taken of her anxiety and guilt in the face of sexual arousal.

Attention has already been drawn to what was probably the predominant sexual organization of the prepsychotic period — an active phallic sexuality. While the mother remained alive, this organization, with its heterosexual aims, found a limited conscious expression and led to conscious conflict. The exhibitionistic aspects of the phallic sexuality were repressed and replaced by shyness and sensitivity with others. However, these exhibitionistic tendencies found a free outlet during the psychotic attacks. Homosexual (masculine) wishes were not in evidence either directly or indirectly prior to the illness.

As has been mentioned, there was a continuing conscious conflict about masturbation, and at one time Miss M. enlisted her mother's help to overcome this. At times there was anger against the mother and evidence of unconscious death wishes. It does not seem that these death wishes were part of the Oedipus complex but rather a reaction to frustrations imposed by the mother. Her attitude to her father suggested that he was a narcissistic object representing an idealized, wished-for masculinity, rather than a true oedipal object. It is likely that this young woman never reached the oedipal phase of development and that the libido was arrested at the phallic phase, with her object relations being characteristic of the pre-oedipal situation.

11. ASSESSMENT OF SOME GENERAL CHARACTERISTICS, ETC.

In the acute psychotic attack it was quite impossible to establish any kind of therapeutic alliance because of the extensive dissolution of mental structures. After the psychotic attack passed an attempt was made to establish a psychotherapeutic relation. At this time Miss M. had come to recognize that she had been mentally unwell, but she was unable to maintain the integrity of the ego organization necessary for a psychotherapeutic treatment. During the sessions, which could only be held once a week, she was usually silent from a reluctance to speak. She freely admitted she did not want to come.

Some weeks after leaving hospital Miss M. started work in a factory. This proceeded satisfactorily for a while, but then she reported that one woman was referring to her as a lesbian. From this time on she talked more freely, perhaps because she felt under pressure to describe her experiences. The references to homosexuality by her fellow workers continued, according to the patient, so that she had to give up the work.

When discussing the circumstances under which the psychotic ideas emerged, she revealed that a young man had come to work next to her. She recalled that she had felt attracted to him. She wondered if there could have been a connection between his presence and the women calling her a lesbian. She was reminded of the fact that just before her previous attack she had been at a party and had been sitting on a young man's knee. She wanted to know if there was a relation between heterosexual and homosexual feelings. At the meeting following these revelations she appeared in a disturbed mental state. She reported that she was hearing voices to the effect that she masturbated and was a homosexual. Her father reported that she would not leave the house because she believed people in the street were looking at her and talking about her. This occurrence of yet another acute psychotic attack required a further admission to hospital.

PROFILE III

This profile is based on data obtained from the patient over a three-month period during which time an attempt was made to initiate a psychotherapeutic treatment.

1. REASON FOR REFERRAL

The patient, Mrs. N., a married woman of 45 years of age, was initially seen by the author at her home. She had become a source of anxiety to her family as a result of her irrational thinking and behavior. Recently she had taken to accusing a woman neighbor of causing her to be subjected to unwanted sexual experiences and of corrupting her sons. As a reprisal she threw a stone at the neighbor's house and smashed a window. Later Mrs. N. complained that this neighbor, who lived in a house immediately behind her house, had given her some drug that put her into a state where men could come into the house and have sexual intercourse with her. Mrs. N. did not know what it was or how it had been administered. The men involved were usually prominent local politicians, but even the Prime Minister had been with her. Mrs. N. believed that perhaps it was the result of a hypnotic influence exerted on her by the neighbor. She also believed the world would shortly come to an end.

Mrs. N. was very critical of her husband. He did nothing to stop the persecution. He was the one who was insane and needed treatment. She had the feeling that he had become involved with the persecution and was assisting its progress. According to Mr. N., his wife had been unwell for several years. He could not give details of her ideas, but she had complained about her neighbor for some time past. About two years ago Mrs. N. had refused to have coitus with him any longer.

Mrs. N. was admitted to the mental hospital in December 1973. She refused to concede she was ill and therefore had to be admitted as a formal patient.

2. DESCRIPTION OF THE PATIENT

When Mrs. N. was seen at her home, she was both agitated and aggressive. She regarded the author's presence as an intrusion. She said, "I'm not sitting here like a fool.... I'm not going to be treated.... He [the husband] should be treated." At this time she did not divulge any of her delusional ideas, confining herself to criticisms of her husband.

In the hospital, when Mrs. N. was approached by a female psychiatrist, she was pleasant in manner, cooperative, and most willing to describe all that happened to her. Although continuing to deny that she was in any way unwell, she did not object to having regular interviews. At all times she was neat and tidy in her dress, revealing concern for her appearance. As will be described later, she came to admire the ward sister and was always pleased to talk to her.

3. FAMILY BACKGROUND AND PERSONAL HISTORY

Much of the information detailed here was obtained during attempts to initiate a psychotherapeutic treatment. This was undertaken by a female psychiatrist, because Mrs. N. was unwilling to express anything other than superficialities to the author. The following data are of significance. Both Mrs. N.'s parents were dead. Her father was killed in a traffic accident in 1968 at the age of 68. In 1966 and 1968 he was a patient in a mental hospital because he had developed paranoid ideas. He had lived alone from the time of his children's marriages.

He had been a gardener and had a good work record. In 1965, just before the onset of his illness, he had moved to a flat from his house. He thought the people in the flat below were talking about him and watching all his movements. A stranger was spreading a rumor that he was a member of the IRA, while in fact he was a law-abiding citizen. These ideas disappeared after treatment but recurred in 1968. After his first discharge from hospital he lived for about a year with Mrs. N. He was knocked down and killed shortly after his second discharge from hospital. Mrs. N.'s father drank but not to an extent that interfered with his work.

In 1939, when Mrs. N. was 11 years of age, her father joined the Army and served until 1945. Mrs. N. was fond of her father and recalled weeping when he went away. However, she was more attached to her mother. Mrs. N. said she was about four years of age when her mother had a still birth, followed by a severe hemorrhage. Mrs. N. claimed that she remembered this and recalled her fear. Subsequently the mother suffered from uterine bleeding, which required treatment in hospital. In addition, the mother suffered from valvular heart disease. Her repeated hospitalizations distressed Mrs. N., who remembered praying for her mother every night — "If she dies let me die too." When Mrs. N.'s father came home from the Army on leave, Mrs. N. resented his sleeping with her mother. She was aware of their having coitus. After her father's discharge from the Army she was able to persuade him that he should not sleep with the mother because of her poor health. Eventually Mrs. N. resumed sleeping with her mother and did so until shortly before her mother died. Mrs. N. was 24 years of age at the time.

Mrs. N. had a brother two years younger than herself.

They fought a good deal. The parents quarreled quite a lot, particularly if the father had been drinking. Mrs. N. believed she had been a shy, retiring child, given to daydreaming. On one occasion she said, "I was an odd child — I used to run into the street at night and shout, 'Murder.' " At another time she described herself as a "special child."

Her schooling was uneventful and she left at 14. She then had several jobs, mostly in factories, although she was also in domestic service. During her early adult life she kept the company of a young man, and this continued after her mother's death. Mrs. N. terminated the relation after seven years. She had been on the point of marrying him when she heard her mother's voice saying, "You must throw him over." This was because he was of a different religion. Mrs. N. also recalled that at about 16 years of age she was very attracted sexually to another girl with whom she worked. At the time she wished she had been a boy. She had never disclosed her feelings but it was a long time before they disappeared.

Mrs. N. met her husband some time after the end of her first love affair. She told him he was her second choice. She married when she was 28 years of age. There were three sons, aged 16, 13, and 10 years respectively. The marriage had been a disappointment to Mrs. N. She said it started badly. Her husband did not have coitus on the wedding night: "He was too small and did not think he was strong enough." Later he never seemed to want her sexually — "Often I used to be begging him for sex but he would say, 'You make me sick.' It was unnatural for a man. He didn't want it for months often. I felt like leaving him and we had rows over it." Mrs. N. also had difficulties with her mother-in-law, who interfered with the upbringing of the children. She did not get support from her husband — "He was so tied to his mother he did not want sex with me."

Finally, note should be made of the fact that an uncle died in a mental hospital.

4. POSSIBLY SIGNIFICANT ENVIRONMENTAL CIRCUMSTANCES

(a) The father's death was probably the immediate cause of the illness. Death wishes against him, present from childhood, were realized (see her dream predicting his death) and this led to the psychosis.

(b) The presence of an unconscious homosexuality adversely affected the "heterosexual libido." This led to a chronic disturbance in the marriage relation and to a constant state of libidinal frustration.

(c) Childhood factors include: the absence of the father, the mother's chronic ill health, a homosexual seduction, and the libidinal attachment to the mother.

5. ASSESSMENT OF THE DRIVES

A. *The Libido*

(1) *Problems of Libido Distribution*

(a) *Cathexis of the Self:* The libidinal cathexis of the self was heightened, which resulted in the hyper-cathexis of certain elements of the self-representations while others were not so affected. This situation was reflected in the following statement made by Mrs. N.:

I'm perfectly well. . . . You may need tablets but I don't. . . . There's a part of me which isn't me that needs tablets, but you need to give them to that part and not to me. I don't know who this other part of me is unless it's my husband but there hasn't been any [coitus] with him for a long time. It may be my son. I've seen tears in his eyes at the same time as I've had tears in mine. It has all to do with tears, tear drops, it's all in space, visions in space, and I may have sad thoughts; they are not mine they are the other me.

On another occasion she said, "I thought the other soul, which had entered my body, had left me today, but it's here now when I'm talking to you. Can you see the tear in my eye?... I wondered if it was a woman patient in here because she was crying earlier."

As the above illustrations show, the disturbance of the libidinal distribution upset the differentiation between self- and object representations. At another time she said, "I had tears in my eyes and so did Sister D. [the ward sister].... She must be part of it all. We all seem to be mixed up. We're all part of each other, I think it's my husband who is ill.... He's been odd for a long time, long before I married him."

The confusion of self- and object representations (identification) due to the loss of object cathexis led to the following phenomena:

I have discovered I have the power to take over bodies and voices. I take them into myself, and my voice can change so that I talk with their voices. I've taken over some of the nurses in here. My niece in Australia, she's about 20, I've taken over her body lots of times. I dreamt about her last night [see Affects]. ...I can look at her and she becomes part of me. The last time she was home I thought she could read my mind.

The tendency to assimilate external objects into the self

(object cathexis giving way to identification) was also to be observed in the case of those political personages with whom she had coitus in fantasy. Mrs. N. said, "Mr. C. [a leading political figure] came to me [coitus] and was a part of me after that.... I was the government." Such "introjections" added to the cathexis of the self, resulting in grandiose delusions (see Regression of sexual organization).

The hypercathexis of masculine representations of the self led to a series of clinical phenomena: "I was young Dr. W." (a man); "I am Jesus"; "I am God"; "he's [husband] a bull but I'm a bull too, tough and strong." There were also ideas of omnipotence and omniscience. The result of the cathectic disturbance was a confusion about her real identity. This confusion was naturally enhanced whenever certain self-representations were hypercathected and acted under the influence of the primary process. She said, "I've been wondering lately who I am.... I think I'm next to God; of course, I don't know who God is; I could be Sister D. or Dr. W." At other times, conceivably when the hypercathexis of these self-representations lessened due to a diminution in drive (libidinal) pressure, other reality-oriented self-representations came to the fore—"The occupational therapist came up this morning; she reminded me of Linda [a friend]; she looked well in nice shoes and a nice skirt and jumper. I felt envious; I've always loved clothes and would like plenty of them. I like to look nice."

(b) *Cathexis of Objects:*

i. *Cathexis of real persons (current relations)*

There was nothing in Mrs. N.'s behavior to indicate that the libidinal drives retained need-satisfying characteristics. Real persons were cathected with advanced forms of libido. Nevertheless, as has been described and will be further illustrated below, the primary process dictated the form and content of much of Mrs. N.'s cognitive functioning. The result was that periodically object constancy was not maintained.

(i) Husband: Mrs. N. blamed her husband for not protecting her from the persecutor. She said, "My husband let it all go on." On another occasion, when referring to her husband's failure to take her part, she unconsciously alluded to the danger his impotence had provoked: "My husband should have been able to stand up for me." Mr. N. was also criticized because he had exposed her sons to moral corruption:

> I know a lot of things are to do with homosexuals. I saw a film on TV, a very "arty" thing all about homosexuals, and one of the men screamed in it when he was shot, and my son was in the bathroom and he screamed at exactly the same time, and I think it's because he has inclinations that way. I told my husband and the neighbor that if they had interfered with him I'd kill them, and I threw a brick at the woman on one side [of the house]. When he [the son] was little my husband was holding him and squeezing him in a sexy way and I told him off about it. I think my husband was homosexual at one time.

This tendency to identify individuals as homosexual was also to be seen in a remark about another patient: "Mrs. X. is a lesbian. I saw her kiss and cuddle this other girl. I heard her say she had taken down her knickers" (see Results of Ego Disorganization).

(ii) Nursing Staff: Mrs. N. admired the ward sister

and wished to be like her. The ward sister was the object of homosexual wishes, which were not far from consciousness. The trend toward the merging of self with the representations of the ward sister and certain other nurses may be regarded as a regressive expression of the homosexual wishes. Mrs. N. also found one of the male nurses attractive. This came to light through dreams Mrs. N. spontaneously reported.

The first dream was as follows:

> I dreamt about John S. [the male nurse]; it was about him being or becoming my husband. I'm not sure how that could be because he's a young man compared with me. He's in here at night sometimes; last night he sat on my bed and said he was Lucifer. I kept thinking of the name Nicky. My mother was in the dream. She was ill and I was looking after her. I took her for a walk along a lane and saw John S. coming toward me. He put his arms round me and kissed me and pushed me up against the wall of the house where I was born. I woke up suddenly, my heart was racing and I felt breathless.

She added that that had happened before "when I dreamt Mr. Heath was kissing me and I felt the impression of his lips so strongly against my lips that I wakened breathless."

The second dream had the following content:

> John S. was giving me an injection. One of the other patients was pregnant to John and I said, "He'll have to marry her and do the right thing, even if I do like him."

Mrs. N. confided in Sister D. that she liked John S. and

he was "involved" in her thoughts. She believed he could read her mind because he uttered her thoughts just as they came into her mind.

(iii) Sons: It is possible that Mrs. N. had incestuous wishes for her eldest son. This hypothesis is based on her reaction to her husband embracing the boy and her fear that her husband would excite the child sexually.

ii. Cathexis of representations of real and fantasy objects

Local and national politicians were the objects of sexual drives. These wishes were unacceptable to Mrs. N. She said:

> My neighbor gave me stuff that she'd got for her wee girl and I don't remember anything after that. . . . I'm afraid I was put under hypnosis and they came into the house and had sex with me. I was singing and dancing. The neighbors were certainly involved; they've been buttering my husband up. I asked them who it was and they said, "That's an awful thing to say." It all started in 1968 [the year father died]. They wanted to find out what sort of person I was, what strength I had. They had no right to do that. . . . That Lord X. for one, he calls himself a Lord, and Mr. Z. and my minister, I'm not too sure about Dr. W., but they took films of it and my husband let it all go on.

Mrs. N.'s utterances showed that when a man had coitus with her in fantasy he became part of herself (see Cathexis of the self).

Mrs. N. had difficulty in maintaining the separation between representations of real persons and fantasy objects. She believed on occasions that Sister D. was God and that she was Dr. W. These delusional ideas can be understood as following from an externalization of the belief that she was both God and Dr. W. — aspects of her masculine images of herself.

(2) *Libidinal Position*

During the psychotic attack a phallic (active) sexual organization with both heterosexual and homosexual aims was predominant. This formulation is based on speech content and on dreams, some of which have been described. The expression of the former was in part determined by the action of defenses, while in the latter case the phallic sexuality had a symbolic representation. The wish to be a man was observed in the following dream: "I dreamt I was young Dr. W. I was sitting like this [she demonstrated the posture] like him." In another dream: "I dreamt about him [a prominent physician] again and I belonged to his family. We did a lot of horse riding and there was a wee man there, he was very 'country' and wore rough country clothes." Later that night she had the dream of the injection given by the male nurse.

The defense against the overt expression of the phallic wishes was almost completely successful, although on one occasion homosexual feelings came near to consciousness. One day Mrs. N. said she had been teasing Sister D. in a provocative way — "I was dancing behind her but she ignored me." Then Mrs. N. went on to say she had, the previous evening, been watching two women patients lying in bed making love. The reality of this report is doubtful. That night Mrs. N. dreamed: "It was at the back of our house. It was about homosexuals, it took place in an old shed. There were sticks which we used, and the thicker the stick, the more thrill I got." The absence in the manifest content of any reference as to whether the excitement was generated by active or passive experiences is noteworthy.

B. *Aggression*

While in hospital Mrs. N. never showed any sign of aggression in speech or action. The only exception to this was her threat to kill anyone who tried to interfere sexually with her sons. Her potential for violence was shown by her action in throwing a brick through her neighbor's window. Death wishes against her husband must certainly have been present. Death wishes against the father were certainly present before his death. He was a burden and an unwanted responsibility for Mrs. N. She said she was not surprised when he died: "I had a dream which predicted he would die."

Externalization was probably the principal mechanism operative in regard to aggression, and it is doubtful if it served a defensive purpose.

6. ASSESSMENT OF EGO AND SUPEREGO

(1) *Ego Functions*

Speech, thinking, attention, and concentration were intact, except when drive pressure led to primary-process functioning (see Regression of Ego Functions). Mrs. N.'s capacity to reflect on her experience (reflective awareness) remained, and thus she was able to describe the various "merging" experiences to which she believed herself subject.

(2) *Ego Reactions to Danger Situations*

Mrs. N. experienced danger with regard to external objects (neighbor, husband). Their purpose was to undermine her moral standards. The inner dangers, represented by the persecutors, arose from both heterosexual and homosexual wishes. The response to these dangers was some degree of superego anxiety. Mrs. N. regarded the persecution as, in part, a test of her moral integrity. The nature of the delusional objects and the strength of the wish for maleness suggest the presence of an intense castration complex.

(3) *State of Defense Organization*

The defense organization was composed of advanced (repression, projection) and elementary (externalization) mechanisms. Repression was successful against the awareness of depressive affects. It was not as effective in barring sexual feeling from consciousness, but the manifest content of the dreams suggests it played an important role in the distortion of libidinal wishes.

The heterosexual wishes became conscious with genital sensation, perhaps with the remembrance of past acts of coitus. A conscious wish for sexual experiences with men was repudiated (barred from consciousness), as was responsibility for the sexual feeling. Here attribution of responsibility led to the delusional content.

The wish to be a man was countered by externalization of aspects of the self. Mrs. N. admired the tall, slim, athletic physique of Sister D. Homosexual interests were externalized onto her husband, son, and other patients. The homosexual wishes were met with by projection. As a result, Mrs. N. remained unaware of her homosexual feelings except in one dream. The persecution had been initiated by a female neighbor with whom Mrs. N. had previously been friendly. The persecution was the end product of the defense against the homosexuality. Using this hypothesis as a basis, it is possible to envisage that the heterosexual delusions acted as a further defense against the intrusion of homosexual wishes into consciousness.

(4) *Affects*

Reference has already been made to the occasions when Mrs. N. described the tears in her eyes, her son's eyes, and in the eyes of other persons, as she thought. One such reference occurred after talking about her father's death. While she was never conscious of a sad feeling, the somatic expression of the affect made itself manifest. A dream may be quoted here: "Last night my niece's [the one referred to above] parents had gone on holiday by bus or train and left her by herself. She was very unhappy." She continued, "I only have to look at her and she becomes part of me."

The other affect noted was jealousy. When talking about her niece, Mrs. N. said, "The last time she was home [from Australia] there was a whole row because I thought she was putting thoughts into my son's mind and I just told her she couldn't take over as his mother."

(5) *Superego*

At the onset of the psychosis the superego appeared to be externalized, leading to the delusion that she was being tested to see if she could withstand temptation (an identification with Christ may have been present at this point). Later, phenomena explainable on the basis of an externalization of the superego disappeared. Self-reproach was not apparent at any time.

7. ASSESSMENT OF REGRESSIONS AND POSSIBLE FIXATIONS

(a) *Regression in Object Relations:* The data available only allow some tentative formulations with regard to the possible regressions in object relations that occurred with the onset of the psychosis. In the sphere of fantasy, as expressed in the erotic delusions (coitus with the Prime Minister and leading politicians), positive oedipal wishes can be discerned. In reality, Mrs. N. quite conceivably repeated with her husband and her neighbor different aspects of her mother relation. Although altered by projection, the neighbor represented the mother as an object toward whom active and passive libidinal wishes were directed. The homosexual dream is in line with this and points to a possible childhood (homosexual) seduc-tion. Mr. N. could well represent the mother both in the role of seducer (Mrs. N.'s belief that her husband might seduce the sons) and as a protector against sexual wishes (masturbation). Mrs. N.'s anger against her husband may have reflected anger against her mother for failing to provide her with an adequate outlet for her phallic excitations (penis envy).

(b) *Regression of Sexual Organization:* While Mrs. N. may have succeeded in achieving genitality prior to the psychosis, the clinical phenomena indicate that during the attack a phallic sexuality predominated. Assuming a genital-phallic heterosexuality was reached, Mr. N.'s lack of sexual drive (impotence?) imposed a frus-tration, which led to a regression to homosexuality with active, masculine tendencies (the wish to be a man).

(c) *Regression of Ego Functions:* Many of the

clinical phenomena illustrate the way in which the primary process altered the functioning of the ego. This occurred in thinking as well as in visual perception and memory. Under the influence of the primary process, homosexual wishes led to a recathexis of memories of childhood sexual play, resulting in auditory hallucinations or misinterpretations of overheard speech—for example, the remark: "I heard her say she had taken down her knickers," attributed to another patient. The primary process led to the condensation of self- and object representations with the result that Mrs. N. could possess the loved or admired object as part of herself (regression from object cathexis to identification).

(d) *Regression of Superego:* At the onset of the psychosis there was an externalization of the superego.

(3) *Fixations:* The clinical data point to fixations at the phallic and oral phases of sexual development.

8. RESULTS OF DRIVE AND EGO DISORGANIZATION

While most of the clinical data can be satisfactorily explained on the basis of regression, this does not apply to all the phenomena. For example, the auditory hallucinations or falsifications of overheard speech can be understood as resulting from the recathexis of childhood memories now experienced as percepts (see Regression of Ego Functions).

9. ASSESSMENT OF CONFLICTS

(a) *External Conflicts:* The external conflict consisted of Mrs. N.'s struggle to free herself from the sexual temptation imposed by the persecutor. This external conflict represented an externalization of her internalized conflicts (presumably present prior to the psychosis) over heterosexual and homosexual wishes.

(b) *Internalized Conflicts:* The internalized conflicts resulted from the homosexual wishes directed to the neighbor. This was unconscious. The conflict over heterosexual wishes was probably preconscious.

(c) *Internal Conflicts:* Internal conflicts centered around passivity and activity and masculinity and femininity (homosexuality and heterosexuality).

10. THE PREPSYCHOTIC PERSONALITY

This account of Mrs. N.'s prepsychotic personality is inevitably fragmentary and incomplete. Nothing is known of her experiences and behavior immediately prior to the outbreak of the psychosis (the prepsychotic phase). The available evidence favors the view that she retained a strong libidinal cathexis of the mother. In spite of this homosexual object cathexis, after her mother's death she made a heterosexual object choice. This turned out to be disappointing and unsatisfying. It is impossible to decide whether this outcome was the result of the libidinal fixation to the mother or whether it was due to Mr. N.'s limited genital potency. Mrs. N.'s accusations against her husband because of his poor sexual performance could well have been caused by an externalization onto him of her own limited heterosexual interest. However, her vivid description of the early period of the marriage supports the theory that lack of genital satisfactions resulted in regression and the recathexis of the homosexual wishes.

Assuming that an unconscious homosexuality was active during the later parts of the marriage, it is likely that Mrs. N. consciously wished for a man who would be more satisfying sexually. Such wishes might very well have been used to reinforce the repression of the homosexuality. Attention has already been drawn to the likelihood that at this stage of her life her sexuality had a phallic orientation with its concomitant admiration of masculinity (reference her adolescent wish to be a boy and her homosexual love for a girl friend). This admiration of masculinity was to be seen in the pride she took in her sons. She regarded her husband as ineffectual, revealing her disappointment in him as a phallic object. Finally, it should be recalled that Mrs. N. was always ambivalent with regard to her father. She had found him a burden after his first mental illness.

11. ASSESSMENT OF SOME GENERAL CHARACTERISTICS, ETC.

Mrs. N. was able to talk freely to a young woman psychiatrist and gave details of her illness and life experiences. However, she did not acknowledge that she was mentally ill and retained a complete belief in the reality of her fantasies. She refused to take any medications and this attitude was respected. Everything was done to ease her fear of the hospital and the medical and nursing staff. During the three-month period on which this profile is based, Mrs. N. did not show any sign that she had re-created her persecutory complex with members of the hospital population as part of the content.

From time to time data emerged that might well have had a transference signficance—for example, her references to her niece in Australia and her reminiscences of her friend who enjoyed dressing nicely. These possible references were not taken up. It seemed that Mrs. N.'s attitude to the psychiatrist was friendly and appreciative that the latter was willing to listen to her problems. This limited interest on Mrs. N.'s part may have been due to the fact that almost all of her libidinal cathexes invested her delusional reality.

DYNAMIC AND ECONOMIC ASPECTS

The patients whose profiles have been presented differ in a number of important respects. These descriptive differences can be attributed to changes in the dynamics and economics of the underlying mental processes. The drives, the ego, and the superego are variously affected by regression. This had its maximum effect in the case of Miss M. and its minimal effect in the case of Mrs. B.

The profiles show that in each case the psychotic attack was precipitated by an external stress, which resulted in an internal frustration that came to act as a danger. In the three cases the mode of reaction to the danger differed in accordance with the state of the libido distribution prior to the appearance of the stress situation. In the cases of both Mrs. B. and Mrs. N., libidinal cathexes had invested heterosexual object representations. These cathexes were not withdrawn in their entirety with the onset of the psychopathological process, as occurred in the case of Miss M. The available evidence suggests that the immediate response to the danger, by both Mrs. B. and Mrs. N., was the creation of a "neurotic-like" response (see Chapter 5). Only later was there a break with reality. It is possible that the prior capacity to establish an object choice acted as a break on the withdrawal of libido onto the self and the tendency for regression.

The metapsychological assessment of Mrs. B.'s case

revealed that the danger was created by unsatisfied phallic (heterosexual) libido and this resulted in superego anxiety. Externalization of the superego relieved the sense of guilt. This externalization could only have come about through a preceding redistribution of libido between self and objects. While the effect of this redistribution was not catastrophic, it led to a pathological narcissistic state. The clinical phenomena suggest that the intensity of the hypercathexis of the self (the pathological narcissism) decides the extent to which the superego, the ego, and its identification systems will be dedifferentiated. In paranoid syndromes, of which Mrs. B. is an example, the redistribution of the libido is limited. There is a dissolution of the ego-superego relation, with the latter being replaced by its precursors — namely, by those external objects of childhood once involved in conflicts over drive expression.

The effect of the failure to consistently maintain the cathexis of objects was observed in the cases of Mrs. N. and Miss M. In the former the resulting hypercathexis of the self was such as to lead to the dissolution of self- and object boundaries (identification) as well as the superego. As a consequence of the changes within the ego, signs of primary-process activity were to be observed in the content of the delusional ideas. The primary process did not find such an expression in Mrs. B.'s case. With Miss M. the changes in libido distribution were even more widespread and the hypercathexis of the self such as to result in phenomena arising from an extensive dissolution of the ego and the superego.

The danger situation identified in Mrs. B.'s case followed from the frustration of the heterosexual drives. The ensuing instinctual regression led to a heightening of homosexual drive cathexes, which remained in repression both in the prepsychotic period and during the psychotic attack. Similarly, homosexual wishes had been activated by heterosexual frustrations in the case of Mrs. N. These wishes also remained unconscious but found an indirect expression in her sensitivity to the "homosexuality" of other women. The danger of which Mrs. N. was consciously aware was that of heterosexuality. In both Mrs. B. and Mrs. N., heterosexual and homosexual wishes were active, each bearing a different relation to consciousness. In the former the homosexual wishes were further from consciousness than the latter. This observation was consistent with the lesser degree of psychic dissolution in the case of Mrs. B. Both sexual currents were available to Miss M.'s awareness but on different occasions. The auditory misinterpretations and hallucinations, attributable to the externalized superego (women calling her a lesbian), indicate that the danger for Miss M. arose from the homosexual drive cathexes (A. Freud, 1974).

During the acute psychotic attack all three patients revealed, either directly or indirectly, that their sexuality had phallic characteristics. Only in the case of Miss M. did this phallic sexuality have an overt expression. Not only was there unconcealed masturbation, but also genital exhibitionism and a masculine attitude toward homosexual objects. This phallic orientation was also observed during the phase of partial remission, when the homosexual libido had been repressed. Then the heterosexual object relation was characterized by the effects of the rescue fantasy more appropriately found in men and sometimes in female homosexuals (Freud, 1920). For Mrs. B. and Mrs. N. the object choice had already become homosexual in the prepsychotic period. It was the threat imposed by the homosexual wishes which eventually led to the break with reality. The homosexual object choice was successfully screened by the absence of conscious genital interest of any kind in the case of Mrs. B., while with Mrs. N. there was an awareness of hetero-sexual affects but not at all of the homosexual wishes, which had been conscious during adolescence.

The kinds of defense mechanisms occurring in para-noid syndromes are dependent on the speed and extent of the dissolution affecting the psychic structures. This dis-solution proceeds from the alterations in libido distri-bution. Where the dissolution is extensive, as in the case of Miss M., the repression barrier is extensively disor-ganized. At best, the instinctual wishes are countered by such mechanisms as externalization and displacement and by the hallucinatory revival of memories of drive gratification. This last permits the deflection of the instinctual wish from an external object to a fantasy or memory.

When externalization is employed defensively, again as in the case of Miss M., this is expressed in terms of attribution of responsibility. An external object is blamed for causing an unwelcome affect or action. Many psy-chotic patients, previously friendly, accuse nurses, doc-tors, and others for being responsible for their unusual bodily sensations, sexual affects, anger, depression of mood, loss of energy, and inability to concentrate. These accusations usually arise during the course of psycho-therapy or follow some interaction between the patient and a member of the nursing or ancillary staff. The ac-cusation generally follows an awareness of sexual or aggressive affects.

Where the dissolution of psychic structures is extensive, the generalization of affect to an external object can be readily observed. Anger felt is experienced as coming from the other person. This is well illustrated by the patient who said to the author, "I can feel you hating me." A similar outcome occurs with sexual affects. As a rule, these persecutory ideas, based on generalization and arising from disappointments and anxiety, do not persist beyond a few hours. The tendency to attribute responsibility for heterosexual affects was pronounced in Mrs. N.'s case. Her phallic sexuality, directed to homosexual objects, was deflected by projection, with the result that Mrs. N. was unaware of her homosexual wishes, instead believing herself to be persecuted by a neighbor.

It is well known that there are paranoid conditions where the patient does not experience the imposition of unacceptable thoughts or feelings. In these paranoiac psychoses the patient complains of being discriminated against, of being deprived of opportunities in life, and of being the object of prejudice and hatred. A particular individual is held responsible for his misfortunes. These patients frequently engage in litigation to obtain redress for the wrongs they believe they have suffered at the hands of the persecutor. When an opportunity is afforded to study such cases, it becomes apparent that unconscious passive-feminine wishes have led to the action of projection as a defense.

The fact that there are paranoid syndromes that can be distinguished from one another on the basis of whether or not the patient experiences an unacceptable wish or intention as imposed by a persecutor raises the question of the relation between projection and that form of externalization leading to attribution of responsibility. Projection is usually assumed to possess some of the characteristics of repression insofar as the object of the drive is replaced by the self and activity as an instinctual aim turns into passivity. This reversal of aim occurs in cases of the type of Mrs. N., where responsibility for an affect is attributed to the persecutor. The affect is experienced, but the patient is unaware of a wish or intention to carry out the act.

The clinical phenomena also reveal that attribution of responsibility is found in paranoid psychoses where there is a disturbance in the capacity to discriminate between self- and object representation. This defect is absent in cases where projection is the sole defense mechanism. It is of interest in this respect that there are cases of paranoid psychosis that begin with a phase during which the patient believes himself to be subject to a persecution of the kind characteristic for paranoiac states or complains that he will be subjected to "homosexual" abuse and attempts will be made to alter his sexual identity. At this stage of the illness the patient is unaware of homosexual wishes or of a sexual passivity, which he identifies as feminine. During this phase of the illness the phenomena can be understood as arising from projection. Where the illness increases in severity, the patient comes to complain of "made" ideas and actions. Like Mrs. N., he now attributes responsibility for the unacceptable affects and actions to the persecutor. Projection has been replaced by externalization of the drive representation, with an accompanying attribution of responsibility.

Externalization of mental contents is common to both projection and to attribution of responsibility. They differ insofar as the former ensures the repression of unwelcome drive derivatives while the latter does not. When this occurs, the instinctual wishes assume an ego-alien quality. The defense, which facilitates the occurrence of attribution of responsibility in psychoses, disrupts the normal ego-syntonic nature of a drive derivative. Once the patient experiences the affects as foreign it is only one step to the belief that they have been imposed on him against his will. When considered from this standpoint, it is apparent that the attribution of responsibility that forms part of delusional content is something qualitatively different from the attribution of responsibility observed in children and in healthy and neurotic adults. In those instances the conscious or preconscious wish is ego-syntonic, even if it does evoke anxiety or guilt. It is hardly justifiable to regard attribution of responsibility, when it occurs in paranoid psychoses, simply as a form of defensive externalization. The defense in this type of psychosis renders the drive derivatives ego-alien. Any explanation of the phenomena must take account of this fact.

The view presented here is that the defense that comes into play and leads to symptoms of a paranoid syndrome depends on the extent to which the ego and the superego have been subject to dissolution. Under certain circumstances the disorganization of ego is limited, and then projection acts to alter the object and aim of the drive derivatives and keep them repressed. When the ego is more affected, this repression is no longer possible. Instead the drives are altered in such a way as to give them an ego-alien quality. In fact, the principal metapsychological difference between the types of paranoid syndromes exemplified by the cases of Mrs. N. and Mrs. B. lies in the finding that only in the former is there a

major alteration in the drive derivatives. The alteration
of aim and object and the change in quality results in a
break with reality. This outcome suggests that the
mechanism leading to "passivity" experiences (attribution
of responsibility) is qualitatively different from the projection and defensive externalizations occurring in
healthy and neurotic individuals.

This hypothesis is substantially the same as that proposed by Katan (1950), who says, "Within the boundaries
of the psychosis the ego has lost its neurotic mechanisms
of defense; the mechanisms are no longer cathected" (p.
204). Basing his formulation on Freud's (1911) theory of
psychosis, Katan proposes that the loss of the neurotic
mechanisms of defense operative in the prepsychotic
phase results from the merging of the ego and id during
the psychotic attack. According to Katan, it is the
decathexis of the object world that brings about this state
of absolute narcissism. The cathexes withdrawn into that
part of the self affected by the dissolution are used to
create the psychotic reality. New defenses are built up
and some of the neurotic mechanisms recathected. Psychotic projection, in Katan's opinion, leads to the complete externalization of id drives, particularly of those
seeking the satisfaction of both masculine and feminine
wishes. In contrast, the projection occurring in neurosis
does not lead to a break with reality, because the unacceptable wish retains its origin in the id.

Psychotic projection is not a primary defense but a
final step in the course of attempting to resolve a danger
situation (Katan, 1950). In neuroses projection has a
primary role in this respect. Psychotic projection can only
come into play after there has been a redistribution of
libido, resulting in a hypercathexis of the self with an

accompanying dissolution of psychic structure. There is an externalization of ego functions, the superego, and the drive representations themselves—"A part of the mind has been exteriorated (projected) and is treated as outer world" (Katan, 1950, p. 203).

DEVELOPMENTAL ASPECTS

The dynamic and economic assessment of persecutory ideas in the adult is based on conditions existing in the patient's mind during the psychosis. The phenomena are also amenable to a developmental analysis. This provides a further source of information, which can be integrated with the dynamic and economic formulations. Two approaches are possible. The first is to seek out all the connections that may exist between the adult phenomena and possible childhood precursors in the individual case. The second is to embark on studies of those normal and abnormal manifestations of childhood bearing a descriptive resemblance to the delusional phenomena in the adult.

Reconstruction of Childhood Histories

The fact that reality has not been wholly abandoned in some paranoid syndromes facilitates the gathering of data such as that recorded in the profiles of both Mrs. B. and Mrs. N. Unfortunately the content of these profiles is meager with respect to childhood experience. This can in part be attributed to the relatively short period during which the patients were under treatment and observation. It is also true, however, that a psychosis, in contrast to a neurosis, imposes conditions that, in varying degrees preclude the emergence of childhood data (see Chapter 6). It is likely that the patient's behavior and delusional experiences constitute much of the repressed childhood history, but such reconstructions require supporting data if they are to have any reliability.

It follows from such considerations that the possibility of reconstructing significant phases of the childhood of those who in adult life developed paranoid psychoses depends on the extent to which the patient can turn his attention away from his delusional experiences. This capacity varies from patient to patient. It is the occurrence of considerable individual differences in this regard that accounts for the variation in the quantity of childhood data reported by those who work with psychotic patients. In spite of all these limitations, the profiles contain sufficient data, which, when taken in conjunction with what is already known about the decisive stages of mental development in the child, allow the beginnings of a reconstruction of those childhood object relations that bear on the content of the delusional ideas.

An outstanding feature of married women who suffer from paranoid syndromes is their hostility to their husbands. This hostility is generated by disappointments, some of which are conscious while others remain unconscious (the castration complex). Sometimes, as in Mrs. N.'s case, the hostility is reinforced by the belief that the husband either has failed in his duty as a protector or is actively assisting the persecutor. The cause for disappointment does not only lie in a lack of genital satisfactions, although this is a frequent cause of complaint (see Chapter 5). The patient no longer looks to her husband as an object of admiration or regard. He has ceased to fulfill the aspirations embodied in the patient's ego ideal. To this may be added the criticism that the husband is a poor provider of material and emotional needs. Disappointments in both father and mother can be discerned in all these reproaches.

The phallic sexuality of the patients must be attributed in part to the seductions to which they were subjected in childhood. This must have prematurely awakened the phallic libido and encouraged active sexual wishes, resulting in conflict. Traces of the need for the mother to help counter these masturbatory wishes were seen in Mrs. N.'s criticisms of the husband's failure to protect her against the sexual persecution. Other criticisms of the husband during the psychosis must have arisen in childhood, as in the complaints of lack of material necessities, lack of care and attention, and undue interest in others. All must be regarded as a repetition of the need for an exclusive relation with the mother.

As far as can be ascertained on the basis of the available material, the patients who married must, in childhood, have been able to abandon, temporarily as later events revealed, the phallic wishes for the mother and to advance in a limited way into the oedipal phase. In Miss M.'s case, and this may be true of all unmarried patients, evidences of the mother attachment were particularly pronounced, indicating the strength of the pre-oedipal relation. The psychotic attack exposed her phallic (homosexual) wishes. This indicated that Miss M. was less able than the married patients to renounce the mother relation in both its pregenital and phallic aspects. The Oedipus complex must only have received a minimum cathexis, if indeed it was significantly cathected at all.

It is cases such as that of Miss M. that provide the basis for the hypothesis that the wished-for love object is narcissistic and represents a wished-for self. It has also been noted that patients who make a real object choice do so on the basis of narcissism. A quantitative factor must operate with respect to the extent to which narcissism enters into the choice of object. Many writers in the past have pointed out that it is the narcissistic element in the object choice that renders the individual vulnerable, with regression occurring from object cathexis to identification. In the married patients described here the reaction to the injury to narcissism was either to find a substitute object, as in the case of Mrs. B., or to regress to the mother relation, as with Mrs. N. In the former the attempt to find a new narcissistic object led to a superego reaction. In the latter the regression continued until object relating was on the basis of identification (merging). Patients such as those just described provide the kind of data that led Katan (1974) to suggest that in the psychotic attack the paranoid woman patient attempts to bring to fruition her wish to be a man. The persecutor, when a male, is a narcissistic object specifically representing the wished-for penis.

It is reasonable to assume that these patients had only the most precarious hold on the oedipal stage. Once again a quantitative factor differentiates one patient from the next. In several cases, apart from those described here, a limited Oedipus complex may have been contributed to by the father's absence from the home or by his unreliability. This may have accentuated the girl's natural tendency to choose a love object on the basis of narcissism. It is noteworthy that oedipal-like fantasies frequently occur in the content of delusions. Mrs. N., for example, believed that the men with whom she had coitus

were important and influential and so may be assumed to be substitutes for a wished-for father. Following the coital act, she assumed their capacities. The object libido was turned into ego libido.

There is nothing in these reconstructions to distinguish them from the reconstituted childhood histories of patients who suffer from neuroses and character abnormalities. The death wishes Mrs. N. had for her father and which recurred with her husband did not possess special characteristics, nor did they evoke a defense that might have predisposed her to a psychotic development. All that can be claimed, on the basis of clinical observation, is that those destined to develop a psychosis have failed in varying degrees to extricate themselves, partly or wholly, from the earliest narcissistic stage (see Chapter 6). Cathexis of objects was, therefore, not secured on a scale capable of resisting regression. In the present study the retrospective assessments are made even more speculative by the scarcity of remembered childhood symptoms and affects which, if known, would provide a bridgehead for a view of the precursors of the conflicts identified in the clinical phenomena.

The fact that an unequivocal distinction cannot be made, on the basis of reconstruction, between the childhood mental life of those who come to fall ill with a paranoid syndrome and those who remain free of psychosis suggests that the elements necessary for the genesis of delusional phenomena do not exist in the early years of life. On this account it is all the more important to examine all those manifestations of childhood bearing the slightest resemblance to the delusional phenomena of adult psychosis in order to determine whether or not there are dynamic and economic similarities between them.

Comparison with Childhood Anxieties

As far as content is concerned, many descriptive similarities exist between the anxieties occurring in healthy children and the persecutory fears of adult paranoid patients. With the exception of the "archaic fears" (A. Freud, 1965), all later childhood anxieties are an integral part of the continuing changes and differentiations affecting the developing mental life. Bodily needs and the physical expression of wishes belonging to the different libidinal stages are only modified following conflict with the parents. These developmental conflicts are responsible for the different kinds of anxieties associated with the advance from one phase of development to the next. Ordinarily these anxieties subside as each phase is successfully negotiated.

The fact that the different forms of childhood anxiety can be related to developmental phases and to the conflicts arising from them provides the basis for a developmental classification (A. Freud, 1965). First there are the archaic fears — fears of darkness, of noises, and of strangers. They occur independently of real events and bear no relation to conflict or regression. They can be understood as the result in part of a disequilibrium in the generation and discharge of cathexes and in part of the inability to assimilate excessive quantities of external stimulation. Separation anxiety is an aspect of the developmental phase during which the mother and child comprise a biological unity. This anxiety finds expression in fears of starvation, of helplessness, and of annihilation. Fear of loss of love makes its appearance once object constancy has been established, with the concurrent differentiation of self- and object representations. Fear of loss of love is enhanced during the anal-sadistic stage by the externalization of the child's destructive wishes. It is during this stage that conflicts with the mother are pronounced, thus leading to fears of criticism and punishment. The fear of loss of love is expressed in fears of being deserted, of death, of punishment, and of the end of the world.

When the oedipal stage is reached castration fear and other anxieties deriving from the oedipal conflicts make their appearance. Castration anxieties are expressed in fears of illness, of injury, of doctors and dentists. Fears of being poisoned spring from fantasies of impregnation. Over and above these developmental anxieties, there is evidence of yet another form of anxiety, which appears to be the direct result of instinctual pressures (A. Freud, 1970).

The danger situations leading to the various forms of anxiety in childhood are reacted to by different defense mechanisms. The defenses employed depend, once again, on the developmental stage a child has reached. A classification of childhood anxieties can, therefore, also be made in terms of defense activity (A. Freud, 1970).

In the symbiotic phase (see Chapter 6), the reaction to separation from a love object consists of a hypercathexis of the rudimentary object representation. This, not yet being completely differentiated from the self, results in an intensification of wishes for union with the love object. When this defense operates, it leads to phenomena arising from the merging of self- and object representations. While this is appropriate for the early phases of object relations, its occurrence in later periods indicates the presence of a developmental arrest or regression. The same is true for the archaic fears. The persistence of these fears into later childhood indicates that ego development has not advanced satisfactorily. When merging phenomena occur in a defense context, they are accompanied by manifestations resulting from activity of the primary process. The defenses employed to deal with the fear of loss of love and castration fear depend on the extent to which ego-id differentiation has taken place. When the ego is well advanced in development, repression, projection, and reaction formation operate. Where development is less advanced, as during the pre-oedipal period, externalizations, including attribution of responsibility, are the principal defensive measures employed to avoid danger situations.

As has been mentioned, the anxieties of childhood may be transitory, as when they reflect the presence of developmental conflicts, or they may persist beyond their appropriate period. This will occur if, as a consequence of "environmental interferences" (Nagera, 1966), ego development is retarded or the instinctual drives are given a premature impetus. The outcome is a disturbance in the differentiation of ego from id, self from object, and fantasy from reality. This in turn has a profound effect on the nature and stability of the superego.

In the sphere of childhood pathology it is the degree of psychical differentiation that determines the kinds of defense mechanisms that will emerge to meet a danger situation. When ego and id, self and object are incompletely differentiated, either as a result of an arrest in development or because of regression, danger situations arising from the pressure of pregenital drive derivatives lead to conflict with external objects — "The first id-ego conflicts, and with them the first neurotic symptoms as conflict solutions, are produced with the ego under pressure from the environment, i.e., threatened not by guilt feelings arising internally from the superego but by dangers arising from the object world such as loss of love, rejection, punishment" (A. Freud, 1970, p. 166). Under pathological conditions there is an intensification of this state, with the parental objects and others, real and fantasy, with whom the associative connections have been made, becoming the source of severe anxiety. The morbid fears arise from pregenital drives, with their sadistic quality being generalized to external objects.

Berstock (1974) describes the case of an 11-year-old boy who was initially referred because of school phobia. He was afraid to go to school because he said boys were spreading rumors about his contact with a girl and he was afraid the boys would harm him. He did not specify the content of the rumors. In addition, this boy was acutely anxious at home and at night would not remain alone in his room. At times he feared his parents might be involved in an accident. One of his fears was that his father would strangle him. Sometimes he was so afraid that he wanted the police brought to the house to protect him. The boy was also aggressive and difficult to manage. He quarreled with his mother, was violent with a younger brother, and was generally provocative. When his wishes were not immediately met, he flew into a rage, lay on the floor like a toddler, and shouted. He had fantasies in which he was an expert in Kung Fu, attacking his enemies. With the psychiatrist he was friendly and at ease, possibly regarding her as an ally against his tormentors. Prior to the onset of the symptoms, this boy was described as an obedient, conforming child and was regarded by his schoolteachers as perhaps slightly withdrawn, but nevertheless happy and settled in his class.

A striking similarity exists between the symptomatology of this boy and of Mr. B., whose case will be described in Chapter 5. Mr. B. was unable to continue at work because he believed some men wished to kill him. Like the boy, he was panic-stricken at home and would not remain alone in his room at night. He too feared that his father planned to murder him and then drop his body in a sack into the river. Again like the boy, he was taken up with means of countering possible attackers. For several years he had spent considerable time acquiring a skill at judo.

When both sets of clinical phenomena are examined from the metapsychological viewpoint, descriptive, dynamic, and developmental differences become apparent. In the adult patient the persecutory fears were the end product of a projection of homosexual wishes directed to the father — for example, the birth fantasy embodied in the murder plot. The homosexuality (passive femininity) was activated by regression from heterosexuality under the impact of castration fear. Overt aggression was not a feature of the psychotic attack, in contrast to the child's mental disturbance. While some of the boy's aggression was no doubt reactive to anxiety, the greater quantity sprang from the aggressive drives themselves. This aggression was not successfully countered by projection, as evidenced by the fact that it found an outlet in consciousness and action. The persecutory fears can best be understood in the child's case as due to externalization of aggression of which he was aware, quite apart from any libidinal element that might have contributed to the "delusional" fears. Regression from the phallic phase and some degree of ego regression was no doubt facilitated in the boy's case by the relative immaturity of the recently acquired psychic structuralization. Reality testing was impaired and the regressed anal-sadistic drive derivatives reinforced the destructive tendencies, enhancing anxiety. In the case of the adult patient, the ego regression was of such a nature that projection could effectively deal with the danger provoked by the homosexual wishes for the father. This projection established the break with reality.

In childhood disorders where the separation of ego and id has withstood the effects of regression, danger situations are dealt with differently. In the boy regression of the libido from the phallic to the anal phase, under the influence of fixations created at that level, enhances passive wishes for the father. The resulting symptoms — phobias, fears of mutilation, fear of the dead — are the end product of internalized conflict. Where the superego is not effectively differentiated, the danger situation created by the drive activity leads the child to attribute responsibility for his thoughts, feelings, and actions to an external object.

Healthy as well as mentally abnormal children can suffer from "persecutory" fears. In the former these fears are transient, arising from developmental conflicts. In the latter the fears either persist after the appropriate period for their expression or they re-emerge long after a prior appearance. When the fears of mentally abnormal children are examined to assess how far they resemble, descriptively, the persecutory delusions of adult patients, some obvious differences immediately present themselves. Apart from childhood psychoses and severe borderline states, older children who present persecutory fears do so in a context different from that of the adult patient who suffers from a paranoid illness. Such children, as in the following example, cling to their love objects and are dependent on them.

Dare (1974) has reported the case of an 11-year-old

boy, an only child, who, following admission to hospital for an appendectomy, became acutely anxious when left by his parents. When seen by a psychiatrist, it transpired that the boy had suffered from a lifelong sleep disturbance, which resulted in his almost constantly sharing his parents' bedroom. Two years previously he had gone away with the school for one week, but after two days he had phoned his parents asking them to come and take him home. At home he was usually domineering, demanding, and given to indulging in fantasies with an omnipotent content. When seen by Dare, the boy was withdrawn and babyish in manner, in accord with the description given of his behavior at school. He complained of being teased and was afraid of older boys attacking him. He said he was very frightened of traveling on the subway. He was afraid of the way in which the drivers controlled the trains and believed they were somehow aiming directly at him. In particular, he feared the tunnels. In contrast to the traveling phobia of the adult, where anxiety is expressed via somatic channels and is without a conscious object, this boy actually experienced a fear of attack by boys, youths, and train drivers in the same way as is experienced by adult patients during a prepsychotic phase (see Chapter 5).

This boy presented the kind of conflict so frequently found in cases of schizophrenia — namely, that provoked by the danger of passive-feminine wishes. As in the schizophrenic patient, these wishes were concealed behind grandiosity and omnipotence. In contrast to the psychotic patient, however, this boy had not abandoned reality, although reality testing was deficient in certain situations (the subway) that evoked excitement and consequently led to anxiety.

Another fact to be taken into account is that the "persecutory" fears appearing in childhood disorders do so in different metapsychological and developmental settings. There are children whose "persecutory" fears are the expression of a true infantile neurosis. For this to occur mental development must have reached that stage where there already have been ".... decisive advances in structuralisation, in every aspect of ego and superego functioning and in the ego's ability to hold its own" (A. Freud, 1972, p. 87). "Persecutory" fears have quite different concomitants in the borderline states and psychoses of early and late childhood. In the psychoses there is overwhelming evidence of an arrest in ego and instinctual development. It is in these cases that the "persecutory" fears appear in the context of object relations characterized by egocentrism and need-satisfying behavior (Thomas et al., 1966). During acute states of disturbance object constancy is absent, but this can return during periods of quiescence. Signs of the primary process in cognition are constantly evident.

Beres (1956) has described a series of disturbed children ranging in age from eight to 14 years of age, many of whom showed "persecutory" fears. In every case the ego was seriously disorganized. This was reflected in the way in which the children gave free rein, in action, to their instinctual needs — aggressive and libidinal. In one case: "All forms of instinctual drives were expressed: oral drives in biting and voracious eating; anal drives in soiling and defecating on the floor; phallic drives in exhibitionistic displays of her genitals and unconcealed masturbation" (Beres, 1956, p. 189). Des Lauriers (1962) has also reported on similar cases, where the clinical phenomena can only be attributed to the loss of the repression barrier, to egocentrism, and to the effects of need-satisfying behavior.

The "persecutory" fears of borderline and psychotic children arise on the basis of the limited differentiation between ego and id and self and object. During the treatment of these children it is possible to observe how oral- and anal-sadistic wishes are generalized to the therapist (Thomas et al., 1966). Conflict and anxiety occur in relation to the external object. This is in contrast to the situation existing in the child whose "persecutory" fears are part of an infantile neurosis. Here the conflict occurs between an ego already sharply distinguished from the id and the drive derivatives. The conflict is internalized in kind and remains so because of the integrity of the repression barrier and the secondary process. The danger situation alone is externalized through the action of projection.

Only the type of paranoid syndrome represented by the case of Miss M. presents manifestations metapsychologically similar to those of borderline and psychotic children. In Miss M.'s case, dissolution of the repression barrier and the re-emergence of the primary process led to behavior similar to that of the children described by Beres (1956). As with the children, only elementary forms of defense acted against the drives. However, one important difference between cases such as Miss M. and borderline and psychotic children must not be overlooked. This is that prior to Miss M.'s illness progression in mental life was the predominant trend. In retrospect, arrests in mental development must be presumed to have occurred but only in discrete areas of mental functioning. The predominance of progressive tendencies enabled

Miss M. to meet the demands of home, school, and, for a while, university. An extensive dissolution of psychic life had to take place before the paranoid syndrome resembling the childhood conditions could emerge.

Clinical psychiatry distinguishes between the type of case represented by Miss M. and what is sometimes described as nuclear or process schizophrenia on the basis of the presenting symptomatology and the previous personality. When cases of process schizophrenia are thoroughly investigated, it can be shown that the personality is typified by widespread restrictions and inhibitions. In this regard, the pre-illness personality of the schizophrenic patient differs completely from that which characterizes cases such as Miss M. The personality deficits of the potentially schizophrenic patient are due to extensive arrests in both ego and instinctual development. It is of interest that the parents of such patients do not recall the occurrence in childhood of phenomena akin to those found in borderline or psychotic children. There is also the fact that such disturbed children rarely progress spontaneously to the level of personality development achieved by Miss M. and similar cases.

It is the types of paranoid syndrome represented by the cases of Mrs. B. and Mrs. N. that differ most markedly, both descriptively and metapsychologically, from the borderline states and psychoses of childhood. While mental structure is disorganized in different ways in these adult states, psychical differentiation is not entirely lost. Even in Mrs. N.'s case, the effect of the residual ego was to be seen in the considerable synthetic activity (e.g., the delusional system) and in the way projection played a part in the defense. The primary process was restricted to thought and there was no breakthrough of drive derivatives into action. The type represented by Mrs. B. comes closest, metapsychologically, to the infantile neurosis and thus to the neuroses of adult life. In this paranoid syndrome the repression barrier is intact and self- and object images remain discrete. Many writers have remarked on the close connections between the types of paranoid psychosis represented by Mrs. B. and, for want of a better term, psychotic depression. Patients are found who, in successive bouts of illness, alternate between paranoid and depressive states. The clinical condition appears to depend upon the status of the superego.

This survey of the "persecutory" fears in healthy and abnormal children and the persecutory delusions of adult patients indicates that, with the exception of the syndrome resulting from the extensive dissolution of psychic structure, few metapsychological similarities exist between the two groups. While the "persecutory" fears of young children, healthy or ill, arise on the basis of one mechanism (generalization), the infantile neurosis being the one exception, the delusions of the adult patient have several sources of origin. The concept of psychosis includes a wide variety of abnormal mental states in adult life. In only a small number (for example, in process schizophrenia) can the psychosis be attributed to a widespread arrest in development. In the majority of cases the symptomatology follows from a dissolution of mental functions that have achieved a high degree of development. The reaction to the dissolution comprises the dramatic signs of the illness — the delusions, hallucinations, affect and motility disorders. The persecutory ideas are complex in their origins and development when compared with similar ideas occurring in normal and abnormal children. It is surely misleading and an oversimplification of the problem to claim that an identical "psychotic" process underlies both the adult and childhood phenomena.

The identification of a childhood psychosis or borderline state requires the presence of phenomena over and above the occurrence of "persecutory" ideas. There must also be a transient or persistent break with reality, which reveals itself in inappropriate modes of object relation. This kind of childhood data has not been forthcoming from adult psychotic patients who have been under psychoanalytic or an allied form of treatment. All that has been noted is a variety of fantasies (see Chapter 6), indicating that the progressive advance of the developmental line to "emotional independence and adult object relationships" (A. Freud, 1965) must have been hindered throughout the childhood period. The fantasies suggest the occurrence of periodic withdrawals from reality in early life but never a break with reality commensurate with that occurring in childhood psychoses and borderline states. Katan (1954) has vigorously opposed the concept of an infantile psychosis envisaged as providing the prototype for the psychosis of adult life, be it schizophrenic or manic-depressive (see Chapter 6).

It is the belief in the prior occurrence of an infantile psychosis, either as a feature of normal development or as a pathological event, that has led several psychoanalysts (Rosenfeld, 1952b; Searles, 1963) to claim that a special form of transference (a transference psychosis) regularly appears during the psychoanalysis and psychotherapy of adult psychotic patients (see Chapter 6). The expressions of the transference psychosis are manifold and they include negativism, inattention, misidentifications, merging phenomena (transitivism), and persecutory delusions. The concept of a transference psychosis has encouraged the idea that these phenomena have a common source of origin in infantile object relations believed to be intrinsically psychotic. In pursuing this belief, the real differences between the phenomena have been glossed over and obscured. It follows from what has been said earlier that the psychical situations that give rise to transitivism and persecutory delusions, for example, are completely different. In the case of the former an extensive dissolution of mental structures has allowed the reconstitution of a primary identification, whereas in the latter a relatively intact ego is necessary for their expression (i.e., through projection and other mechanisms).

The concept of transference implies the repetition in the therapeutic situation of childhood object relations. The question is whether the psychotic phenomena that may arise in connection with the therapist during the treatment of schizophrenia or a paranoid illness are to be regarded as repetitions of real or fantasied childhood relations. Negativism, withdrawal from others, and even the nonrecognition of love objects are encountered in very young children who have been subject to sudden separation from their mothers (A. Freud, 1939-1945). Minor degrees of negativism are, as has been mentioned previously, a normal accompaniment of the anal phase of libidinal development. However, there is no normal or pathological childhood mental state equivalent to the passivity delusions of the adult psychotic patient, and misidentifications are unknown except in some cases of childhood psychosis.

The extent to which transferences will occur during

the treatment of a psychotic patient depends on the degree to which psychic structures remain intact. Some of the psychotic phenomena that attach themselves to the therapist may be repetitive in nature, as in the case of negativism and withdrawal, but the vast majority of manifestations arise, *de novo*, either as a result of the action of the primary process revived by the dissolution of the ego or as a consequence of measures (projection, etc.) designed to reconstitute the object world. The psychotic patient certainly reacts to the therapist. Some of these reactions spring from the healthy or neurotic residues unaffected by the morbid process, others from the modes of mental functioning exposed by the injury to the ego and superego, and still others from the drive to regain contact with reality (Freud, 1914).

CHAPTER 5

The Prepsychotic Phase and the State of Partial Remission

It is well known that patients who succumb to acute attacks of psychotic illness experience symptoms of different kinds in the weeks or months prior to the appearance of the delusions, hallucinations, and disorders of motility. It is also well recognized that the passing of the acute psychotic attack is usually followed by a period of indefinite duration during which the patient complains of disinterest, lack of energy, and depression of mood; is hypochondriacal; and presents a host of neurotic-like symptoms and inhibitions. This state of partial remission may be succeeded by a return to complete mental health or it may persist unchanged for years. There are many descriptive similarities between the prepsychotic phase and the state of partial remission, but these similarities should not obscure the differences between the two phases of the illness. This distinction is based on the observation that, while the prepsychotic phase is marked by signs of anxiety and compulsive behavior, the partial remission is characterized by a symptom complex including withdrawal and self-preoccupation. The state of partial remission is periodically disturbed by a variety of symptoms, which either disappear or develop into a further psychotic attack. When the latter occurs, the

preceding period is identical in every way to the prepsychotic phase that ushered in the very first bout of
psychosis.

The purpose of this chapter is to study the phenomena occurring during the prepsychotic phase and the
state of partial remission and to try to describe the connections between them and their relation to the acute
psychotic attack.

THE PREPSYCHOTIC PHASE

Katan (1950, 1954) has the distinction of being the
first writer to draw attention to the importance of the
prepsychotic phase and its relation to the acute attack in
cases of schizophrenia. Jacobson (1967) has also described
the connections between the psychotic attack and the
mental states following partial or complete remission.
Jacobson's views, however, are more appropriately discussed in the section dealing with the state of partial
remission. Katan's general hypothesis (1950) is that the
symptoms and behavior of the patient in the prepsychotic
phase can be understood as following from the struggle to
retain the cathexis of heterosexual objects chosen on the
basis of narcissism. The withdrawal of libidinal cathexis
from these narcissistic oedipal objects leads to the recathexis of the pre-oedipal mother relation, resulting in the
wish to be a woman in the case of the man and the wish to
be a man in the case of the woman. It is Katan's opinion
that men who are destined to develop schizophrenia have
failed, in childhood, to reach a healthy Oedipus complex. The oedipal wishes and objects are based on narcissism. The mother, in the case of the boy, represents his
wish for femininity.

The male patient's wish to be a woman in the pre-psychotic period causes castration fear. Strenuous attempts are made to reinforce the failing masculinity as well as efforts to ward off feminine wishes. The former consist of repeated heterosexual intercourse, masturbation, and other forms of behavior described below. The latter comprise symptoms and inhibitions whose aim is to avoid arousal by homosexual objects. The man's wish for femininity cannot be contained and enters into all those operations created to annul its effect. Hence, heterosexual acts and fantasies are accompanied by sensations, ideas, and affects with a feminine significance. Masturbation and coitus are given up because their practice carries with it homosexual ideas. This is equivalent to the satisfaction of feminine wishes. Castration fear is reinforced. The result is a withdrawal of cathexis from object representations and a further regression, which brings about the loss of differentiation between psychic structures. The primary process becomes dominant and reality testing is no longer possible.

On the basis of clinical observation, Katan (1950) has demonstrated that the bisexual conflict is continued through into the psychotic attack. The wish to be a woman is projected, resulting in delusion formation. This delusional reality is the psychotic equivalent to the attempts at restitution (the move to strengthen masculinity in the male or femininity in the female) in the prepsychotic phase.

Schizophrenia

Katan's metapsychological analysis of the prepsychotic phase in schizophrenia provides a means for classifying the clinical phenomena of this period. It follows from Katan's (1950) formulation that two distinct but interrelated trends operate unconsciously during the prepsychotic phase. There is the defense against the wish for femininity or masculinity, as the case may be, and there is the movement to restore and enhance the failing masculinity or femininity (the process of restitution). One of these will be uppermost in the individual case, but there will also be evidence of the other tendency. The result is a distinctive symptomatology and behavior. Classifying the clinical data in this way does not imply a commitment to the theoretical assumptions. They draw attention to the clinical phenomena, and this ensures a careful examination of the anxieties patients experience in connection with masculinity and femininity, on the one hand, and heterosexuality and homosexuality, on the other.

In the first category the clinical phenomena can be explained on the basis of the attempt to restore a failing masculinity. The patient Mr. A. had suffered from two acute psychotic attacks, each of which was followed by partial remission. Prior to the second psychotic attack, this young man expressed concern about envy and jealousy of his brother, who was six years older and engaged to be married. At this time Mr. A. worried inappropriately about his brother's health and safety. However, within a few days a new series of ideas came to dominate Mr. A.'s mind. He said his brother was annoying him. He realized that his brother was ineffectual, weak, and effeminate. Worst of all, his brother envied his abilities and good looks and was following him around everywhere and imitating him. It seemed to Mr. A. as if his brother wanted to turn into a replica of himself. Mr. A.'s anger mounted and he accused his brother of being evil and of having criminal tendencies. He wished his brother out of his sight and would not have regretted his death.

In this case the patient externalized his femininity, his envy and jealousy. In addition, he projected his wish to possess his brother's masculinity, as in the idea that his brother wanted to be identical to himself. During this period of the prepsychotic phase the patient magically possessed his brother's masculinity and, as a result, felt fit, strong, and virile. He looked back on the previous months of ill health with disbelief and insisted that he was completely healthy. Mr. A. was aware of powerful heterosexual feelings and masturbated frequently with the image of a girl friend of schooldays in mind. In Katan's (1950) terms the identification with the brother kept at bay the homosexual (passive-feminine) attraction to him.

Identical restitutional phenomena occurred during the prepsychotic phase preceding Mr. A.'s first acute psychotic attack. He had felt unusually confident then and believed that he was especially attractive to women. He regarded his physique as particularly manly. This wishful thinking, springing from the desire for a masculinity that would dissipate a threatening femininity, was also observed in another case (Mr. B.). The patient was a young man of 23. He had been injured in a fight and had been absent from work for some months. Shortly after commencing a new post, he too experienced a well-being and confidence in himself. When walking down the street near his home or in the town, he was conscious of the admiring glances of passers-by. He gained the impression that a girl in the office had fallen in love with him and wanted to marry him. Quite soon after this an acute psychotic attack characterized by persecutory delusions and hallucinations made its appearance.

Somewhat similar phenomena occurred in the case of Miss M., whose psychotic attack was described in Profile II. Prior to the fourth relapse, she fell in love with a married man and a relationship developed. During the acute psychotic attacks Miss M. was disturbed by homosexual as well as heterosexual feelings. A heterosexual relation had seemed to her to be the solution to her homosexual conflict. The wish for femininity and the repudiation of her phallic homosexual wishes only lasted as long as the relation with her man friend continued. When he abandoned her, a psychotic attack occurred with the same homosexual content as on previous occasions.

The second category includes all those cases in which the symptoms of the prepsychotic phase are principally due to efforts to dissipate the wish for femininity or masculinity. In the male cases homosexuality is understood as equivalent to behaving like a woman with wishes for passive sexual experiences. Anxiety arising from this passive femininity frequently makes its appearance following a period when the patient's behavior arose from determined attempts to achieve the restitution of masculinity. In other instances the anxiety arising from feminine wishes is present from the start of the prepsychotic phase and no movement toward restitution takes place.

An example of the former is provided by Mr. D., a young man of 19, whose acute psychotic attack was preceded by a phase during which he entered into a competitive situation with a friend over a girl. During this period he masturbated frequently with heterosexual fantasies. Some time later he renounced his claim for the girl, saying he would not hurt his friend's feelings any longer by continuing to compete with him. From then on he became moody and unwilling to mix with others. He was also disinclined to go to work. Later Mr. D. told a psychiatrist he was afraid to go to work because, having just completed his apprenticeship, he was due to submit to an initiation ceremony. He felt inferior to his workmates and was uncomfortable when they made references to sexual matters. He thought that he did not stand up for himself and there were occasions when he should have challenged one of them to a fight. Following the decision to withdraw his claim for the girl friend, he abandoned masturbation. His nervousness increased, and one day while driving he suddenly felt the car was no longer responding to his control. He felt himself being carried along as a passive agent. This experience may well have reflected the pressure of passive feminine wishes threatening to break through into consciousness.

In some cases the feminine wishes find a conscious expression in heterosexual masturbatory fantasies or a homosexual thought occurs during coitus. When this happens, efforts are made to abandon sexual activity. Mr. A. reported that when masturbating and thinking of his girl friend of schooldays her image changed into that of a male friend. This was followed by a fantasy of having homosexual relations with the friend, the patient taking the passive role. This led to his stopping masturbating immediately and condemning the practice as well. Observations such as these support Katan's (1950) hypothesis that masturbation and coitus represent the gratification of feminine wishes and thus lead to castration fear.

Avoidance behavior, preoccupation with the appearance of the body, and obsessive-compulsive symptoms may also appear during the prepsychotic phase of young patients who develop schizophrenia and paranoid illnesses. In all cases these phenomena appear to arise from the fear of femininity. Avoidance of human contact is part of a wider symptom complex in which ideas of reference play a leading part. Sometimes the patient has insight into the irrational nature of his behavior, but such an awareness is usually transient. The patient refuses to leave the house and remains alone in his room, often with the blinds drawn. All attempts to get him to join in family activities are met with hostility. In one case the patient believed that when out in the street men looked at him because he had a girlish appearance. As long as he remained in the house he could acknowledge that this idea must be erroneous, but once in the street the conviction of its truth returned.

In other cases the fear of femininity is concealed from consciousness and instead there is hypochondria. Complaints are made about parts of the body or its function. Some patients insist that their appearance causes them to be ridiculed or criticized. Sometimes it is sensitivity about the shape of the nose, the quality of the hair, or the manner of walking. At other times the patient's anxiety springs from a belief that his body emanates an unpleasant odor. In all these instances, the patient shuns the company of others because of his belief that he is the object of contempt or derision. The appearance of these symptom complexes does not always herald an acute psychotic attack, although this is often the case. Frequently these symptoms continue unchanged over many years without the development of a psychosis.

Paranoid Syndromes

A prepsychotic phase is not peculiar to cases of schizophrenia, whether this begins in late adolescence or early adult life. Such a phase is also found in the paranoid syndromes whose onset is in the fourth decade of life. The symptomatology of the prepsychotic phase in these states differs from that described for schizophrenia. The greatest differences are found in those cases where the patient is married and has been relatively free of mental symptoms from adolescence onward. There are, of course, married patients for whom the content of the delusions is identical to that found in established cases of schizophrenia.

Depression of mood, loss of self-confidence, insomnia, and loss of appetite are nearly always present in the months preceding the start of a paranoid illness occurring for the first time in middle life. Hypochondria is common with patients fearing cancer or heart disease. There are usually complaints about one or more bodily systems. Headaches and unpleasant sensations in the head are often reported. Accompanying such symptoms are loss of the power of concentration and a feeling of fatigue. A common complaint is of a burning sensation, which may be limited to the scalp or the back or may extend over the whole body surface. A change in attitude toward other persons is present. There is an extreme sensitivity and a fear of meeting people, and inappropriate ideas about them may appear.

Two cases will be briefly referred to. The first is that of Mrs. B. (see Profile I), who presented with ideas of reference and misinterpretations of overheard speech. She believed that an older woman, with whom she had previously worked, was spreading rumors to the effect that she, the patient, was promiscuous. In the months before the psychotic attack this patient was depressed in mood, irritable, and bad-tempered. She suffered from a burning sensation in her genitalia and from frequency of micturition. No physical cause was found to account for the latter. Later the burning sensation spread all over the body.

The second case is also of a married woman, aged 31. At first she complained of fatigue and a loss of interest in her home and family. Housework was a burden and she took progressively longer to complete her various tasks. She too expressed the belief that her neighbors were unfriendly and inclined to criticize her needlessly. She attributed the criticisms to protests she had made about her children being bullied by other children. Eventually she refused to go out to shop; the house and the children were neglected. If the husband commented on this, she became enraged. Angry outbursts against the husband frequently occurred. On one occasion she threw a knife at him. Immediately prior to the outbreak of the paranoid attack, she accused her husband of being unfaithful with some of the neighboring women.

In the two cases referred to and in others, the husband is the object of anger and sometimes of hate. He is a source of disappointment for which different causes are cited. Mrs. B. criticized her husband because he was reserved in manner and undemonstrative. She thought he was no longer interested in her and made no effort to understand her problems. When under the influence of the delusion, she blamed him for not causing the interference to be brought to an end. In the second case the patient criticized her husband for not taking her out and for not satisfying her sexually. She accused him of being too mean to buy condoms; she found coitus interruptus unsatisfying. She also blamed him for forcing her to live in an area she disliked. In cases such as these, the prepsychotic phase is initiated by a danger created by an internal frustration. This has two sources: loss of love and loss of sexual satisfactions, both genital and pregenital. These frustrations arise from different childhood object relations but find a conscious outlet in the husband. He is both a heterosexual and a homosexual object insofar as he represents the mother.

In another case, that of a married woman of 36 years of age, the predominant feature was the patient's fear that her husband would be killed or die from overwork. This idea caused much distress since she believed her whole existence depended upon him. On the other hand, she was critical of her husband. She criticized him because he spent too much time at work, because he visited his mother too often, and there were occasions when she doubted his fidelity. This ambivalence could be traced to her childhood relations with her mother and her aunt. The affectionate dependency belonged to the aunt and the distrust, fear, jealousy, and anger were part of the mother relation.

A metapsychological formulation of the prepsychotic phase in paranoid syndromes is complicated by the fact that patients, prior to the onset of the symptoms, differ as to how far they have completed the developmental line to "emotional self-reliance and adult object relationships" (A. Freud, 1965, p. 64). In the cases cited it can be safely assumed, on the basis of their having made a real object choice, that the libido had cathected the phallic-genital level and possibly an oedipal stage in object relations had been reached, even if precariously.

The clinical phenomena, particularly as they appear during the psychotic attack, suggest that most patients are characterized by a phallic organization with active sexual aims and either heterosexual or homosexual objects (see Chapter 4). Whether this phallic orientation is an integral aspect of the pre-illness object relations resulting from a fixation of the sexual instincts or from a regression brought on during the prepsychotic phase could not be established. However, the presence of a phallic organization may explain why some patients react to sexual frustration with wishes for a more satisfying sexual partner. These wishes either reach consciousness, are repressed, or are projected. This last defense would account for the occurrence during the prepsychotic phase of the belief that the husband is unfaithful. Katan (1974) interprets the occurrence of jealousy and the belief in the husband's infidelity as indicating that unconscious homosexual wishes—specifically the wish to be a man—are active in the patient. He believes that during the prepsychotic phase of a paranoid psychosis heterosexual needs are heightened, the aim of which is to ward off the homosexuality (the wish to be a man in relation to a woman).

The symptoms of the prepsychotic phase can be understood as following from defensive measures initiated to combat the dangers provoked by disappointment (the castration complex) and sexual frustration. The loss of interest and the withdrawal from others are a consequence of repression. Repression involves a decathexis of phallic-genital and aggressive drive representations and thus provides the necessary conditions for libidinal regression. At this stage (i.e., in the prepsychotic phase) object representations remain cathected. The patients' complaints about the unsatisfactory nature of the husband as provider point to the regression that has taken place in the sphere of object relations. It is possible that the cause of the repression and the subsequent loss of self-confidence in these paranoid syndromes springs from the fact that the husband is no longer valued as a narcissistic object (see Profiles I and III). The patients described here, in light of their phallic sexuality, probably selected their husbands on the basis of an abnormally increased narcissism. Anxiety about the husband and concern for his health concealed death wishes, which may have had their origin in the father or mother relationship. In some cases the preoccupation with illness and the reference to specific body organs appears to be based on an identification with a sick or complaining mother. In the prepsychotic phase externalization and displacement act against the aggressive wishes.

The remaining symptoms — the sensations of burning, accusations of infidelity, frequency of micturition — are derivatives of the repressed libidinal wishes. It may be safely assumed that what are repressed are regressed libidinal wishes — namely, of active (phallic) heterosexual or homosexual tendencies. The frequency of micturition is a masturbatory substitute. The fear of the husband's infidelity, arising initially from the wish for another man, may be reinforced by the unconscious homosexuality provoked by the libidinal regression. While the prepsychotic phase continues, the conflicts leading to the symptoms remain firmly internalized.

Further Metapsychological Considerations

A fundamental difficulty stands in the way of formulating a metapsychology of the prepsychotic phase that will find general agreement. This is because the reconstruction of the prepsychotic phase preceding a first psychotic attack is based almost entirely on data obtained during the psychosis (Katan, 1954). The possibility always exists that the conflicts discerned during the psychosis need not be those that initiated and sustained the prepsychotic phase. This problem can be circumvented, however, in those patients who, having reached a state of partial remission and continuing under treatment, succumb to a further psychotic attack.

Katan (1954) bases his formulation on the observation that psychotic patients easily abandon objects in favor of the self. This alteration in the balance between self- and object cathexis results in a pathological narcissism, which has different forms of expression. The presence of conflicts over femininity and masculininity in male and female patients led Katan to the opinion that the heterosexual interests of the prospective schizophrenic patient are not derived from an existing Oedipus complex but that the situation is, in Katan's words, "only a counterfeit of an oedipus complex" (1950, p. 186) and the heterosexual wishes are based on a narcissism with the object embodying the wished-for femininity or masculininity. The prepsychotic conflict revolves around the tendency to decathect this narcissistic Oedipus complex and the struggle to maintain its cathexis.

The symptoms of the prepsychotic phase in schizophrenia and other psychoses can also be regarded as having metapsychological affinities to neurotic symptomatology. The potential psychotic patient may have reached the oedipal phase, but the cathexis of the complex remains weak because of the prior occurrence of extensive pregenital fixations that had a profound effect on the development and regulation of narcissism and hence of object relations. The heterosexuality of the prospective schizophrenic patient can thus be regarded as arising from a true Oedipus complex, but the fear of the heterosexual libido becomes so great as to lead to regression and to a psychotic resolution of the conflict.

When the symptoms of a prepsychotic phase are examined in terms of the metapsychological model of the neuroses, it is apparent that the similarities and the differences vary depending on the type of psychosis under consideration. Katan's (1950) observations demonstrate that the prepsychotic phenomena of schizophrenic patients are more in the nature of behavioral manifestations than of symptoms. These behavioral changes and the accompanying affects do not result from repressed compromise formations but instead follow from drive (heterosexual) activities whose purpose is to stave off unacceptable and dangerous (homosexual) wishes. Externalization and projection play a part in vitiating the anxiety-provoking ideas.

The remaining symptomatic phenomena appearing during the prepsychotic phase of schizophrenia also fail to fit the model for the neurotic symptom. The hypochondria, phobic and obsessive symptoms, and concern about the body and its appearance have a different structure. As with the behavioral changes, the hypochondria arises against the background of an alteration and redistribution of libido between self and object, itself the consequence of an attempt to bring about repression. The failure to establish a stable repression barrier accounts for the fact that the fear of femininity is never far from consciousness in these patients. The phobic and obsessional phenomena are a means of avoiding consciousness of or the translations into action of libidinal and aggressive impulses. It is well known that there are occasions when a compulsive sadistic thought is replaced by a destructive act in cases of schizophrenia.

When the clinical data of paranoid syndromes in women are studied with a view to reconstructing the way in which dynamic and economic factors contribute to the prepsychotic symptoms, disappointments and frustrations emerge as the principal sources of danger. These disappointments have their source in disillusionment with the husband as a narcissistic (ideal) object. This leads to a return (regression) to the frustrations implicit in a phallic sexuality (Freud, 1925), which heightens the danger situation. In these cases the initial defense is by way of repression, with the result that sexual wishes lose their cathexis (see Profile I). There is no conscious masturbatory conflict. Repression weakens the cathexis of current object representations, with resulting clinical withdrawal. In the case of Mrs. B. (Profile I), the effect of regression was for the urethral erogenous zone to provide the outlet for sexual excitations.

The depression of mood, self-criticism, and loss of self-confidence in these cases can be understood as due to a superego reaction to death wishes accentuated by the influence of the regressed phallic sexuality. Insofar as internalized conflicts can be inferred as providing a basis for the prepsychotic symptomatology, these phenomena can be regarded as having greater metapsychological similarities to those of the neuroses than to the manifestations of the prepsychotic phase of schizophrenia. Insufficient data preclude corroboration of the theory that the hysterical (descriptive) symptoms of the prepsychotic phase in the paranoid syndrome have a similar structure to that found in the hysterical neurosis, where the compromise formation finds a form of representation through identifications with ambivalently regarded love objects.

The idea that the symptoms of a neurosis and those of

a prepsychotic phase of a paranoid psychosis may have an identical metapsychological basis is completely rejected by Katan (1969, 1974). References have already been made to his belief (1974) that during the prepsychotic phase a woman's wish to be a man rapidly gathers momentum. In contrast to a neurosis, this homosexual wish is not countered by a defense with a resulting compromise formation but evokes, as in the prepsychotic phase of schizophrenia, an increase of the heterosexual libido, the aim of which is to strengthen contact with reality. The breakthrough of the homosexuality results in the psychotic attack.

The comparison between the prepsychotic phase of schizophrenia and that of paranoid syndromes can be widened by taking economic concepts as a guide for the extension of clinical observation. A most valuable concept in this context is the state of the libidinal distribution between self- and object representations. When the prepsychotic phases of both schizophrenia and the paranoid syndrome are examined in terms of this concept, descriptive differences immediately present themselves.

A striking feature of the prepsychotic phase of schizophrenia is provided by the phenomena indicating that a greatly increased libidinal cathexis of the self has already taken place. In the cases described, fantasies of a wish-fulfilling kind (e.g., that women were in love with them) were hypercathected and at times commanded belief. This transfer of libidinal cathexis from objects to the self can be regarded as part of the process whereby masculinity in the male patient and femininity in the female patient is strengthened. Insofar as this is a defense against the dangers of femininity or masculinity, the movement (withdrawal) of libido constitutes the attempt at repres-

sion (see Chapter 6). The clinical phenomena indicate that the withdrawn cathexis is not used to bar instinctual wishes (for femininity or masculinity) from consciousness through the establishment of an anti-cathexis, as in neurosis, but instead invests wishful fantasies, which are used in the restitutional manner already described.

The alteration in libido distribution in the prepsychotic phase of a paranoid syndrome would appear to be different, perhaps similar to that redistribution occurring in a neurosis. There is an increased cathexis of the self, the outcome of which is a preoccupation with the self and a loss of interest in real objects. There is a withdrawal but not a break with reality (Katan, 1969). This withdrawal is the result of the drive decathexis that is part of the process of repression.

In schizophrenia the break with reality occurs whenever the defense described above can no longer match the pressure of the drive cathexis. There is dissolution of both ego and superego. The primary process causes the failure of reality testing. In a paranoid syndrome the break with reality results from a different sequence of intrapsychic events. The response to heightened drive pressure is a limited dedifferentiation of mental structures. The superego is externalized. The clinical phenomena point to the possibility that, with the superego out of commission, repression and cathexis of object representations can be maintained in the face of the increased drive activity.

Paranoid states of the kind described are more common in women than men (Forrest, 1975). This observation may throw light on the fact that it is the superego that is most affected in the psychosis. Freud (1933) has pointed out that the Oedipus complex in girls, in contrast to boys, is initiated by the castration complex: "In the absence of fear of castration the chief motive is lacking which leads boys to surmount the Oedipus complex. Girls remain in it for an indeterminate length of time; they demolish it late and, even so, incompletely. In these circumstances the formation of the super-ego must suffer: it cannot attain the strength and independence which give it its cultural significance . . ." (p. 129).

With this as a basis, it is possible to imagine that a paranoid syndrome would be more likely to occur in individuals in whom there had been only a partial internalization of the oedipal objects (see Chapter 6). Under these circumstances, drive cathexis would continue to invest the oedipal figures and their substitutes in reality. The superego would then have only a rudimentary development. The fixation to the oedipal objects would leave such a superego vulnerable to dissolution through regression. Identifications would be replaced by the original object relations. In paranoid psychoses object cathexis is largely retained and the delusional ideas consist of conflicts relating to the parents. Is this observation related to the defective superego structure postulated as a feature of the personality of potentially psychotic individuals?

THE STATE OF PARTIAL REMISSION

States of partial remission are so called because they are characterized by an incomplete return to healthy mental life. They are most commonly found in patients who have suffered from an acute psychotic attack during which persecutory delusions were the leading manifestation. However, during the partial remission there is no longer any sign of delusions or hallucinations and the patient's behavior does not appear to be governed by psychotic ideas. Negative symptoms predominate. There is a lack of drive, initiative, and interest, although this may vary from time to time. Emotional expression is limited except for irritability and occasional anger. Insight into the fact of having been mentally ill may be present or absent. The most common positive symptoms are hypochondria and depressive manifestations, which can become extremely severe.

Description of Two Cases

Two of the cases reported in the first part of this chapter will now be referred to, but this time in the context of the state of partial remission. Both patients had been under treatment for periods of three to three and a half years since the occurrence of the first psychotic attack. In the first case the patient Mr. B. had only intermittent psychiatric supervision but was in regular casework with a psychiatric social worker over a period of two years. The second patient (Mr. A.) was treated by systematic psychotherapy over a three-and-a-half-year period. Neither patient ever achieved a complete remission of symptoms. The data drawn from these cases will be supplemented by clinical observations made on other patients in a similar partial remission.

Mr. B. was an only child, whose acute psychotic attack occurred shortly after he returned to work following an injury to his eye. During the attack he feared he would be killed by men who were friends of a girl he believed wished to marry him. He heard the voices of these supposed attackers in the garden of his house. He was afraid to be alone at night and slept with his father.

Toward the end of the psychotic attack, the fear of the unknown persecutors was replaced by a fear that his father wanted to kill him and planned to drug and drown him in the sea.

Although the acute symptoms abated, Mr. B. remained fearful of leaving the house unless accompanied. Arrangements were made for him to have regular meetings with a female psychiatric social worker. This was done because Mr. B. appeared to be apprehensive of men and of the author, whom he identified with his father. He responded well to the psychiatric social worker and talked freely to her. He appeared to recognize that he had been mentally unwell and was willing to discuss the acute episode. He explained that he was frightened of hurting himself and so had not resumed his motorcycling. He was worried about his health, which he felt was not very good. In the months after the acute attack his mother reported that he was irritable, depressed, and argumentative, preferring to remain in the house rather than go out. This irritability and withdrawal disappeared following the start of the meetings with the psychiatric social worker.

Three months after the psychotic attack Mr. B. decided to resume body-building and judo classes, which he had attended before he fell ill. He agreed to go to a mental health club, which met twice a week. Sometimes he appeared overconfident and talked in a loud voice. Meetings with the psychiatric social worker often began in this way, but soon the elated mood gave way to complaints of boredom and of difficulty in getting on with people. He could find no interest in them and was distrustful. Sometimes he feared he might attack someone just to show his physical strength. Then he feared he might be attacked and injured.

He stopped going to the mental health club after six weeks. The occasion for this was meeting a girl who told him she was unhappy because she had recently broken with her boy friend. Mr. B. thought she was too interested in him. He felt she was watching him all the time — "to see what she can get out of me," he surmised. When with the psychiatric social worker, he was concerned with finding the cause of his breakdown. He spent time going over his childhood memories with the hope that they might reveal some clue. He wondered if he was oversensitive, if it was this that made him vulnerable. His mother complained that he was rude and unpleasant to her, especially if they were in the company of others. Later he confided to the psychiatric social worker that he was oversexed and had been so since puberty. At school this preoccupation with sexual feeling had disturbed his concentration and his schoolwork had deteriorated. His father had criticized him on this account. Mr. B. worried because he could not overcome the need to masturbate. He discussed this with his parents and caused them much embarrassment. He attributed his lack of stamina and weakness to masturbation.

During the next months Mr. B. became increasingly abusive to his mother. There were moments when he was at the point of striking her. He became especially angry when his mother expressed a wish to, or tried to, speak to the psychiatric social worker. Mr. B. told her his mother was the aggressive one and had kept him down when he was a child. He explained how frightened he had been of her. Concurrently he talked of his sexual "frustrations" and of his fear of masturbating to excess. He believed he was particularly attractive to women. He wanted to have a girl friend but was too suspicious to trust one. Marriage worried him. He feared the idea of having to deflorate the woman and asked the psychiatric social worker if the hymen could be perforated surgically prior to marriage. He had tried to have coitus once but failed. At this time he was depressed in mood, seeing himself as a failure in everything, including coitus.

The meetings with the psychiatric social worker had to be interrupted for four months because she was pregnant. Mr. B. was persuaded to see the author as a temporary measure, and meetings occurred about once every two weeks. Shortly after the separation from the psychiatric social worker Mr. B. became anxious and unsettled. He told the author, "I have not been so nervous since I was 14." He recalled fears of the dark and of being attacked when out alone in the street. It was because of these fears that he had taken body-building and judo classes. Mr. B. continued in low spirits and in an anxious state for the next three months. He complained of lack of energy and of feeling self-conscious and conspicuous in company. Lack of strength made him unfit for work, which as yet he had not found. During this period there was a brief spell of overconfidence and the aggression, which had disappeared, returned. His mother reported him as "aggressive and high." Soon he was again depressed in mood and anxious. Instead of arguing with his parents, he accepted their decisions.

As soon as the meetings with the psychiatric social worker resumed, he refused to see the author any more. Information obtained later revealed that the depression and anxiety were caused by the loss of the social worker. Mr. B. had not reacted with psychotic symptoms. Such a development was observed in another patient when regular meetings with his psychiatric social worker ended after she was transferred to a senior post. This patient,

Mr. L., had fallen ill at the age of 23 with acute psychotic symptoms. The attack subsided and was replaced by a mental state characterized by apathy, withdrawal, and egocentrism. He had to be under constant surveillance, otherwise he did not take care of his appearance or remember to attend meals, urinate, or defecate. He was greedy and lacked consideration for others. Whatever was on the table at mealtimes he would swallow voraciously.

After discharge from hospital, Mr. L. remained withdrawn and without interest in himself or others. He was seen at an out-patient clinic shortly after discharge; he still retained some persecutory ideas—he said his throat was to be cut because his neck was too long. No further contact was made with Mr. L. until he was 25 years of age, when he had to be readmitted to hospital. On this occasion he presented with depressive symptoms, but there were also indications of persecutory fears. The previous year he had been working as a farm laborer but had to stop because of difficulty in concentration. He remained in hospital for one month and was treated by electroshock therapy.

Mr. L. was seen regularly at an out-patient clinic and after several weeks was able to return to work. He broke off contact with the clinic about a year after discharge from the hospital. About a year later he reappeared, now aged 27, complaining once more of depression of mood, inability to concentrate, and a lack of interest and energy. He had stopped working. He was readmitted to the mental hospital, where he was noted to be "listless and withdrawn." He believed he was physically ill: first that he had tuberculosis and second that he had jaundice. This hypochondriasis was connected with fears that he had injured himself through excessive masturbation. He had struggled to give up the habit and had, in fact, done so during the eight weeks prior to being readmitted to hospital. Once again he was treated by electroshock therapy and discharged.

No more was heard of Mr. L. until he reappeared at the out-patient clinic three years later. The symptoms of which he complained were identical to those of the previous attacks. During the three years he had been working as an agricultural laborer while living at home with his mother. His father had died a number of years earlier. Arrangements were made for his case to be supervised by a psychiatric social worker and he was encouraged to attend the mental welfare club. He was asked to come to the out-patient department and did so for some weeks. Then he asked to stop attending as he felt better. However, he agreed to continue seeing the psychiatric social worker. Periodic reports about the patient were submitted by the psychiatric social worker to the psychiatrist in charge of the case.

Eighteen months later the psychiatric social worker, Miss P., left to take up another post and a colleague took over the interviews with Mr. L. Quite soon she reported that Mr. L. was seriously disturbed. He had told her that he was married to Miss P. and that the reason she had left was because she was pregnant by him. He explained that some years earlier, possibly at the time of the first psychotic attack, he had been very attached to a girl but the relationship had broken up. This occurred because he had found himself in a conflict of loyalties between his mother and the girl friend. He was convinced that Miss P. was the girl he had rejected all those years ago. Mr. L. said that Miss P. came to his bed each night and they had some form of sexual relation. He did not specify what this was. She disappeared during the day, but they remained in mental contact. He could hear her voice and she advised him how to conduct himself. All this was agreeable to Mr. L., but he was unhappy because Miss P. was absent in the daytime. He wanted the psychiatric social worker to find her. He had been searching for her and making what inquiries he could. As the months passed, the references to Miss P. decreased, but there was nothing to believe that he was not still preoccupied with the delusional ideas.

Mr. B., though, did not develop wishful delusions of this kind while separated from the psychiatric social worker with whom he had been working. On resumption of the sessions, she noted that he was preoccupied by the fact that he had been ill and that he was still nervous. He told her that he intended to write a book about his illness and he was sure it would be of great interest to others. In a few weeks he obtained work as a van driver. His parents now considered that he had recovered and discouraged Mr. B. from continuing his meetings with the psychiatric social worker. The result of this action by his parents was for Mr. B. to threaten to give up work. Mr. B.'s mother telephoned the psychiatric social worker and asked her to come and see him. Both parents criticized Mr. B. for laziness. Mr. B. said the reason he was giving up his job was his inability to get work done to the satisfaction of his employer. In fact, he left and found another job.

A new development was Mr. B.'s wish to leave home and live elsewhere. The psychiatric social worker suggested a hostel, and at first he was enthusiastic about this idea. Arrangements were made for him to look over the hostel. His reaction was critical, and he decided not to take the offered vacancy. He said later that he had refused because he was afraid he might be attacked when alone or, if he complained of being nervous, he would be rushed off to a mental hospital of which he had a dread.

After working at his new job for three months he gave it up. It was during this time that he struck up a friendship with a young woman. He brought her along to a meeting arranged with the psychiatric social worker and announced that they were engaged to be married. He then asked his "fiancée" to leave the room while he talked to the psychiatric social worker. He told her that his "fiancée" had been married but the marriage had been annulled because it had not been consummated. Later it transpired that his "fiancée" was only separated from her husband. Once again he expressed a fear of impotence. When he was younger, "any old thing" would cause him to have an erection. Now he could not have an erection even when making love with his "fiancée." He had obtained her promise that, before they married, she would enter hospital to have her virginity "removed." When Mr. B. discovered his "fiancée" was still married, he became very anxious. He feared the husband would seek him out and attack him. While talking about these fears, he recalled a period of childhood when his father had taken alcohol to excess. He would come home drunk and there would be violent scenes with the mother accusing him of infidelity.

Mr. B. began a new job, but it soon ended. A workmate accidentally spilled some paint over Mr. B., who immediately thought it was a deliberate act arranged by his "fiancée's" husband. He said, "I could have sworn someone said, 'That will be a warning to him.' " Mr. B. left his job immediately. It was particularly unfortunate that this incident coincided with the psychiatric social worker leaving her post for a new one in a different part of the country. Mr. B. reluctantly agreed to come and see the author from time to time.

The first apparent consequence of the loss of the psychiatric social worker was an intensification of the hostility against his mother. He was reluctant to go out except when persuaded to by his "fiancée." Usually he lay in bed until late in the morning and was inactive during the rest of the day. He continued to fear attack by his "fiancée's" husband. After three months he began to show some interest in his motorcycle, went out occasionally, and eventually found a new job. However, this improvement was short-lived. He was reluctant to go to work. At first he complained that he was finding it difficult to get up in the morning and later that he was afraid to go out alone. He remained at home for two weeks and them managed to return to work. He soon stopped, saying that his fellow workers were tormenting him. He did not specify in what way. At home he did not express persecutory ideas but was irritable and unapproachable.

At this time Mr. B.'s mother told the author she had not realized how much her son had benefited from the relation with the psychiatric social worker and she wondered if a similar arrangement could be made. As for Mr. B., he complained of being nervous for no apparent cause, but he was afraid to go out alone and to make love to his "fiancée," in case her husband should find out. Mr. B. added that this fear of being punished occurred after any occasion when he had made love to a girl. Arrangements were made for Mr. B. to have regular appointments with a female psychiatrist. As with the psychiatric social worker, Mr. B. responded well. He talked freely and told her he had lost all sexual feelings for his "fiancée" and could neither have an erection nor an emission. In fact, he preferred his motorbike. The improvement in his mental state was quite striking. He was friendly at home, took to working at his motorbike, and recommenced attending the "vintage" motorcycle club of which he was a member. When not working, he went out alone and was helpful to his mother in the house. This was the position at the end of 1973.

The second case is that of Mr. A. Following the second psychotic attack, which lasted for about three months, there was a brief period during which Mr. A. was able to resume his work as a farmer and occasionally go out with a friend. Quite soon he noticed he had lost confidence in his ability to carry out his work. He worried when he had to milk the cows, feed them, or clean out the barn. He was frightened when his brother was not there to help. He said he felt himself to be without energy and every undertaking required effort. He could not concentrate on anything. At the same time he was worried about his health. If he had a pain in his chest, he was sure he had heart disease. At times he had an uncomfortable feeling in his genitalia and, then, he feared that his penis was not properly attached to his body. He turned to his mother for reassurance, but this did not help. He feared that his brother and parents would fall ill. He was frightened at the thought of having to be alone in the house.

The depression of mood deepened and it was accompanied by self-criticism as well as by anxiety. Wherever he turned there was a cause for worry. The grass did not seem to be growing profusely enough. He feared there would not be enough food for the cattle and worried lest the price of fodder rose so high that his father would be unable to afford it. The cattle would starve and die. The cows looked thin. The calves he had to wean did not seem to be thriving. He blamed himself for this. He expected them to fall ill. When a cow was due to calve he was acutely anxious. His father would have to sell the farm to meet increasing debts because he, the patient, was not working properly. During this period he reported two dreams. In the first he dreamed that a neighbor had cows with large udders. In fact, this man did not keep cows. In the second dream children were born in the shape of calves. One turned into a monster with a large horn and a long tail and began to destroy everything. Mr. A. woke up in fear. It is of interest that toward the end of the first psychotic attack Mr. A. expressed the fear that he had a destructive bug inside him.

It was several months before this period of illness subsided. As long as the depression continued, Mr. A. remained preoccupied with his suffering. Slowly the depressive symptoms lessened in intensity, and he returned to that state present just after recovery from the acute attack. Then his brother became ill with a severe hand infection. During the three weeks that the brother was away from work, Mr. A. successfully carried out the tasks of both. He was completely free of symptoms. He resumed social activity, going to dances and to a social club of which he was a member. Sexual feeling, which had been absent during the depression, returned. He resumed masturbation with the image of his girl friend of schooldays in mind. Even in this improved state, he still feared some ill would befall his brother or his parents.

About two months later an acute mental disturbance

occurred, although less severe than the second psychotic attack. It was confined to a repetition of the phenomena of the first prepsychotic phase. A number of immediate causes for the disturbance could be immediately discerned, apart from those the patient later described himself. Just preceding this acute upset, arrangements had been made for his brother's marriage. Plans were also drawn up for a house, which was to be built on grounds adjacent to the farm and in which the brother and his wife would live. These events upset Mr. A. They resulted in resentment, jealousy, and envy. Within days Mr. A. was accusing his brother of envying him and wanting to be like him.

After the acute attack subsided, Mr. A. recalled that a young woman had visited the farm just before he had become disturbed. She had married about two months earlier. Mr. A. had known her for a long time and had always found her sexually stimulating. Mr. A. had been invited to the wedding but had not felt well enough to go. On the day of the visit Mr. A. found the woman especially attractive. He believed she was also attracted to him. Later that day he masturbated with her in mind. The same night he thought he was being watched by the television. This idea passed and did not recur. A revulsion against masturbation appeared. He declared it to be an evil practice and the equivalent of homosexuality. This idea was based on the fantasy of a penis suddenly appearing on the girl he was imagining during masturbation.

The disturbed phase, during which he felt hostile to his brother and wished him dead, only lasted for about two weeks. After this he was at pains to disclaim all the hateful thoughts and expressed regard for his brother and

a need for his help. It was during this period of relative
well-being that the brother married. Mr. A. was the best
man and carried out his duties at the wedding quite
efficiently. However, a few weeks later Mr. A. began to
complain again about depression and difficulty in working. Immediately prior to this he complained of a pain in
his chest, the cause of which was a muscular strain. He
decided to see his general practitioner and had his chest
x-rayed. No abnormality was detected.

Once again, there was a rapid development of the
depressive symptom complex. He was frightened to work
lest he make a mistake. He was afraid that he might not
get the cattle into the barn, that he would not be able to
get the cows off the road into the field, that they would
break out of the field onto the road, that he would not be
able to spread the bales of hay, that when the bull had to
be loaded on to the truck it would break out. From time
to time he would burst into tears, either when working or
when in the house. He lost his appetite and this caused his
mother distress. On more than one occasion he said the
"silly" ideas of the psychotic attacks were preferable to
the mental distress he had to endure.

The depressive symptoms recurred after the brother's
marriage and during the period when the house was near
completion. There was some improvement after the
newlyweds entered the house, but this did not continue
for long. The depression of mood eased, but in its place
there appeared a series of compulsive thoughts, the
content of which comprised the idea of killing his parents
and his brother. These ideas were initially provoked by
watching a crime film. The ideas distressed him because
he really wanted to be on good terms with his brother and
parents. This was Mr. A.'s mental state in February 1974,

three and a quarter years after the onset of the first psychotic attack.

Metapsychological Considerations

When the phenomena appearing in the state of partial remission are examined from the metapsychological viewpoint, they can be seen to represent an alternative means of dealing with the dangers that in the psychotic attack find expression in delusions and hallucinations. In this respect, a continuity exists between the two phases (partial remission and acute attack), similar to that which Katan (1954) has demonstrated as existing between the prepsychotic phase and the acute psychotic attack. The significant change leading to the establishment of the partial remission is the restoration of the ego-id differentiation and the lessening of the influence of the primary process. As the latter recedes, reality testing returns. The resolution of the acute psychotic attack must therefore be dependent on the emergence of a form of repression that deprives the dangerous drive representations of access to consciousness. The restoration of the ego proceeds hand in hand with a recathexis of real object representations.

The phenomena described in this chapter and in the literature support Jacobson's theory (1967) that the "repressive barriers" in patients who recover from a psychotic attack are less stable than those found in neurotic patients. Jacobson has drawn attention to the fact that in those patients who are in a partial remission self- and object representations are not as sharply differentiated as in cases of neurosis. When the patient is confronted with an internal danger, this blurring of the self-object boundaries promotes the strengthening of a defense (externalization) that, in view of the weakened repression barrier, is only partly effective. Waelder (1951) has proposed a similar idea in terms of denial. The author has also suggested that during the partial remission the cathexes withdrawn from the drive representations may not be converted into an anti-cathexis ensuring the stability of repression (Freeman, 1973).

Mr. A.'s wish for femininity and his death wishes against his brother were dealt with quite differently in the psychotic attacks and in the partial remission. In the latter anxiety over "homosexuality" was virtually absent. Much more pronounced was the oral content of his anxieties; this was consistent with the oral-sadistic nature of the delusions during the psychotic attack. None of the anxiety was bound in symptoms of a phobic, obsessional, or hysterial character. This suggests that the structure of the symptoms during the partial remission is of an entirely different nature from that presenting in neurotic symptomatology. Mr. A.'s anxiety symptoms can be regarded as a direct response of the ego to unacceptable instinctual wishes. The symptoms did not act as substitutes for regressed wishes and an ego reaction to them.

Many of Mr. A.'s fears can be classified under the headings of object loss and fear of loss of love. The fears for his parents and brother and the fears for the cattle and farm can be understood as reactions to death wishes and to the greed briefly expressed in the prepsychotic phases of the illness and later in the dream of the cows with large udders. Mr. A. did not fear his own starvation, instead this danger was externalized to the animals. He represented his phallic destructiveness by the dream image of a monster calf and in real life externalized these wishes to the cattle: the animals would break out and damage property. Again his fear of being unable to wean the young calves, that they would starve, develop infections, and die, resulted from an externalization of his own anxieties. Here he probably identified with his over-anxious mother, the calves representing himself. This tendency to externalize was matched by a series of passing identifications with those who suffered from physical diseases. This was in part, at least, the cause of his periodic hypochondria.

The phenomena described demonstrate that in the partial remission regression affected Mr. A.'s object relations as a result of alterations in the drives and the ego. This regression differed from that of the psychotic attack. During the partial remission a regression to oral (sadistic) fixations took place to relieve the dangers provoked by the active and passive (masculine and feminine) genital conflicts observed during the prepsychotic phase. The regression led to new anxieties. In contrast to the psychotic attack, repression, with the aid of externalizations, allowed reality testing to be maintained. Periodically the regressive defense did not suffice because of a progression of the libido to the phallic phase with the re-emergence of anxieties about "homosexuality."

The anxiety symptoms from which Mr. B. suffered during the partial remission can also be regarded as a direct response of the ego to the danger of mounting drive tension. Mr. B.'s street fears were not genuine neurotic symptoms but a direct expression of castration fear. Mr. A.'s predominant anxieties were of separation and loss of love. Only when there was a libidinal progression from orality did castration fear make its appearance in the guise of a dread of "homosexuality." This occurred in the period immediately following the end of the history of the illness described above. In Mr. B.'s case, however, castration fear appeared to be the sole response to the danger created by drive pressure.

Castration fear was reflected in almost all of Mr. B.'s anxiety symptoms. Its most striking and direct expression was in his distrust of women and his fear of the female genitalia. This fear extended to all women with whom there was a possibility of physical contact. In this regard, the social worker was exempt, although, as was learned later, he believed she was physically attracted to him. Mr. B. equated body and penis and, on this account, every threat to the integrity of his body had to be met with precautions or steps taken to revitalize it. He was afraid of hurting himself and, as a result, gave up the excitement of motorcycling. He feared the loss of strength and complained of lack of stamina. To rectify this, he briefly returned to the body-building classes but had to abandon them in the face of homosexual excitement and the resulting castration fear. The fear of loss of virility was connected with his fears about masturbation.

Castration fear was also evoked whenever he was sexually aroused by a woman. At such times he became frightened and genital wishes disappeared from consciousness. Mr. B. differed from Mr. A. in that he was able to establish a nongenital relation with a woman. Once there was a heightening of the genital libido, it was followed immediately by falsifications of reality experience. During the partial remission there were periods of psychotic misinterpretation, as when he believed that a workmate had intentionally spilled paint over him. These misinterpretations were "superego phenomena" and the threat — in the instance cited above — a memory from childhood. With Mr. A., on the other hand, the superego maintained its internalized status throughout the partial remission. This possibly accounts for the presence of self-blame and the maintenance of reality testing in the one case and not in the other.

It would appear that, in patients who have sustained a severe psychotic attack and pass into a state of partial remission, psychic instability is not limited to the "repression barrier" but extends to the ego and the superego, to their relation to each other, and to the id. In some cases the ego retains a fair degree of integrity and the drive derivatives that have undergone regression from the cessation of the psychotic attack are held in check. The amount of anxiety experienced by the patient depends on the activity of the regressed drives. The ego and the "repression barrier" only become threatened when there is a libidinal progression to genitality, which may be heterosexual or homosexual (masculine or feminine) in its orientation.

Some such development must be considered in the case of Mr. L., where the depressive phenomena in the partial remission were replaced by a wishful delusional system during the period of his contact with the social worker Miss P. A similar sequence of clinical events has been reported by the author (Freeman, 1963) in the case of an unmarried female patient, whose depressive symptoms following a psychotic attack led her to seek treatment. In other cases, and Mr. B.'s is illustrative, the faulty reality testing occurred whenever there was a dissolution of the superego, presumably precipitated by

the heightening of drive tension. Prior to this dissolution
and externalization of the superego, repression effectively
contained the drive derivatives at whatever regressive
level they had reached at the end of the psychotic attack.
The state of partial remission is one where some form
of real object relation is restored. Jacobson (1967) has
suggested that the presence of such relations is essential
for the maintenance of whatever psychic health has been
regained. She says, "I am inclined to believe that a large
group of psychotics highly invest and frantically adhere to
a carefully chosen type of work, personal objects, and
activities. . . . Actually, such activities protect them for
long periods from manifest psychotic episodes" (Jacobson, 1967, p. 38). She demonstrates that these objects are
narcissistic in type and, insofar as this is so, they can be
employed for both drive and defensive needs. The lack of
definition of self- and object representations facilitates
the action of externalizations and merging mechanisms.

In Mr. A.'s case the brother was a narcissistic object,
which in the partial remission was a means whereby there
could be a vicarious satisfaction of wishes (masculinity,
heterosexuality). During the prepsychotic phases the
brother served as an object onto whom unacceptable
drive and self-representations were externalized. Mr. B.'s
"fiancée" can also be envisaged as a narcissistic object
onto whom was externalized the femininity he so despised. Not only did Mr. B. denigrate his mother, but he
also criticized his "fiancée" freely—she was stupid and
unattractive. It is noteworthy that the periods of falsification of reality, which occurred during the partial
remission, appeared when he decided, for his own safety
as he thought, that he had better abandon the relation-

ship. The relationship allowed Mr. B. to believe in his masculinity and so kept from consciousness his passive-feminine (homosexual) tendencies.

SOME CONCLUSIONS

The acute psychotic attack comprising delusions, hallucinations, and affect and motility disorders is only one episode in the course of a mental illness. Neglect of the phenomena comprising the prepsychotic phase and those following the acute attack has led to confusion and controversy over what constitutes the basic psychopathology of the psychoses. Only when a psychosis is examined in its entirety is it possible to reconcile the views of those who follow Freud (1911) in believing that the essential internal change is the loss of object cathexis and those who maintain that object cathexis is retained in psychoses. During the acute attack the loss of object cathexis cannot be disputed. However, during the state of partial remission object cathexis is restored in varying degrees. Its maintenance is precarious because the underlying dangers have by no means been overcome.

The data presented in this chapter and those found in the literature demonstrate unequivocally that the different phases of a psychosis are interconnected both descriptively and metapsychologically. The phenomena characterizing the acute psychotic attack and the state of partial remission arise from mental processes that have the common aim of containing internal dangers, the signs of which are to be most clearly seen during the prepsychotic phase. This phase, which can only be reconstructed in the case of a first psychotic attack, can be observed at first hand during relapses from states of partial remission.

With the recognition, initially made by Katan (1954), of the importance of the prepsychotic phase for the future development of a psychosis, the profile schema for the psychotic patient (Freeman, 1973) has to be suitably amended to accommodate a full descriptive and meta-psychological account of this decisive stage of the illness.

CHAPTER 6

The Predisposition to Schizophrenia

Those who come to develop a psychotic illness in adult life do so because they possess a special vulnerability to these abnormal mental states. This vulnerability is in the nature of a predisposition to which, it is generally agreed, both hereditary and environmental factors contribute. There is, however, controversy over the relative importance of these factors and particularly over the part adverse childhood experiences play in promoting mental illness in adolescence or adulthood.

All attempts to explain the nature of the predisposition to psychotic illness rest on the concept of faulty mental development derived from Freud's theories of the libido and symptom formation in the neuroses. According to the libido theory, the sexual instincts, in their course to maturity, are subject to varying degrees of inhibition of their development. This may affect the instinct representations, their aims, and their objects. The inhibition of development (fixation) may be complete or partial. In the latter instance the sexual instincts only attain an incomplete maturity and thus are liable to regression. The occasion for such regressions occurs whenever, and for whatever reason, the precariously-held genitality is denied an outlet. Under such circumstances, the libidinal cathexes regress and invest a preliminary stage of sexual development.

Regression and fixation bear a close relation to one another. The presence of fixations is the necessary condition for regression, which occurs in those cases where there were fixations during the evolution of the sexual instincts. According to Freud, it is the libidinal fixations that provide "the predisposing internal factor in the aetiology of the neuroses . . ." (1917, p. 346). The fact that regression and fixation are part of Freud's biologically-based libido theory carries important implications for the nature of the predisposition to mental illness.

Fixations of the libido are created by the arousal of some aspect of infantile sexuality as it passes through the developmental sequences. The site of the fixations and their subsequent establishment depend on an interaction between the inherited characteristics of the sexual instinct representations and the kinds of external stimulation to which the child was subjected. Fixations contribute the inherited elements to the predisposition as well as representing the way in which innate sexual tendencies are transformed by "developmental interferences" (Nagera, 1966). The scene is set for the appearance of neurotic symptoms when the fixations, which are cathected by the regressing libido, result in conflict. The wish to satisfy childhood sexual wishes clashes with the moral standards already adopted by the ego. The resulting symptoms are a compromise between the conflicting forces. Regression to the fixation points brings the libidinal cathexes, which sustain the wishes, under the influence of primary processes. This and the activity of the ego alter the form of representation of the childhood sexuality, providing it with a substitute expression — namely, the symptoms of the neurosis.

THE CLASSICAL THEORY OF PSYCHOSIS

The concepts of regression and fixation play an equally important role in Freud's (1911) theory of psychosis. Again it is a conflict arising from libidinal frustration that initiates the process of symptom formation. In the case of a paranoid psychosis, it is "an unconsciously reinforced current of homosexuality" (Freud, 1911, p. 59). The predisposition to the illness is provided by fixations established at early phases of libidinal development. At this time the libido, for whatever reason, is prevented from taking the representation of the mother as its real object. Instead, representations of the self permeate the object, wholly or in part, with the libidinal cathexis moving easily from self to object and vice versa. Thus, in the case of paranoid psychoses, the predisposition consists of a fixation of the libido at a phase when the object, already differentiated from the self, acts as a vehicle for the self-representations. This narcissistic fixation is to be distinguished from the fixation providing the predisposition to schizophrenia, which is established at an even earlier period when self and object have only achieved the most rudimentary differentiation — that is, at the phase of autoerotism.

Libidinal frustration is the immediate cause of the psychotic attack. In contrast to the neuroses, the regressive movement effects a dramatic alteration in the distribution of libido between self- and object representations. This redistribution is of such an order as to lead to a break with reality. Libidinal cathexes are withdrawn from objects and concentrated in the self. The cathectic withdrawal by itself does not lead to psychosis; such libidinal movements also occur in both healthy and neurotic individuals. It is the return of the libido to the self, facilitated by the fixations established at narcissistic levels, that is unique to the psychotic attack—"On the basis of this clinical evidence we can suppose that paranoiacs have brought along with them a *fixation at the stage of narcissism,* and we can assert that the length of *the step back from sublimated homosexuality to narcissism* is a measure of the amount of *regression* characteristic of paranoia" (Freud, 1911, p. 72).

Throughout this discussion, "narcissism" is used in its metapsychological sense and as such bears no relation whatsoever to personality traits described as "narcissistic." An individual may overvalue his mental and physical qualities and exhibit all the signs of self-love yet still cathect object representations with libido and so maintain his ties with reality.

Repression in the psychoses, both paranoia and schizophrenia, was identified by Freud (1911) as the process whereby libidinal cathexes are withdrawn from objects. The extent of the detachment depends on the need for repression in much the same way as libidinal cathexes in both healthy and neurotic individuals are withdrawn from drive representations as a means of dissipating a danger situation. In psychoses a partial detachment of libido from objects is more common, but, as in the case of Schreber (Freud, 1911), this can become complete. Such an outcome follows when the object of the prohibited wishes continues to attract libidinal cathexes, for then repression will only succeed when the libidinal detachment is total. "End of the world" delusions and the conviction that only the self survives are the result. Where there is only a partial detachment, the patient retains the capacity to relate in a realistic way to relatives, friends, doctors, nurses, and other patients.

The detachment of libido means nothing other than the loss of object cathexis. When that occurs, there is an immediate identification with the object. This identification is of a primary kind, in the nature of a merging of self and object. The clinical phenomena reflecting this process have been described in detail, initially by Federn (1952) and later by Freeman, Cameron, and McGhie (1958). In all acute psychotic attacks, whatever the subsequent course of the illness, the pathological process begins with a limited withdrawal of object cathexis as a means of defense. In those cases where the acute attack does not lead to an extensive dissolution of mental life, it is possible to observe that an object has been given up and an identification has taken its place. The patient whose libido has cathected a heterosexual or homosexual object, for whatever reason (see Chapter 5), reveals, in the psychotic attack, features belonging to the abandoned love object. Delusional ideas will be based on this identification, which has replaced object cathexis. Whether there will be a further detachment of libido from objects or whether the detachment will be confined to the one object depends on factors not yet understood.

Nunberg (1921) was the first psychoanalyst to present a detailed account of the relation between schizophrenic symptomatology and the underlying libidinal changes. In the case he described there was only a partial detachment of the libido from objects. Nunberg became the focus of the patient's homosexual urges. There was a wish to repeat a homosexual relation of childhood. Strenuous attempts were made by the patient to establish and maintain an object relation. A homosexual transference made a transient appearance. The danger provoked by this libidinal movement resulted in a further detachment of libido (repression, according to Freud). The effect was a merging with the object—object cathexis having given way to primary identification. This phase was followed by the patient believing that Nunberg was his persecutor. The persecutory ideas, brought about by projection, allowed distance to be created again between the patient and his object.

Where there is only a partial detachment of the libido, as in Nunberg's case, object relations of different kinds become manifest. Phenomena similar to the transferences of the neurotic patient appear alongside transitivistic (merging) and persecutory manifestations. The former result from repression (the detachment of libido), while the latter represent the return of the repressed, now altered as a result of the projection.

However, in psychoses, repression, as envisaged by Freud (1911), is of a different nature from that conceived for neuroses. While the aim of repression is the same — namely, the resolution of a danger through its removal from consciousness — the consequences are different. In neuroses the libidinal cathexes, while being withdrawn from the drive representations, remain attached to their objects. In psychoses repression, consisting as it does of the detachment of libido from object representations, results in an extensive dissolution of the self. There is, in Freud's words, an "internal catastrophe" (1911, p. 70). The effect of this catastrophe is to deprive the individual of those measures whereby instinctual wishes can be contained in the form of neurotic symptoms based on the compromise achieved between the regressed wishes and the opposition of an ego that is part of an intact self. Freud (1911) did not regard the delusions and hallucinations of paranoia or schizophrenia as compromise formations but as direct results of an alteration in the direction and aims of libidinal wishes as they tried to regain their objects. In paranoid psychoses this alteration was brought about by projection. In schizophrenia the libidinal wishes were subject to the primary process.

REVISIONS OF THE CLASSICAL THEORY

The study and treatment of psychoses has been a continuing activity of psychoanalytic psychiatrists since the presentation of the classical theory. As a result, there has been a gradual accumulation of clinical data and information about the patient's pre-illness personality, about his family background and childhood circumstances. This additional material has led to modifications of the classical theory. Some have been of a limited kind, while others have been of a more radical nature. The radical revisions always involve the metapsychological basis of the classical theory of psychosis. In every case conceptualization of the clinical data dispenses with the libido theory, with the result that the concepts comprising the theory no longer have their original meaning. Regression, narcissism, fixation, etc., may be retained but, as they are torn from their original context, it is often difficult to decide whether they are being used in a descriptive or metapsychological sense. For example, most revisions make free use of psychological regression as an explanatory concept to describe how the object relations and cognitive disorders of the psychotic patient come to expression.

While some theoretical expositions continue to interpret the clinical phenomena in terms of changes affecting the drive representations, there is no mention of the economic factor on which so much depends in the classical theory. Although the occurrence of mental conflict depends on changes in mental economics, the revisionists of classical theory are content to confine explanations of clinical phenomena to dynamic grounds without reference to the economic principle. Conflict, which occupies a central place in every formulation, is disconnected from the "energy" sources that make its presence possible.

The major modifications of the classical theory also consider predisposition to result from adverse infantile and childhood experiences. While allowance is made for constitutional factors, rejection of the biologically based libido theory deprives these new theories of a concept that can embrace psychobiological inheritance. In some revisions predisposition is thought of as a partial arrest in psychological development. This provides a focus for later regression. The concept of arrest is to be distinguished from fixation which, being an integral aspect of libido theory, applies only to the sexual drives and not to the functions of the ego.

The data on which all theories of predisposition are based have several sources. There are the phenomena of the illness which can be observed at first-hand. There are the data supplied by friends and relatives. Then there is the information obtained during psychoanalytic and psychotherapeutic treatment. This material has been evaluated from different standpoints. The result has been a number of divergent views on the nature of predisposition in psychosis all of which differ from the classical theory.

Descriptions will now follow of the clinical observations and hypotheses which are based on the newer theories of predisposition. First there are those psychoanalysts who use some metapsychological concepts but do so within their own general theory. Rosenfeld (1952b; 1954) and Searles (1958, 1959a, 1959b, 1961, 1963) belong to this category. Second are those represented by the writing of Lidz et al. (1966) and Bowen (1960). These writers eschew theory, only retaining a general developmental orientation to the clinical phenomena. According to Lidz and Fleck (1960) the clinical data must be ordered only "in their own transactional frame of reference."

The clinical phenomena repeatedly described are withdrawal, disinterest, negativism, outbursts of rage, dislike of physical and emotional closeness, various expressions of faulty differentiation between self and objects, misidentifications, disturbances of identity, disorders of syntax, word form and memory, persecutory ideas relating to the therapist, delusions of grandeur, and anxieties about sexual identity. There are also patterns of relating in which the patient expresses anxieties and sexual wishes. He looks to the therapist for reassurance and to gratify or restrain his sexual needs.

The Kleinian Theory of Psychosis

In an early paper Rosenfeld (1952b) describes a typical sequence of events at the outset of treatment of a schizophrenic patient. The patient, a young man of 20, was initially friendly, but by the third session he became

hostile and restive. During the first session he talked freely after some preliminary hesitancy, expressed through disconnected thoughts about previous treatment. He talked about his sexual difficulties. Then he recalled a boy at school who had sat next to him in class. When Rosenfeld said that he had started to like him as he had his school friend, the patient rose from his chair and wanted to leave. He was restless until the end of the session. In the second session the patient was unsettled and preoccupied with his thoughts. For a time he ignored Rosenfeld but later said he was unsure whether it was right to like him too much. In the third session the patient was restless and aggressive in manner. He was inattentive and unresponsive. Rosenfeld describes how, in a session some weeks later, the young man confused himself with his father and also with a psychiatrist who had previously treated him. Rosenfeld inferred that this self-object confusion also applied to himself and the patient.

This merging phenomenon was described by Rosenfeld in a later paper (1954). This time the patient was a girl aged 17, who also suffered from schizophrenia. She would only agree to be seen if her mother was present. At first she ignored Rosenfeld's presence. At the end of the fourth session she touched his hands and then kissed them. In the fifth session she had an outburst against her mother, who was still present. She accused the mother of wanting to have Rosenfeld to herself. Following this session, the patient, who had previously ignored her father, began to fuss over him and sit on his knee. At night she was excitable and would run into her parents' bedroom. When Rosenfeld raised the fact of her sexual excitement, she asked him not to talk about sex. At home there were occasional lucid periods, but she was mostly disturbed. She was negativistic and did not want to attend for treatment. During one session she asked if the room was the same as it had been before and how she had got there. She said she had been walking in the park and found she was in someone else's coat. Rosenfeld responded by saying she was mixed up with him as she was with other persons. She then asked him why he was imitating her. Following a further intervention on Rosenfeld's part, she became frightened and asked if he was going to phone the police. After this she refused to come for sessions and Rosenfeld had to visit her at home. One day she asked him why he was keeping her under his jacket and why he was playing about with her. She then put her hand in his jacket.

The Kleinian theory of psychosis asserts that schizophrenia occurs when there is a regression to a hypothesized infantile (psychotic) mental state described as the paranoid schizoid position. This position provides the predisposition to the psychosis if it is not outgrown in the course of development. Innate tendencies, particularly destructive and sadistic elements, are possibly decisive in determining how far the paranoid position retains its influence over later developmental achievements. In all this there are affinities to the concept of fixation.

After birth, according to Melanie Klein (1932), anxiety is caused by the infant's capacity to generate destructive fantasies. These are countered by primitive ego defenses — namely, projective identification and splitting. It is these defenses that give the paranoid schizoid position its special characteristics. The destructive tendencies contaminate the mental representations of the various parts of the self and of the object (the breast).

The bad parts of the self as well as the bad parts of the breast, already introjected, are pushed into the mother (projective identification). Splitting of both object and self occurs simultaneously in order to disperse the concentration of the destructive wishes. Good and bad objects are created. The bad parts, whatever their composition, are projected into the external object. This causes a dread of the object's retaliation. A continuing process of introjection and projection of good and bad objects occurs until the advent of the depressive position.

Rosenfeld, in common with other Kleinian writers (Segal, 1950; H. S. Klein, 1974), believes that the clinical phenomena are a repetition of the nuclear elements of the paranoid schizoid position. The analyst is immediately drawn into this complex of unconscious mental events. According to these authors, it is therefore justifiable to utilize the clinical phenomena as material for transference interpretations. For instance, the indifference, unresponsiveness, and negativism which the schizophrenic patient presents are not seen as the result of a widespread withdrawal of object cathexis, as the classical theory would maintain. Instead they are viewed as the outcome of a primitive form of object relation where the patient, by pushing the bad, destructive parts of his self into the analyst, converts him into a malevolent figure from whom he must withdraw. The merging of patient and therapist results from introjection of the bad parts as well as from their projection into the analyst. For example, when Rosenfeld's patient (1952b) confused himself with his former psychiatrist, Rosenfeld told him that he (the patient) had put his depressed and suicidal self into the psychiatrist, into his father, and into Rosenfeld himself. This made him mixed up and confused. Having put himself into Rosenfeld, he was frightened of losing Rosenfeld and himself as well.

In another case (Rosenfeld, 1952a), the patient was looking at his hand; "it looked as if he was holding something there" (p. 122). When Rosenfeld asked about this, the patient responded with the word "crater." Rosenfeld said the patient was afraid that he (Rosenfeld) was in the crater and was dead. The patient then squeezed his own hand tightly. Rosenfeld interpreted this as meaning the patient was imprisoning and crushing him. At this point the patient ran out of the room. He was brought back by nurses. The fantasy of imprisoning him had the effect of making the patient believe the room was a prison from which he must escape. Having introjected the imprisoned Rosenfeld, he must escape before he himself was crushed to death. The next day the patient had two cataleptic attacks during which he fell to the ground as if dead. Rosenfeld said that the patient, having killed him in the crater, was now killed in retaliation.

The construction of the infantile paranoid schizoid position is largely based on the merging phenomena that are such a striking feature of schizophrenic psychoses. The clinical phenomena are then interpreted in terms of the theory. According to the Kleinian authors, the hypothesized destructive fantasies of infancy, which may be oral, anal, or phallic, constitute the most important ingredient of the predisposition. This results in these workers accepting at face value whatever sadistic ideas or fantasies the patient may reveal and believing that these data confirm their basic assumptions. This tendency is particularly true with regard to childhood memories. For example, H. S. Klein (1974) reports that a young schizophrenic man recalled that when he was a boy he had been in a relative's house. He had been about to touch the keyboard of the piano when suddenly he felt himself surrounded by howling wolves. He was panic-stricken. Klein told the patient that the keys, symbolizing the mother's teeth, would bite and devour him and that this destroying, internalized mother had been pushed (projective identification) into Klein. Now the patient feared Klein lest he eat him up. Some might rightly regard this childhood recollection as a memory screening masturbatory fantasies and anxieties of the oedipal period.

Searles' Concept of Symbiosis

Searles, in a series of papers (1958, 1959a, 1959b, 1961, 1963), describes phenomena identical to those reported by Nunberg (1921) and Rosenfeld (1952a, 1952b, 1954). Searles has worked predominantly with patients suffering from chronic schizophrenia and, like the Kleinian analysts, he believes that the psychotic patient compulsively repeats in the treatment situation the significant object relations of his infancy. Unlike the Kleinian authors, however, Searles (1963) finds that these infantile transferences (transference psychosis) are not immediately discernible by the analyst. They have to be gradually isolated from the mass of delusional content. Here Searles appears to follow the classical view regarding the identification of the transference in the neurotic patient. According to Searles, the analyst can, as with a neurotic patient, only gradually come to recognize the transferred reactions as they apply to himself. Up to this point they are widely disseminated through the course of the patient's daily life. It must be stressed, however, that

Searles (1963) attributes this difficulty in discovering the transference in schizophrenia to the fact that it expresses an infantile mental state where subject and object, reality and fantasy, and ego and id are not yet differentiated.

Searles bases his etiological views on schizophrenia on the symbiosis concept introduced by Mahler (1968) to account for the emergence of psychoses and borderline states in childhood. Searles (1959b) regards the faulty differentiation and lack of integration characterizing schizophrenia as due to a regression to that infantile state where self and object are undifferentiated. In his opinion, the predisposition to schizophrenia is created under two sets of circumstances. The first is when the infant is unable to establish "symbiotic relatedness" with the mother on account of her ambivalence to him. In the absence of the symbiotic phase, there is a complete or partial arrest in development, which allows undifferentiated mental processes to persist within the growing personality and thus render it vulnerable to regression. The second condition for predisposition occurs when the symbiotic phase is established but its resolution and replacement by progressive development in later childhood fails to take place. Persistence of the symbiotic relatedness causes a pronounced instability of the boundaries of the self, even when other aspects of mental functioning achieve some degree of maturity. Again a vulnerability is created, which may lead to psychosis under the conditions of regression. Searles (1959a) has suggested that the persistence of the symbiotic phase into adult life can be traced to the patient's need to sacrifice his own personality integration in order to save the parent from mental illness.

In two papers Searles (1961, 1963) has systematically

categorized his clinical observations on the basis of the etiological assumptions just described. In one paper (1961) the data are organized in accordance with the phases of patient-therapist interaction which, in Searles' view, repeat the vicissitudes of the infant's relation with the mother. In the second paper (1963) the clinical observations are ordered in terms of the psychotic transference manifestations. In all his papers Searles devotes considerable space to an account of his reactions to the speech and behavior of the patients. These data will not be described here, important as they are in revealing the considerable stresses to which the therapist of the chronic schizophrenic patient is exposed.

The clinical phenomena are most comprehensively described by Searles in his paper on transference psychosis in schizophrenia (1963). The phenomena that emerge within the context of the patient-therapist situation are viewed as transferences. This being so, it is considered appropriate to regard particular manifestations as characteristic of specific forms of transference psychosis. The first form of transference psychosis described is one whose expression leads to a situation "in which the therapist feels unrelated to the patient" (Searles, 1963, p. 257). In this "out of contact phase" (Searles, 1961) of the therapy, the patient is thought to be living through an infantile autistic state where the animate, inanimate, human, and nonhuman are indistinguishable from one another and where only parts of the self and the mother have a mental representation. This hypothesized infantile autistic phase, derived from the phenomena presented by chronic schizophrenic patients, resembles rather closely the stage of need satisfaction that has been postulated to precede the establishment of object constancy in infancy

252 CHILDHOOD PSYCHOPATHOLOGY — ADULT PSYCHOSES

(A. Freud, 1952a). The phenomena that, according to Searles, reflect the presence of this "out of contact" transference consist of misidentifications, disorders of identity and autonomy of the self, the free expression of needs and wishes, and the belief that the therapist is psychotic.

The second form of transference psychosis described by Searles (1963) is one where the phenomena follow from the patient's regained capacity to acknowledge himself as an entity distinct from others. The object relations that occur are colored by an intense ambivalence. Searles understands this kind of transference psychosis as a repetition of a phase of infantile development where self- and object representations are differentiated but where the relation is marred by ambivalence. It is this ambivalence that prevents the patient, in infancy, from advancing "from identification with mother to the subsequent establishment of successful individuation . . ." (Searles, 1963, pp. 260-261). The infant's ambivalent feelings are such as to lead to a regressive withdrawal to the earlier autistic (part-object) state.

In this form of symbiosis, repeated as transference, the patient wishes to regain an ambivalence-free symbiotic relation with the therapist (mother) but fears that the consequence of this step will be the annihilation of the self and the mother. For example, Searles (1958) describes the case of a 38-year-old female schizophrenic patient who remained antagonistic and contemptuous of him for a period of two and a half years. During this time she was, in his opinion, taken up with destructive fantasies and was often on the point of attacking him. Later on in the therapy she revealed that the purpose of her hostility was to protect both him and herself. Expressing her fear of closeness to the therapist, she said, " 'If we got together, we might kill one another' " (Searles, 1958, p. 582).

Searles (1963) describes a third form of transference psychosis, which arises when the patient repeats with the therapist his childhood efforts to deal with a parent who was unable to allow the dissolution of the symbiotic relation. The patient attempts to restore the therapist-parent's personality to enable him to become, once again, a "separate and whole person" (Searles, 1963, p. 263). The anxiety, which the patient is envisaged as experiencing in infancy and in repetition with the therapist, consists of a dread that the achievement of independence will cause the parent's death. The wish for separateness is construed as the equivalent of murder. Searles (1963) illustrates this form of transference with a number of clinical examples. In all of them he interprets the patient's behavior as representing a need to build up a parental figure with wished-for attributes. In one case incomprehensible speech and indecisive behavior represent the repetition of a childhood wish for the father-therapist to be explicit and definite. Similarly, a female patient's seductive behavior is seen as her wish to make the father-therapist a man by his having coitus with her. Searles suggests that the bizarre speech and behavior that may appear at any time during a schizophrenic illness is motivated by the patient's wish to evaluate the therapist's mental stability and/or relieve his supposed depression.

The fourth variety of transference behavior that Searles (1963) claims to have identified consists of confused, irrational behavior. This has a two-fold aim. It is an attempt by the patient to get the therapist to do his thinking for him and so maintain a state of symbiosis. It is also a means of destroying the therapist's efforts to help and, as such, an expression of the patient's need to be an independent functioning individual. In these cases the patient, in childhood, both accepted and repudiated a parent's omniscient attitudes. Searles (1963) cites the case of a female patient whose father, believing that she was intellectually subnormal, had taught her to act, think, and speak. This was reflected in the psychosis in her belief in an omnipotent delusional figure. During the therapy a confusional state continued for a long time. Searles considered that the purpose of the confusion was to nullify all his efforts to help. The patient had to demonstrate the fallibility of the father-therapist. When she came to recognize the motive for her behavior, she was able to cooperate in the therapy. It is on the basis of cases such as this that Searles asserts that the behavior of the parents was regarded by the child as intrusive and, as such, interfered with the development and establishment of a true sense of self.

The limited range of concepts Searles uses in his theory of psychosis follows from his belief that the predisposition to schizophrenia is the result of disturbed interpersonal relations in infancy. Omnipotent delusions and "narcissistic" withdrawal, for example, are explained as a defense against excessive dependency needs. Seeing no need to go beyond such dynamic explanations, Searles is freed, as are the Kleinians, of the necessity to make use of the economic principle.

Searles uses the concept of symbiosis quite differently from Mahler (1968). According to the latter, the symbiotic phase, which follows the stage of normal autism, begins from the second month of life when the infant is beginning to be aware of the mother in her need-satisfying role. At this time "the infant behaves and functions as though he and his mother were an omnipotent system — a dual unity within one common boundary" (Mahler, 1968, p. 8). During the phase of normal symbiosis, self- and object representations are not clearly differentiated. The emergence of a coherent and stable sense of self and identity are dependent on a smooth passage through the symbiotic phase. Persistence of the symbiotic phase into childhood results, according to Mahler (1968), in a symbiotic form of childhood psychosis. Self- and object representations are confused and need-satisfying kinds of behavior predominate in object relations.

The patients treated by Searles did not suffer from such childhood mental disturbances. Prior to the psychosis the individual patient had attained a sense of identity and the ability to differentiate self and objects; need-satisfying behavior had been largely given up. Thus, in postulating the persistence in vulnerable individuals of a tendency to relate symbiotically to others, Searles is describing something other than Mahler's concept of symbiosis. Searles is suggesting that while the patient-to-be is clearly aware of the boundaries of his physical and mental self, object and self-representations still retain a syncretic character in the unconscious. It is difficult to understand how this could comprise a potential for a pathological symbiotic relatedness when account is taken of the fact that in the system unconscious representations of the self and of objects are subject to condensations and displacements (primary process) as in the dreams of healthy individuals.

In categorizing the clinical data according to the different forms of a transference psychosis, Searles (1963) portrays the manner in which the symbiotic state is believed to persist and find a repetitive expression in the treatment situation. In the three latter forms of transference psychosis described by Searles, the patient no longer confuses himself with others, as he does in "the out of contact phase" (Searles, 1961), when mental functioning proceeds in accordance with the primary process. The clinical illustrations drawn from these latter three categories of transference psychosis indicate, as Searles intended they should, the way in which the patient externalizes aspects of the self onto the therapist, how he identifies with the therapist, and how he displaces onto the latter important figures of the past. Only in the first form of transference psychosis — the "out of contact phase" — does the patient believe in the reality of these "repetitions" and does he display the merging of self and objects typical of the symbiotic childhood psychosis.

Much of the difficulty in understanding Searles' views on etiology arises from his unwillingness to commit himself to a coherent theory of mental functioning. While he acknowledges the difficulty of distinguishing phenomena resulting from transferences (as in the neuroses) from manifestations due to a "transference psychosis," his lack of concepts causes him to employ the one term to describe phenomena with different developmental origins. Symbiosis is equated with identification, but the identification to which Searles (1963) refers is the primary identification preceding object cathexis. Searles then proceeds to use the concept of symbiosis (identification) to describe phenomena resulting from the translation of secondary identifications into transferences, either direct or reversed.

By locating the predisposition to schizophrenia in the autistic-symbiotic phase of infancy, Searles regards the later childhood experiences that come to light through the transference as merely a further expression of the pathological symbiotic relatedness. On this account, data that can be regarded as reflecting conflicts of the oedipal and pre-oedipal periods and might be contributory to the predisposition are ignored. As with the Kleinian psychoanalysts, childhood memories and the manifest content of dreams are used to confirm the etiological hypothesis. For example, Searles (1959a) describes the case of a male patient who said he had never seen his mother kiss his father. As in many other instances, the oedipal background of such memory falsifications is passed over.

Family Studies of Schizophrenia

During the last 20 years a wealth of new information bearing on the problem of predisposition has been obtained from the intensive study of the families of schizophrenic patients (Lidz et al., 1966; Bowen, 1960) and from conjoint and other forms of family therapy (Jackson, 1961; Alanen, 1972; Rubinstein, 1974). In contrast to individual psychotherapy, the conditions of family therapy obstruct the development of the patient-therapist relation and transferences. As a result, most of these additional data have been derived from the observation of the interactions between the parents and between one or other parent and the patient. These transactions are believed to be specific for the families of schizophrenic patients.

While the developmental and dynamic viewpoints are fundamental to Lidz's theory of schizophrenia (1972; Lidz and Fleck, 1960), his research experiences have led him to consider metapsychology as inadequate for the task of providing comprehensive and realistic explanations of the schizophrenic psychoses. Since the family exerts continuing pressure, albeit of different kinds, on its members from infancy to adolescence. Lidz finds it difficult to accept as at all likely that the vulnerability to mental ill health results primarily from adverse experiences limited to the first years of life. On this account, he finds no need for concepts describing the contribution made by instincts and the emerging ego to the beginnings of object relations or for concepts portraying the consequences of traumatic events.

The observations Lidz and his colleagues (1966) made during their family studies led them to propose that there are certain types of families that generate the predisposition to schizophrenia. This is essentially the position adopted by Bowen (1960). The over-all effect of the "skewed" and "schizmatic" families identified by Lidz and his colleagues (1966) on the patient-to-be is to impair the establishment of that autonomy of the self on which satisfactory interpersonal relations and a realistic judgment of environmental events depend. The "skewed" family is characterized by an unobtrusive father and a mother who has a compulsive tendency to intrude into the lives of the family members and into the life of the patient in particular. This leads to special reactions on the patient's part, which come to form the core of the predisposition to the psychosis. In the "schizmatic" family the parents are constantly at loggerheads. The patient is exploited either as a support or as a means of vicarious satisfaction for both father and mother. Again the reaction to this behavior creates a vulnerability to psychosis.

Family studies of schizophrenia (Wynne, 1972; Laing, 1971; Stierlin, 1972) have led to the introduction of new concepts to describe the specific parent-patient interactions believed to be schizophrenogenic. Wynne (1972) describes two types of familial interactions he believes lead to a restriction and distortion of the growing individual's capacity for psychical differentiation (self and object, fantasy and reality). He terms these interactions the "injection of meaning" and the "concealment of meaning." While these interactions are not unique for the families of schizophrenic patients, they occur more frequently and with greater intensity than in nonschizophrenic families. Wynne also acknowledges that the involved individual is one whose sensitivity to these interactions is heightened by an innate tendency to psychosis.

"Injection of meaning" (Wynne, 1972, p. 182) denotes that kind of interpersonal contact where one person puts ideas and feeling directly into the mind of another person, believing this is in his best interest. The initial reaction of the recipient may be one of rejection and hostility, but eventually there is acceptance. Wynne gives an illustration of this process as he observed it during marital therapy. Mrs. A. was angry. Mr. A. said, " 'You're not *angry*. You're feeling *hurt*,' " and Mrs. A. replied, " 'I don't feel in pain. I feel like killing you' " (1972, p. 182). Mr. A. told her that her reaction was excessive and that it sprang from her disturbed mental state. She needed help. Mrs. A. succumbed in tears. When Mr. A. comforted her she no longer protested against the interpretation of her subjective state. The effect of "injection of meaning" continued over many years is to weaken the recipient's belief in his own feelings, ideas, opinions, and judgments. His autonomy becomes limited and gradually he comes to depend on the instigator of the injections to validate his experiences, intentions, and awareness of reality. This state of dependency has been designated "binding" by Stierlin (1972). "Binding" causes the child to become entirely dependent on his parents and prevents him from creating new relations outside the family.

"Concealment of meaning" (Wynne, 1972, p. 187) describes the situation where one individual withholds affectively significant information from others at a moment when they are in need of this communication. As an example of this form of family interaction, Wynne cites the behavior of a mother who was involved in conjoint family therapy with her husband, a daughter, and the patient, her 16-year-old son. A disagreement about the potential hazards of hitchhiking arose between the father, on the one side, and the daughter and the patient on the other side. The mother did not join in the discussion. She was asked for her opinion but did not reply. After several fruitless attempts to get her to participate, the others fell silent, the father saying, " 'I'm talking down a blind alley' " (Wynne, 1972, p. 188). Just as the discussion revived, the mother intervened, implying she had special knowledge of hitchhiking. The other members of the family were deeply impressed, indicating that they acknowledged her superior insights.

"Concealment," like "injection of meaning," promotes an overdependency based on the belief that the concealer is in possession of special powers of understanding. These powers are not explicitly claimed but are inferred by remarks and statements designed to promote such an impression on vulnerable individuals. This overdependency, which develops during childhood, has the effect of disturbing and limiting the emerging capacities for self-differentiation and independent thinking.

Wynne's concepts can be accommodated within the

scope of what Stierlin (1972) describes as "psychological exploitation." According to Stierlin, this form of exploitation can be witnessed at first hand during family therapy. Stierlin has identified patterns of relating that, he believes, are instrumental in promoting the predisposition to schizophrenia. What he calls "binding" has three basic causes. The first results from the excessive indulgence of the child's wishes, which vitiates his capacity to be separate from the need-satisfying object. The second results from those family interactions that limit and disorganize psychical differentiation (see Wynne above). The third cause follows from the exploitation of the child's loyalty to the parents. This form of "binding" is akin to Searles' (1963) transference concept of the patient's compulsive need to preserve the parent's (therapist's) mental and physical integrity.

Two other transactional modes are described by Stierlin (1972): the "mode of delegating" and the "mode of expulsion." Neither has the significance of "binding" for the development of a schizophrenic psychosis. The adolescent becomes a "delegate" when, already selectively "bound," he separates from the family to perform a specific mission. Conflict may arise when the wish to separate further occurs. The nature of the mission may also be a source of conflict. This conflict may be so severe as to result in symptoms that are often indistinguishable from an acute schizophrenic attack. However, it is "binding" that leads most frequently to schizophrenia. Where the "binding" has a three-fold base — on the need-satisfaction level, the cognitive level, and the loyalty level — the child remains psychically undifferentiated with poor "ego boundaries." His need for a permanent symbiotic relation invalidates all attempts at separation from others and from the family. A schizophrenic psychosis ensues and usually proceeds to chronicity. Stierlin (1972) also envisages a schizophrenic outcome in children who are victims of neglect and then of "expulsion."

All those who have written on schizophrenia within the context of family studies acknowledge the weaknesses inherent in their etiological formulations. There is the matter of the intrafamilial phenomena that have been observed and on which so much emphasis is laid. Are they a replica of the interactions that occurred during the patient's childhood and adolescence or are they a reaction to the patient's illness? The authors cited are satisfied that what is observed represents the special kinds of interactions that occurred in the patient's family in his earlier, pre-illness years. There is also the difficulty of reconciling the etiological hypotheses with the fact that the transactional modes found in the schizophrenogenic families are also observed in families where there is no evidence of psychosis. This suggests, in spite of Wynne's (1972) assertion that the transactional modes are more intense in schizophrenic than in nonschizophrenic families, that these interactions are fundamentally nonspecific and do not contribute decisively to the predisposition or immediate cause of the psychosis.

The theory of predisposition just described is based on reconstructions of the family life of the schizophrenic patient as it is believed to have been during his childhood and adolescence. Little attention is paid to the instinctual components of object relations. Influenced by the structural aspects of psychoanalytic theory, Lidz, Wynne, and others base predisposition on the grounds of ego weakness and faulty identification. Parents of "skewed" and "schizmatic" families (Lidz et al., 1966) fail to provide the models on which a stable personal and sexual identity can be based. According to their view, patients who develop delusions about sexual identity have been predisposed to this outcome by identifications with parents whose sexuality had an overt or latent pathology. However, where delusional content consists of conflicts about sexual identity, there are additional phenomena that render the structural approach insufficient as a means of explanation. Some patients go beyond fearing that their sexual identity has been altered by persecutors to claiming an identity properly belonging to the opposite sex. A case in point is the woman who believes she is Christ and simultaneously shows a heightened genitality expressed in masturbation and sexual overtures to both men and women.

Young girls may find themselves in a conflict over masturbation with fantasies of a heroic kind. They picture themselves as the redeemer, a famous doctor, an adventuress, etc. Certain influences are at work causing a pubertal girl to entertain active and/or masculine fantasies. Is it likely that the reasons are to be found solely in the disturbed sexual identity of parents? Pubertal daydreams cannot be separated from the instinctual wishes promoting their representation. It is active phallic wishes that cause the conflict, and the pubertal fantasies are the successors of earlier instinctual aims and objects, which gave way to repression. Any explanation of delusions about sexual identity must take all such data into consideration.

Further Considerations

The major revisions of psychoanalytic theory have taken place at the hands of those who have worked predominantly with psychotic patients or with very young children. The nature of the clinical states and the methods of treatment have had a decisive influence in leading to dissatisfaction with the classical theory. The behavior of the psychotic patient is not only different from that of the neurotic patient but, under the conditions of therapy, the direction of his thinking is different as well. Having accepted the rule of free association, the attention of a neurotic patient is taken up with accounts of current relations, dreams, and memories of adolescence and childhood. These data give the psychoanalyst a first orientation regarding future transferences and an opportunity to learn more about the patient's life history. Such developments do not occur during the psychotherapy or psychoanalysis of the psychoses, even after the acute attack has passed. For long periods, the literature on the subject reveals, the cooperative patient is entirely preoccupied with relating his various physical and mental experiences. Only occasionally does he make reference to his childhood or adolescence. He sees no need for this, and so there is a continuing repetition of the same information. The psychoanalyst has to seek out new material by using as a stimulus some aspect of the patient-therapist relation.

The Kleinian analyst makes free use of this maneuver and employs as stimulus an interpretation based on his theory of psychosis. Sometimes this method is effective, for Kleinian as well as for other therapists, and the patient will talk about his life, past or present, and perhaps report a dream or fantasy. It is all too easy, then, to believe these new data have some important transference significance. The writings of Searles (1963) and others (Boyer and Giovacchini, 1967) show that from time to time the patient brings forward contents similar to those presented by a neurotic patient but in a different context.

It is not just that the psychotic patient deprives the psychoanalyst of dreams, fantasies, memories, and useful transferences. The precondition for the analysis of these phenomena is usually absent also. The psychotic patient cannot, even with the analyst's help, mobilize the concentration essential for the resolution of the resistance that stands in the way of an understanding of the mental contents presenting to consciousness. These obstacles have directed the attention of Kleinian and other psychoanalysts, including the family workers, from clinical observation to theory construction. As a result, the hiatus, created by lack of knowledge of the determinants of the fantasies and memories, has been filled with unsubstantiated theoretical concepts.

A thorough exploration of the early childhood of psychotic patients presents great difficulties. The few systematic reconstructions that have been made of these early years have been derived from delusional content (Katan, 1959, 1975) and from the dreams and associations the patient has brought forward (Nunberg, 1921; Róheim, 1955). These reconstructions contain as their central element experiences that, having provoked intense excitement, interact with the child's phase-appropriate instinctual behavior and ego state. The ensuing object relations, real and fantasy, can then be seen as focal points from which the pathological mental contents of later childhood and adolescence are derived. The reliability of these reconstructions has been repeatedly questioned and their credibility has not been improved by the lack of contributions to the subject. Further studies, essential as they are, are insufficient in themselves. They need to be supplemented by data from other sources — from the results obtained from analysis of neuroses in adults and children and by information gained from the borderline states of childhood where the patients have been able to cooperate in therapy.

The material obtained from these sources has shown that the fantasies and memories of later childhood are no different from those found in psychotic patients. The neurotic symptoms have their origins in the sexual conflicts that are an integral element of the object relations of the early childhood period. It is difficult to avoid the conclusion that the reluctance to investigate those childhood years of the psychotic patient when cognition is rapidly establishing itself springs from an unwillingness to acknowledge the central role sexuality plays, for good or ill, at this critical period of mental development. It is the repudiation of infantile sexuality that provides the mainspring for the assertion that the libido theory is irrelevant for an understanding of psychotic illness.

THE PREDISPOSING FACTORS

The several revisions of Freud's (1911) theory of psychosis have failed to answer the question of whether there are specific factors, other than constitutional ones, that act together to form the predisposition to psychosis in adult life. Those who look to the classical theory as a basis for the study of the predisposition believe that this unsatisfactory state of affairs has resulted from psychoanalysts' losing interest in metapsychological concepts and failing to recognize resistances that counter the attempts to penetrate the childhood amnesia of psychotic patients. This is not to underrate the difficulty that such a task imposes. In the neuroses the reconstruction of early childhood is based on dreams, transferences, and the analysis of screen memories. This, as already has been stated, is facilitated by the patient's active participation in the work of the analysis and his ability to tolerate and resolve the resistances caused by repression. Even when the psychotic patient has passed out of acute phases of illness, the phenomena appearing in connection with the therapist are bereft of the supporting evidence that would confirm them as transference repetitions. Neither memories of childhood relations nor confirmatory dreams make an appearance.

There is no disagreement about the kinds of phenomena that occur during the course of a psychotic illness. The controversy is over the designation and significance of the phenomena. There is little to favor the view that every patient's response is a repetition and therefore a transference. It is more likely that many so-called transferences arise as a consequence of the patient's reactions to behavior, thought, or feeling in the therapist, which has been evoked by some aspect of the psychotic symptomatology. All the phenomena cannot be accorded an equal importance and only some manifestations are relevant to the problem of predisposition.

Freud's (1911) theory offers a means of distinguishing between the different kinds of psychotic symptoms and signs. There are those which result from drive or ego regression (the negative symptoms) and those which are restitutional (the positive symptoms). If there are acquired elements in the predisposition to psychosis, they must be reflected in the form and content of the clinical phenomena. In an acute phase a psychotic patient cannot relate to an affectively significant person in a normal way. When the patient is invited to participate in a therapeutic relation, he either rejects this, behaving in a negativistic and unresponsive manner, or he shows that he cannot sustain a separateness from the therapist and becomes mixed up with the therapist. The latter state of affairs only occurs when the patient welcomes the therapist's interest and shows that he wishes to be like him. Within a short time the patient comes to regard the therapist as a persecutor (Nunberg, 1921; Burnham, 1961; Rosenfeld, 1952b; Searles, 1963; Freeman et al., 1965).

In the cases referred to above, the patients harbored homosexual wishes, which were converted into persecutory fears. In metapsychological terms the sequence of events can be described as follows: The cathexis of the homosexual object reached a level where conflict occurred. The immediate response was a detachment of object cathexis and identification with the object (primary identification). This defense occurred because the acute attack had exposed a state where the primary process was in ascendancy. Cathexes could move easily from object to self, self to object, and object to object — hence the expression of wishes in thought and action, the formal disorder of speech and thinking, the misidentifications, and the merging phenomena. The conversion of the wish to be like and to be the therapist into a fear of his persecution occurred when the primary process receded and there was a return of some degree of psychic structure. Then the defense against homosexuality was by projection.

The psychiatric and psychoanalytic literature attests to the high degree of reliability characterizing the phenomena just described. They therefore provide a firm groundwork on which to base inferences about predisposition. Two sets of phenomena must be singled out: the specific modes of relating and the thought content through which some of this relating finds expression. Both sets belong to the category of positive symptoms. Insofar as this is so, they can be thought of as having been exposed to view by the psychopathological process.

The psychotic patient's incapacity to retain autonomy of the self due to loss of "ego boundaries" has been seized upon by every writer (see above) to provide an observational base for etiological theories. The phenomena resulting from merging or identification could not occur in the absence of an inbuilt weakness of the function ordering the differentiation of self and object prior to the onset of the illness. What is known of patients who come to develop psychoses indicates that this vulnerability varies quantitatively from case to case. The clinical findings suggest that the breakdown of the "ego boundaries" is a consequence of an inability to sustain the libidinal cathexis of an object. The events preceding the onset of an acute psychotic attack are consistent with this hypothesis. A danger situation created by libidinal wishes is countered by regression to primary identification.

An instability of object cathexis must then constitute a major factor contributing to the predisposition to schizophrenic and paranoid psychoses. This instability can be detected in the kinds of object relations that characterized the patient throughout his previous life. Where information has been sufficiently extensive, reconstructions of the previous personality have indicated that real object choice, when it occurred, was based on narcissism. This finding has led to the theory that it was an increased ego libido that acted as the predisposing factor facilitating the regression to narcissism. Katan's (1950) work on the prepsychotic phase of schizophrenia reinforced the idea that the instability of the object cathexis was related to pathological narcissistic development.

The narcissistic basis of the object libido can also be noted in the fantasies that come to light as delusions and as "transferences" in cases of schizophrenia. These fantasies must have been active in the patient's childhood and in early adolescence. The content of the first group of delusions comprises the patient's denial of his parentage and/or claim that he is the child of exalted or important persons. These delusions, reported by numerous authors, are identical to the fantasy of the family romance (Freud, 1909), which has its principal origin in the Oedipus complex arising from the child's recognition of his parents' sexual life. In subsequent fantasies of the mother's infidelity, the mother's lover "almost always exhibits the features of the boy's own ego, or more accurately, of his own idealized personality, grown up and so raised to a level with his father" (Freud, 1910, p. 171). The child, while still cathecting the parental objects, has, metapsychologically speaking adopted a narcissistic position in that the self has become the recipient of libidinal cathexis. The self has increased in significance at the expense of real objects.

Every detail of the family romance, from its forerunners to the final version, can be found in schizophrenic patients. The mother is believed to be promiscuous, the father a criminal and even a murderer. Later the parents are replaced by others more acceptable to the patient's grandiosity. The contents of all the fantasies reveal hatred and a wish for revenge. Both male and female schizophrenic patients frequently express a hatred for the mother; the denial of her reality is a reflection of this. This hatred, previously repressed, must have been a vital element in the childhood mental life of these patients. Hatred provokes and intensifies the withdrawal of libido, thus reducing the cathexis of the love objects and of reality. Fantasies based on this narcissism would, as Freud (1910) points out, become ingrained as a consequence of the masturbation activated by the parental behavior. Here there is a meeting point between the classical approach and the family theories of schizophrenia (Lidz and Fleck, 1960). Parents of schizophrenic patients unwittingly accentuate, to pathological proportions, reactions that are integral features of the healthy child's mental development.

Rescue fantasies comprise the content of the second group of delusions. They are most often found as a counterpart to "end of the world" delusions, where the patient claims that he has saved the world or humanity from disaster. Quite apart from these dramatic assertions, patients believe that they have saved the life of another patient, of the therapist if in treatment, or, as Searles (1963) has described, they are preoccupied with the task of rescuing a parent from mental illness or suicide. These delusions occur equally among men and women patients.

The wish to rescue a loved one from a life of promiscuity is, as Freud (1910) described, a characteristic of men who make "a special type of object choice." However, this conscious wish is only the expression of a constellation of unconscious ideas derived from the Oedipus complex. The boy's fantasy of rescuing the mother signifies giving her a child, like himself—"All his instincts, those of tenderness, gratitude, lustfulness, defiance, and independence, find satisfaction in the single wish *to be his own father"* (Freud, 1910, p. 173). On the other hand, the fantasy of saving the father's life is an expression of defiance. In the case of women, a rescue fantasy represents giving birth to a child, but under certain conditions it reflects the masculine wish to give a child, as in the case of the boy.

Rescue fantasies occurring as part of delusional content must have figured prominently in the childhood mental life of schizophrenic patients. The birth of a sibling, for example, regarded by the child as betrayal, leads to a withdrawal of object cathexis and to a heightening of narcissism. This does not cause a break with reality but again encourages the tendency to withdraw from others. In some cases of schizophrenia it is possible to trace out the connections between delusions of rescue and birth fantasies based upon childhood experiences.

A young man fell ill with schizophrenia ostensibly after failing to establish a love relation with a woman. In the psychosis, which assumed a chronic character, he continued in a state of identification with her. He claimed that they were to marry but she could not bear children. She was sacred and pregnancy would destroy her beauty. He had been beautiful himself, but his beauty had been sacrificed by his rescue of the hospital patients from a disaster. His wife must not be disfigured by pregnancy and childbirth. This man hated his mother, yet his identification with her was pronounced. When he was four years of age, she had thrown him out of the family car. This memory expressed his belief that he was rejected in favor of his sister, who was born when he was about three years of age; it represented the act of birth. His birth fantasies also found representation in his claim to poetic creativity. By insisting that a particular poem and himself were both masterpieces, he revealed the claim that he had fathered himself.

There is a third category of delusional content, which is related to the twin fantasy (Burlingham, 1952) and to the fantasy of the imaginary companion (Nagera, 1970). These conscious fantasies, like those already described, are derivatives of the Oedipus complex. Again the narcissistic element is predominant: "A child who feels himself thwarted and forsaken is thrown back upon himself. He cannot imagine finding anyone more satisfactory than he is. He therefore creates a twin, an image of himself that he can love. This solution acts as a cover for self-love and as a means of avoiding guilt for self-love. In the disguise of the twin the daydreamer loves himself; narcissism is hidden, and self-love appears under the mask of object-love" (Burlingham, 1952, p. 5). This same narcissistic element is to be found in delusions arising from the fantasy of the imaginary companion (Freeman, 1973).

The narcissistic reaction that affects the young child in the face of disappointment in the parents, and the consequences of this, must disturb those processes promoting the transition from the primary to the secondary process, in particular the establishment of object constancy. It is this function that is deranged in both acute and chronic schizophrenic states due to the action of the primary process. The question is whether such an outcome results from an inherent weakness in object constancy that has been present since early childhood. In the healthy child the beginnings of object constancy and its ultimate stability and integrity depend on a continuing diminution of the narcissistic quality of the libidinal cathexes (Hoffer, 1952). As Burgner and Edgcumbe (1972) point out, the establishment of object constancy or, as they call it, "the capacity for constant relationships" only has its beginnings in late infancy. It is not, in their opinion, a developmental phase. The capacity for constant relationships evolves slowly over a long period of time and includes progressive changes in both the drives and the ego. It is quite possible that a continuing reinforcement of narcissism militates against the emergence of a reliable capacity for object constancy.

When the psychoanalytic treatment of severely disturbed young children has been possible (Fraiberg, 1952; Furman, 1956; Sperling, 1952), information has been forthcoming demonstrating that the evolution of the secondary process was obstructed by the pressure of libidinal drive activity. The libidinal arousal usually followed a seduction or overstimulation. Sometimes these events were accompanied by reactions to the birth of a sibling. The emerging capacity for object cathexis was weakened under these circumstances, and the tendency was for the narcissistic condition to reinstate itself. This libidinal movement was, in these cases, reflected in the clinical withdrawal. Even more significant was the loss of object constancy at the height of an affective crisis.

Cases such as these reveal unequivocally how the premature arousal of infantile sexuality, in any of its forms, can lead to an arrest in the development of the secondary process, with all the consequences this has for future object relations and reality testing. At the same time, the psychoanalytic treatment of adult neuroses has shown that once the infantile amnesia is lifted the factors that led to the libidinal fixations and created the vulnerability to illness become manifest. The psychotic patient no less than the neurotic shows signs of disturbances of his sexuality. The sexual content of delusions and of transferences occurring in psychoses can be regarded as evidences of the kinds of sexual conflict that occurred in childhood. It is flying in the face of common sense to explain the homosexual wishes of a female schizophrenic patient on the basis of the infant-mother relation (unresolved symbiosis) when, for example, the patient demonstrates that she is spurred on to act the part of a man by intense phallic excitations.

Much of psychical significance affects a child between infancy and later childhood. Outstanding in the case of the girl are her active sexual (phallic) wishes for the mother. The prevalence of a phallic orientation in female psychotic patients cannot be unrelated to childhood clitoral masturbation. Similarly, the frequent occurrence of passive feminine wishes in male patients must be connected with the homosexual seductions frequently reported or discovered as having occurred during childhood.

It is data from the severe nonpsychotic childhood disorders that suggests a pathological sexuality may arise in early years which is sufficiently influential to bring about the kinds of deviation of sexual aim and object characterizing young schizophrenic patients. Most easily observed is the reaction of these patients to genital arousal, which evokes the most intense affects. This is illustrated by the case of a young man of 22, who had been ill for three years with a schizophrenic psychosis. He disliked and distrusted psychiatrists because of their tolerant attitude to masturbation. He criticized his parents because they had ignored the evidence of his unremitting masturbation and his later sexual activities with a girl friend. If the parents had been vigilant, he would have been spared much suffering. He said masturbation was a crime and should be severely punished. When reactions of this kind are taken together with delusional ideas regarding sexual identity, cases like this provide support for Katan's (1974) belief that genital excitation, and in particular orgasm, must be avoided at all costs by those who are possessed, unconsciously, with the wish to be a woman. Orgasm signifies the fulfillment of their wish and, in vulnerable individuals, leads to a break with reality. The avoidance of genital arousal is not confined to periods during the prepsychotic phase but also continues into later stages of the illness.

Whatever the impact of genitality on the psychical apparatus at puberty, the direction the libidinal cathexes will take must depend on the kind of sexual organization established at the end of the infantile period. Katan's theory of schizophrenia (1950, 1954) brings together the predisposing factors just referred to. In approaching the problem of origins from a metapsychological viewpoint, he gives prominence to the narcissistic disposition of the schizophrenic patient-to-be. Katan acknowledges that the sexual instincts pass through their developmental sequences even in the vulnerable individual. These phases are, of course, subject to the influence of adverse chance events ("environmental interferences"), which create fixations, enhance narcissism, and influence the formation of the Oedipus complex. This is an Oedipus complex where the mother represents aspects of the boy's femininity and the father the girl's masculinity. The advent of genitality at puberty sees the start of a conflict between the patient's masculine and feminine strivings. It is under the conditions of disease that the "counterfeit of the oedipus complex" (Katan, 1950, p. 186) finds its representation in the rescue delusions, where the male patient assumes the parturient role and the female patient the part of procreator.

A theory of predisposition that leans heavily on the concept of narcissism is faced with the fact that everything that can be discerned in the history of a schizophrenic patient and that contributes to a pathological narcissism and to a preference for passive sexual aims in the male and active sexual aims in the female can also be found in sexual deviations and in certain forms of neurosis (Freeman, 1964). The treatment of these states shows that in the face of childhood disappointments and frustrations there is a withdrawal of object libido and a hypercathexis of the self. As in the narcissistic state envisaged for the potential schizophrenic patient, the detached libidinal cathexes "innervate" the wishful fantasies (see above). They condense within themselves the frustrated sexual and aggressive drive derivatives (Freeman, 1963). In adult life these nonpsychotic patients base their object choices on narcissism.

Two possibilities present themselves as to why narcissistically disposed individuals develop a psychosis rather than a sexual deviation or a neurosis. It may be that the narcissism predisposing to psychosis has its basis in a persistence of the primary form with its accompanying lack of attainment of a stable mode of object constancy. The adverse circumstances attendant on the child in his first years may limit the transition to secondary narcissism because of the failure of the object representations to consolidate themselves. In their absence, secondary identifications cannot achieve stability and the individual is left without a firm sense of identity. This may lead to transient identifications with those who become affectively significant to the patient. On the other hand, in individuals destined to develop sexual deviations, the secondary identifications are firmly established and the narcissism is founded on these mental structures (secondary narcissism). The other possibility is that the narcissistic dispositions of both psychotic and sexually-deviant individuals are identical and that divergence only begins to appear after puberty. At this time, hereditary and constitutional influences would play a decisive part. Whichever view happens to be favored, these innate tendencies must be given a central place in the predisposition to psychosis.

A theory of predisposition that gives a prominent place to narcissism finds most favor with this writer, in spite of all the difficulties arising from its usage. It is an unfortunate fact that studies of predisposition based on treatment of psychotic patients will never yield results that will find universal approval. Nevertheless, comfort can be taken from the knowledge that the hypothetical factors that have been isolated so far have already had their influence on the work of those concerned with the prevention and treatment of mental disorder in children and young people.

REFERENCES

ALANEN, Y. O. (1972), The benefits of family psychotherapy in hebephrenic schizophrenia. In: *Psychotherapy of Schizophrenia*, eds. D. Rubinstein & Y. O. Alanen. Amsterdam: Excerpta Medica Press, pp. 194-200.

BERES, D. (1956), Ego deviation and the concept of schizophrenia. *The Psychoanalytic Study of the Child*, 11: 164-235. New York: International Universities Press.

BERSTOCK, R. (1974), Report of the Hampstead Clinic, London (unpublished).

BORNSTEIN, B. (1935), Phobia in a 2½-year-old child. *Psychoanal. Quart.*, 4:93-119.

BOWEN, M. (1960), A family concept of schizophrenia. In: *The Etiology of Schizophrenia*, ed. D. D. Jackson. New York: Basic Books, pp. 346-372.

BOYER, L. B. & GIOVACCHINI, P. L. (1967), *Psychoanalytic Treatment of Characterological and Schizophrenic Disorders*. New York: Science House.

BURGNER, M. & EDGCUMBE, R. (1972), Some problems in the conceptualization of early object relationships. Part II: the concept of object constancy. *The Psychoanalytic Study of the Child*, 27:315-333. New York: Quadrangle Books, 1973.

BURLINGHAM, D. (1952), *Twins: A Study of Three Pairs of Identical Twins*. New York: International Universities Press.

BURNHAM, D. L. (1961), Autonomy and activity-passivity in the psychotherapy of a schizophrenic man. In: *Psychotherapy of the Psychoses*, ed. A. Burton. New York: Basic Books, pp. 208-236.

DARE, C. (1974), Report of the Hampstead Clinic, London (unpublished).

279

DES LAURIERS, A. M. (1962), *The Early Experience of Reality in Childhood Schizophrenia*. New York: International Universities Press.

EKSTEIN, R. & WALLERSTEIN, J. (1954), Observations on the psychology of borderline and psychotic children. *The Psychoanalytic Study of the Child*, 9:344-369. New York: International Universities Press.

ELKAN, I. (1973), Report of the Hampstead Clinic, London (unpublished).

FEDERN, P. (1952), *Ego Psychology and the Psychoses*. New York: Basic Books.

FORREST, A. D. (1975), Paranoid states and paranoid psychoses. In: *New Perspectives in Schizophrenia*, eds. A. D. Forrest & J. Affleck. Edinburgh: Churchill Livingstone, pp. 32-44.

FRAIBERG, S. (1952), A critical neurosis in a two-and-a-half-year-old girl. *The Psychoanalytic Study of the Child*, 7: 173-215. New York: International Universities Press.

FREEMAN, T. (1963), The concept of narcissism in schizophrenic states. *Internat. J. Psycho-Anal.*, 44:293-303.

_____ (1964), Some aspects of pathological narcissism. *J. Amer. Psychoanal. Assn.*, 12:540-561.

_____ (1971), Observations on mania. *Internat. J. Psycho-Anal.*, 52:479-486.

_____ (1973), *A Psychoanalytic Study of the Psychoses*. New York: International Universities Press.

_____ , CAMERON, J. L., & McGHIE, A. (1958), *Chronic Schizophrenia*. New York: International Universities Press.

_____ _____ _____ (1965), *Studies on Psychosis. Descriptive Psychoanalytic, and Psychological Aspects*. New York: International Universities Press, 1966.

FREUD, A. (1939-1945), Infants without families — reports on the Hampstead Nurseries. *The Writings of Anna Freud*, 3. New York: International Universities Press, 1973.

_____ (1952a), The mutual influences in the development of ego and id: introduction to the discussion. *The Writings of Anna Freud*, 4:230-259. New York: International Universities Press, 1968.

_____ (1952b), The role of bodily illness in the mental life of children. *The Writings of Anna Freud*, 4:260-279. New York: International Universities Press, 1968.

_____ (1960), Discussion of John Bowlby's work on separation, grief, and mourning. Part II. "Grief and mourning in infancy and early childhood." *The Writings of Anna Freud*, 5:173-186. New York: International Universities Press, 1969.

_____ (1965), Normality and pathology in childhood. *The Writings of Anna Freud*, 6. New York: International Universities Press.

_____ (1970), The symptomatology of childhood: a preliminary attempt at classification. *The Writings of Anna Freud*, 7:157-188. New York: International Universities Press, 1971.

_____ (1971), The widening scope of psychoanalytic child psychology, normal and abnormal. Report of the Hampstead Clinic, London (unpublished).

_____ (1972), The infantile neurosis: Genetic and Dynamic Considerations. *The Psychoanalytic Study of the Child*, 26:79-90. New Haven, Conn: Yale University Press.

_____ (1974), Personal communication.

_____ & BURLINGHAM, D. (1943), *Infants Without Families*. New York: International Universities Press, 1944.

_____ &DANN, S. (1951a), Observations on child development. *The Writings of Anna Freud*, 4:143-162. New York: International Universities Press, 1968.

_____ _____ (1951b), An experiment in group upbringing. *The Writings of Anna Freud*, 4:163-229. New York: International Universities Press, 1968.

FREUD, S. (1909), Family romances. *Standard Edition*, 9:235-241. London: Hogarth Press, 1959.

_____ (1910), A special type of choice of object made by men (contributions to the psychology of love I). *Standard Edition*, 11:163-175. London: Hogarth Press, 1957.

_____ (1911), Psycho-analytic notes on an autobiographical account of a case of paranoia (dementia paranoides). *Standard Edition*, 12:1-82. London: Hogarth Press, 1958.

―――― (1914), On narcissism: an introduction. *Standard Edition*, 14:67-102. London: Hogarth Press, 1957.

―――― (1917), Introductory lectures on psycho-analysis. *Standard Edition*, 16. London: Hogarth Press, 1963.

―――― (1920), The psychogenesis of a case of homosexuality in a woman. *Standard Edition*, 18:145-172. London: Hogarth Press, 1955.

―――― (1925), Some psychical consequences of the anatomical distinction between the sexes. *Standard Edition*, 19:241-258. London: Hogarth Press, 1961.

―――― (1933), New introductory lectures on psycho-analysis. Femininity. *Standard Edition*, 22:112-135. London: Hogarth Press, 1964.

FURMAN, E. (1956), An ego disturbance in a young child. *The Psychoanalytic Study of the Child*, 11:312-335. New York: International Universities Press.

―――― (1974), *A Child's Parent Dies*. New Haven: Yale University Press.

HARTMANN, H. (1952), The mutual influences in the development of ego and id. *The Psychoanalytic Study of the Child*, 7:9-30. New York: International Universities Press.

HOCH, A. (1915), A study of the benign psychoses. *Johns Hopkins Hosp. Bull.*, 26 (291).

HOFFER, W. (1952), The mutual influences in the development of ego and id: earliest stages. *The Psychoanalytic Study of the Child*, 7:31-41. New York: International Universities Press.

JACKSON, D. D. (1961), The monad, the dyad and the family therapy of schizophrenics. In; *Psychotherapy of the Psychoses*, ed. A. Burton. New York: Basic Books, pp. 318-328.

JACOBSON, E. (1967), *Psychotic Conflict and Reality*. New York: International Universities Press.

KATAN, M. (1950), Structural aspects of a case of schizophrenia. *The Psychoanalytic Study of the Child*, 5:175-211. New York: International Universities Press.

_____ (1954), The importance of the non-psychotic part of the personality in schizophrenia. *Internat. J. Psycho-Anal.*, 35:119-128.

_____ (1959), Schreber's hereafter. Its building-up (aufbau) and its downfall. *The Psychoanalytic Study of the Child*, 14:314-382. New York: International Universities Press.

_____ (1969), A psychoanalytic approach to the diagnosis of paranoia. *The Psychoanalytic Study of the Child*, 24:328-357. New York: International Universities Press.

_____ (1974), The development of the influencing apparatus: a study of Freud's article "A case of paranoia running counter to the psycho-analytic theory of disease." *The Psychoanalytic Study of the Child*, 29:473-510. New Haven: Yale University Press.

_____ (1975), Childhood memories as contents of schizophrenic hallucinations and delusions. *The Psychoanalytic Study of the Child*. New Haven: Yale University Press, in press.

KENNEDY, H. (1964), Report of the Hampstead Clinic, London (unpublished).

KLEIN, H. S. (1974), Transference and defence in manic states. *Internat. J. Psycho-Anal.*, 55:261-268.

KLEIN, M. (1932), *The Psychoanalysis of Children*. New York: Norton.

KRAEPELIN, E. (1904), *Lectures on Clinical Psychiatry*. New York: Hafner, 1968, pp. 68-76.

LAING, R. D. (1961), *The Self and Others. Further Studies in Sanity and Madness*. Chicago: Quadrangle Books, 1962.

LIDZ, T. (1972), Schizophrenic disorders: the influence of conceptualizations on therapy. In: *Psychotherapy of Schizophrenia*, eds. D. Rubinstein & Y. O. Alanen. Amsterdam: Excerpta Medica Press, pp. 9-24.

_____ & FLECK, S. (1960), Schizophrenia, human integration and the role of the family. In: *The Etiology of Schizophrenia*, ed. D. D. Jackson. New York: Basic Books, pp. 323-345.

____ ____ &CORNELISON, A. R. (1966), *Schizophrenia and the Family*. New York: International Universities Press.

MACCURDY, J. T. (1925), *The Psychology of Emotion (Morbid and Normal)*. New York: Harcourt, Brace.

MACHLUP, M. R. (1974), Seth. In: *A Child's Parent Dies* by E. Furman. New Haven: Yale University Press, pp. 149-153.

MAHLER, M. S. (1952), On child psychosis and schizophrenia: autistic and symbiotic infantile psychoses. *The Psychoanalytic Study of the Child*, 7:286-305. New York: International Universities Press.

____ & FURER, M. (1968), *On Human Symbiosis and the Vicissitudes of Individuation, Vol. I: Infantile Psychosis*. New York: International Universities Press.

MITTELMAN, B. (1954), Motility in infants, children and adults: patterning and psychodynamics. *The Psychoanalytic Study of the Child*, 9:142-177. New York: International Universities Press.

NAGERA, H. (1966), *Early Childhood Disturbances, the Infantile Neurosis and the Adult Disturbances: Problems of a Developmental Psychoanalytic Psychology*. New York: International Universities Press.

____ (1970), The imaginary companion: its significance for ego development and conflict solution. *The Psychoanalytic Study of the Child*, 24:165-196. New York: International Universities Press.

NUNBERG, H. (1921), The course of the libidinal conflict in schizophrenia. In: *Practice and Theory of Psychoanalysis*. Nervous and Mental Disease Monographs. New York: Coolidge Foundation, 1948.

ROCHLIN, G. (1953), Loss and restitution. *The Psychoanalytic Study of the Child*, 8:288-309. New York: International Universities Press.

____ (1959), The loss complex. A contribution to the etiology of depression. *J. Amer. Psychoanal. Assn.*, 7:299-316.

RÓHEIM, G. (1955), *Magic and Schizophrenia*. New York: International Universities Press.

ROSENFELD, H. A. (1952a), Notes on the psycho-analysis of the super-ego conflict of an acute schizophrenic patient. *Internat. J. Psycho-Anal.*, 33:111-131.

_____ (1952b), Transference-phenomena and transference analysis in an acute catatonic schizophrenic patient. *Internat. J. Psycho-Anal.*, 33:457-464.

_____ (1954), Considerations regarding the psycho-analytic approach to acute and chronic schizophrenia. *Internat. J. Psycho-Anal.*, 35:135-140.

RUBINSTEIN, D. (1974), Techniques in family psychotherapy of schizophrenia. In: *Strategic Intervention in Schizophrenia*, eds. R. Cancro, N. Fox, & L. Shapiro. New York: Behavioral Publications, pp. 99-141.

SCHIFF, E. J. (1974), Jim. In: *A Child's Parent Dies* by E. Furman. New Haven: Yale University Press, pp. 88-95.

SEARLES, H. F. (1958), Positive feelings in the relationship between the schizophrenic and his mother. *Internat. J. Psycho-Anal.*, 39:569-586.

_____ (1959a), The effort to drive the other person crazy—an element in the etiology and psychotherapy of schizophrenia. *Brit. J. Med. Psychol.*, 32:1-19.

_____ (1959b), Integration and differentiation in schizophrenia. *Brit. J. Med. Psychol.*, 32:261-281.

_____ (1961), Phases of patient-therapist interaction in the psychotherapy of chronic schizophrenia. *Brit. J. Med. Psychol.*, 34:169-193.

_____ (1963), Transference psychosis in the psychotherapy of chronic schizophrenia. *Internat. J. Psycho-Anal.*, 44:249-281.

SEGAL, H. (1950), Some aspects of the analysis of a schizophrenic. *Internat. J. Psycho-Anal.*, 31:268-278.

SPERLING, M. (1952), Animal phobias in a two-year-old child. *The Psychoanalytic Study of the Child*, 7:115-125. New York: International Universities Press.

SPITZ, R. A. (1945), Hospitalism: an inquiry into the genesis of psychiatric conditions in early childhood. *The Psychoanalytic Study of the Child*, 1:53-74. New York: International Universities Press.

_____ (1946), Anaclitic depression. *The Psychoanalytic Study of the Child*, 2:313-342. New York: International Universities Press.

STIERLIN, H. (1972), Family dynamics and separation patterns of potential schizophrenics. In: *Psychotherapy of Schizophrenia*, eds. D. Rubinstein & Y. O. Alanen. Amsterdam: Excerpta Medica Press, pp. 169-179.

THOMAS, R. ET AL. (1966), Comments on some aspects of self and object representation in a group of psychotic children: an application of Anna Freud's diagnostic profile. *The Psychoanalytic Study of the Child*, 21:527-580. New York: International Universities Press.

WAELDER, R. (1951), The structure of paranoid ideas: a critical survey of various theories. *Internat. J. Psycho-Anal.*, 32:167-177.

WEIL, A. P. (1953), Certain severe disturbances of ego development in childhood. *The Psychoanalytic Study of the Child*, 8:271-287. New York: International Universities Press.

WOLFENSTEIN, M. (1955), Mad laughter in a six-year-old boy. *The Psychoanalytic Study of the Child*, 10:381-394. New York: International Universities Press.

WYNNE, L. C. (1972), The injection and the concealment of meaning in the family relationships and psychotherapy of schizophrenics. In: *Psychotherapy of Schizophrenia*, eds. D. Rubinstein & Y. O. Alanen. Amsterdam: Excerpta Medica Press, pp. 180-193.

NAME INDEX

SUBJECT INDEX

DATE DUE

JUL 10 '81			
OCT 23 '8			
APR 3 '82			
AP 24 '8			
DE 8 '84			
AP 04 '8			
MY 3 '88			
DE 07 '89			
GAYLORD			PRINTED IN U.S.A.